Create, Edit, and Share Your Digital Photos

DIGITAL PHOTOGRAPHY
SOLUTIONS

David Busch

Digital Photography Solutions

Copyright ©2003 Muska & Lipman Publishing

All rights reserved. No part of this book may be reproduced by any means without written permission from the publisher, except for brief passages for review purposes. Address all permission requests to the publisher.

All copyrights and trademarks used as examples or references in this book are retained by their individual owners.

Credits: Senior Marketing Manager, Martine Edwards; Marketing Manager, Heather Hurley; Associate Marketing Manager, Kristin Eisenzopf; Manager of Editorial Services, Heather Talbot; Acquisitions Editor, Kevin Harreld; Senior Editor, Mark Garvey; Retail Market Coordinator, Sarah Dubois; Production Editor, Estelle Manticas; Copyeditor, Karen Gill; Proofreader, Jenny Davidson; Technical Editor, Lisa A. Bucki; Cover Designer, Chad Planner; Interior Design and Layout, Marian Hartsough; Indexer, Katherine Stimson.

Publisher: Andy Shafran

Technology and the Internet are constantly changing, and by necessity of the lapse of time between the writing and distribution of this book, some aspects might be out of date. Accordingly, the author and publisher assume no responsibility for actions taken by readers based upon the contents of this book.

Library of Congress Catalog Number: 2003104656
ISBN 1-59200-109-2
5 4 3 2 1

Educational facilities, companies, and organizations interested in multiple copies or licensing of this book should contact the publisher for quantity discount information. Training manuals, CD-ROMs, and portions of this book are also available individually or can be tailored for specific needs

Muska & Lipman Publishing,
a Division of Course Technology
25 Thomson Place
Boston, MA 02210
www.muskalipman.com
publisher@muskalipman.com

About the Author

David D. Busch

Two-time Computer Press Association winner David D. Busch has been demystifying arcane computer and imaging technology since the early 1980s. As a writer, photographer, and contributing editor for ten leading computer magazines, he has more than 70 books and 2500 articles to his credit, including eight books on scanners, seven on digital photography, and a dozen on image editing. His most recent books include three in Muska & Lipman's Photographers' Guide series: *Photoshop 7*, *Digital Retouching and Compositing*; and *Digital Techniques*. He is also author of the best-selling *Digital Photography for Dummies: All in One Desk Reference*.

Dedication

As always, for Cathy.

Acknowledgments

Once again thanks to Andy Shafran, who realizes that a book about digital imaging deserves nothing less than a full-color treatment, and knows how to publish such a book at a price that everyone can afford. Also, thanks to editor Estelle Manticas for valuable advice as the book progressed, as well as copyeditor Karen Gill, technical editor Lisa Bucki, and layout designer Marian Hartsough. Due credit also must go to several of the behind-the-scenes masterminds like Heather Talbot and Chad Planner, who were instrumental in getting this book packaged and out on the shelves.

Special thanks to my agent, Carole McClendon, who has the amazing ability to keep both publishers and authors happy.

http://www.muskalipman.com

Contents

Introduction x

Part I: Starting with a Few Good Digital Images 1

1–Introducing Digital Cameras 3
    Correcting misconceptions about the digital cameral................ 4
        Digital pictures are better than you think 5
        The digital camera is not like a film camera 8
        You won't use a digital camera like a film camera 10
        It might (or might not) be cheaper to shoot digital 10
        You can't shoot" everything" with a digital camera 12
        If a digital camera meets your needs now,
            don't wait for new technology 13
        Things to consider when purchasing a digital camera 17
    Do you need a PC to use a digital camera?...................... 24

2–Learning to Take Better Pictures 27
    Why are you taking pictures?................................... 28
        Deciding what to shoot 29
        Choosing how you will present and share you images 29
        Picture-taking is easy, but getting outstanding pictures takes work... 30
        Seeing the "light" 30
    Ten traditional picture-taking approaches that always work 31
        Shoot with the best possible light 32
        Rule of thirds.. 33
        Vary your camera angles 34
        Include an appropriate foreground or background 34
        Silhouette a backlit subject 35
        Bright subject on black background 36
        Create frames around your subjects.......................... 36
        Crop or shoot for "partial images".......................... 37
        Use partial focus to increase the emphasis on part of your image... 38
        Look for strong geometry.................................... 39
    A "starter set" of 15 digital imaging techniques................ 40
        Shoot interesting objects for their own sake 41
        Shoot poses.. 42
        Shoot backgrounds just as a background...................... 43
        Shoot to create fantasy 45
        Shoot just for color 45
        Shoot sequence of images 46
        Shoot panoramas.. 47
        Shoot images for a photomontage 47
        Shoot for specific effects 48
        Shoot personality 49
        Shoot to create Web page images............................. 49

http://www.muskalipman.com

       Shoot knowing that you can fix it 50
       Shoot for varying photo proportions 51
       Shoot for intrigue, conflict, mystery, action, or … 52
       Shoot for a dramatic effect 53
  Ways to improve your picture-taking skills 53
       Know thyself and thy equipment 54
       Know your digital camera settings 54
       Visit art galleries and digital photography Web sites. 55
       Shoot over and over until you get it right 55
       Create for, and share with, others 55

3–Turning Photographs into Digital Images 57

  The basics of digital image files 57
       Pixels and resolution. 58
       Dots per inch (dpi) 61
       Image color depth or number of color bits 61
       Image size 62
       Image compression 63
  Using a scanner to acquire digital images 65
       Should you buy a scanner? 65
       Six easy steps for buying the right scanner for you needs. 66
  Using Kodak digitization services 71
       Kodak Picture Center Online Services 71
       Kodak Picture Disk 71
       Kodak Picture CD 72
       Kodak Photo CD 73
       Kodak Pro Photo CD 74
  Getting digital images from a local photo lab. 75
  Using a photo kiosk to get digital images. 76
  Using mail-order photofinishers. 77
  Getting scans from custom photo labs 78

4–Managing and Storing Images 79

  How much storage will you need?. 81
  What do you want to be able to do?. 83
  Tips for storing and managing image files 84
       Create an organized folder/directory system 84
       Make and follow a plan for digital camera images 85
       Copy images to removable storage media 85
       Save original digital camera images 85
       Consider implementing a backup plan 86
       Create extra copies of some images on an organized basis 89
  Image management with Windows. 90
       Using Windows Explorer. 90
  Using image-management utilities 92
       Midnight Blue Software's SuperJPG 92
       Paint Shop Pro 93
  Using consumer-level image editors and project applications 93
       Roxio's PhotoSuite 94
       Adobe Photoshop Elements. 95

Using advanced image-management applications 97
    Advanced image-management applications to consider 97
    Cerious Software Inc.'s ThumbsPlus 98
    Extensis Portfolio 99
    Adobe Photoshop Album 100
    Ulead's PhotoImpact Album 101
    Other useful things that you can do 102
Saving images to removable media 103
    Choosing removable storage media 103
    Writing image files to CDs 104
    Tips for storing images on CDs 105
    Using photofinishing services 106

Part II: Transforming Ordinary Images into Extraordinary Ones 107

5–Getting Images into Shape 109
Correcting imperfect images 110
    Fixing an image taken with a digital camera 113
    Fixing a scanned image 116
    Fixing a damaged photograph 118
Selecting the proper file characteristics 121
Using software to automate image correction 122
    Batch processing 124

6–Performing Digital Imaging Magic 129
Choosing a digital image editor 130
    Professional-level digital image editors 131
    Advanced consumer or business-use digital editors 132
    Consumer-level digital imaging applications 132
    Professional-level plug-ins 133
A digital imaging techniques sampler 137
    Selecting parts of an image 138
    Adding objects to an image 138
    Transforming parts of images 139
    Changing colors 140
    Layering objects 141
    Painting with an image 142
    Removing objects from an image 144
    Using masks 145
Creating magical images 146
    Putting up the rainbow 147
    The mushroom garden adventure 148
    Adjusting light in the North Sea 150

7–Filtering for Special Effects 153
What can you do with filters? 154
    A "before" and "after" image sampler 154
    Learning more about what filters can do 157

http://www.muskalipman.com

Using applications with filter effects 167
    Adobe Photoshop and Photoshop Elements filters 167
    Broderbund's The Print Shop 168
    Corel Corporation's Photo-Paint 169
    procreate's Painter 170
    Ulead Systems' PhotoImpact 170
Using plug-in filters 171
    Alien Skin Software's Eye Candy 171
    Alien Skin Software's Xenofex 172
    Alien Skin Software's Splat 173
    Andromeda Software Inc.'s Series 3: Screens Filters 174
    Xaos Tools' Terrazzo 174
    Auto F/X DreamSuite 175

Part III: Useful and Cool Ways to Use Your Images 177

8–Displaying Digital Images Electronically 179

Using a photo album to store and view images 180
    Using an album with database capabilities 181
    Create a book-like picture album 185
    Creating a multimedia slide show 189
Displaying images with a screensaver 190
    Creating a screensaver 191
Guidelines for choosing the best application for your needs 194
    Sharing your images with others 194
    Output options 195
    File and program size 195
    Getting images from many sources 195
    Sorting, searching, and ordering images 195
    Adding nonphoto "things" 196
    Applications to consider 197

9–Other Useful and Fun Things You Can Do with Images 199

Image projects for business 200
    Business cards and letterhead 200
    Project quote sheet 205
    Product catalog pages 206
    Postcards 207
    Certificates 208
Image projects for home 210
    Personal letters 210
    Creating a photomontage 213
    Greeting cards 215
    Wine bottle labels 217
Image projects for kids 218
    Birthday party invitations 218
    Flyers 218
    Creating fun pictures 219
    Images for coaches 221
    Sports cards and posters 222

http://www.muskalipman.com

  Image creations just for art's sake. 223
    Artwork to be framed 223
    Images to accompany short stories 224
  Stitching images together to create a panorama. 225
  Other cool things to do with images. 228

Part IV: Sharing & Enjoying Your Images 229

10–Sharing Images 231

  Sharing Images. 232
    Accessibility is everything. 233
    It takes the right kind of viewer to view 234
    File size matters more than you think. 234
  Using e-mail to send images. 235
    Sending images as an e-mail attachment. 236
    Sending e-mail with a URL pointer. 237
    Using HTML-based e-mail to send images 238
  Sharing images with electronic postcards and greeting cards 240
  Sharing images with instant messenger and chat applications 243
  Sharing electronic documents that contain images 245
  Working with Microsoft Office documents. 245
  Using photo labs and online services to share digital images 246
  Getting your own Web space 250
    Getting free or low-cost Web space 251
  Using software that automatically creates image-based Web pages 251
    Creating an online portfolio 252
  Authoring your own Web pages. 257
    A few words about HTML. 257
    Using Microsoft Office to create Web pages 258
    Using WYSIWYG editors. 259
  Uploading files to your Web site 260

11–Turning Digital Images into Prints 263

  Looking into the future. 263
  Ordering prints through the Internet 265
  Getting prints made at a local photo lab. 267
  Using custom photo lab services or specialty printers 269
  Using a desktop printer to make prints 270
    Type of printers 270
    Printer features that might be important to you 271
    Printers for the PC-less environment. 274
  Choosing print media. 274
    Types of paper. 274
    Specialty papers 277
  A few last words 280

Index 281

http://www.muskalipman.com

Introduction

Welcome to Digital Photography Solutions, a practical, solutions-oriented book that is intended to help you get up to speed quickly with digital cameras by learning exactly what you can and cannot do with them. The emphasis here, however, will be on what you can do with your digital images. The goal of this book is to paint a picture of the possibilities that are now available to you when you combine the capabilities of digital camera technology, the Internet, and a computer. After reading this book, you will have a thorough understanding of the many ways you can edit, use, and share your digital images.

This introduction briefly outlines what you will find in the various chapters and describes conventions that we'll use throughout the book.

What you'll find (and not find) in this book

In addition to lots of valuable content to help you learn about digital photography and how to get the most of your digital images, this book also offers the following features:

- ▶ An overview of hands-on projects, showing you what software applications and steps are needed to complete the most common tasks, such as editing images, creating postcards, and so forth. These overviews will provide you with a good idea of what's needed to perform the tasks, including what software you should have and what kind of steps are involved.
- ▶ Broad looks at a wide variety of software applications, from Adobe Photoshop Elements image-editing software to the ThumbsPlus album program, plus surveys of Internet services, photo-processing options, and other resources that will help you get the most from your digital camera and digital images.
- ▶ Hundreds of digital images showing screenshots of various software applications and Web sites, in addition to the results of using specific tools or services.
- ▶ Tips for selecting and buying a digital camera, safely storing your images, digitally enhancing your images, choosing the best application for your needs, and more.
- ▶ Application notes that provide specific examples of how everyday people have used particular products and services for a particular purpose.

http://www.muskalipman.com

▶ Money- and time-saving tips to help you save cash and effort while enjoying and sharing your digital images.

▶ Recommendations for additional sources of accurate and up-to-date information on products and services.

In this book, you will not find detailed product or service evaluations, nor will you find definitive recommendations of one product offering over another. It's difficult to recommend any one product that's best for everyone because needs vary so widely, and the choices change so rapidly. Instead, you will be presented with a wide range of products and services to show you what options are available.

You also won't find complete lists of all the products or services in a particular category. Things move so rapidly in the digital realm that any complete list would probably be out of date by the time this book was published. You'll find the information you need in this book to locate other products by using search engines such as Google (www.google.com) or the product reviews at CNET (www.cnet.com), which might fit your needs as well as, or better than, the ones included here. Although most of the products and services in this book are considered to be among the best of their respective categories, the inclusion or exclusion of any specific product or service should not be construed to mean anything other than the fact that it's here[md]or it's not!

Who this book is for

This book is for anyone who wants to learn about digital cameras and how digital images can be used, enjoyed, and shared with others. It is for beginner photographers as well as those who are more advanced. It is for those who want to use digital images for business or personal use. If you want to learn about creating slide shows, sending images on electronic postcards, digitally editing images, posting images to a Web page, making an image-based product catalog, electronically stitching images together to create panoramas, or using the Internet to share images, this book is for you.

How this book is organized

Digital Photography Solutions is divided into the following four parts, which are further divided into 11 chapters.

Part I: Starting with a Few Good Digital Images

Chapter 1, "Introducing Digital Cameras." Find out about digital cameras, what you can do with them, and why you ought to have one.

Chapter 2, "Learning to Take Better Pictures." Get practical advice and learn more than two dozen techniques to help you take better pictures.

Chapter 3, "Turning Photographs into Digital Images." Find out about the five different approaches that you can take to turn your photographs into digital images.

Chapter 4, "Managing and Storing Images." An introduction to software applications and image storage media that you can use to make managing and safely archiving your digital image files easy.

Part II: Transforming Ordinary Images into Extraordinary Ones

Chapter 5, "Getting Images into Shape." Gain first-hand experience in digitally editing images, and learn about digital image files.

Chapter 6, "Performing Digital Imaging Magic." Learn all about digital image editors and what they can do. Digitally enhance three images on a step-by-step basis.

Chapter 7, "Filtering for Special Effects." Investigate the use of digital image filters and how to apply them to transform your ordinary images into outstanding images.

Part III: Useful and Cool Ways to Use Your Images

Chapter 8, "Displaying Digital Images Electronically." See how you can use digital photo albums, slide shows, and screensavers to enjoy and share your pictures electronically.

Chapter 9, "Other Useful and Fun Things You Can Do with Images." Find out about many image projects you can complete for home, for business, or just for fun.

Part IV: Sharing and Enjoying Your Images

Chapter 10, "Sharing Images." Examine ways that you can share your images electronically with e-mail, e-postcards, e-greeting cards, chat, instant messaging, and online picture services.

Chapter 11, "Turning Digital Images into Prints." Learn where to go to get prints made from your digital images and find out about desktop printers and their media.

Conventions used in this book

The following conventions are used in this book:

All Web page URLs that are mentioned in this book appear in boldface, as in **www.dbusch.com**.

This book also features the following special displays for different types of important text:

TIP
Text formatted like this offers a money- or time-saving tip that is related to the topic being discussed in the main text.

NOTE
Text formatted like this highlights a specific application of one or more of the products or services discussed in the main text.

http://www.muskalipman.com

Part I
Starting with a Few Good Digital Images

1   Introducing Digital Cameras 3

2   Learning to Take Better Pictures 27

3   Turning Photographs into Digital Images 57

4   Managing and Storing Images 79

1
Introducing Digital Cameras

Digital cameras are everywhere. As of early 2003, as many as 60 percent of U.S. households have at least one digital camera, according to InfoTrends, the leading imaging research group. There are close to 50 million digital cameras in North America alone. You'll find them used in schools to document school projects, slung around the necks of tourists hoping to capture pixel pictures of precious vacation memories, or on the sidelines at amateur and professional sporting events. If you don't think digital cameras are pervasive, consider that in Japan, more than 5 million people carry cell phones with digital cameras embedded in them.

Our love affair with picture taking is rapidly growing in intensity because digital cameras are faster, less expensive, potentially offer better quality, and are more versatile than film cameras of the recent past. Do you want to see your pictures right away? With a digital camera, you can view your image a split second after taking it and, if necessary, correct your mistakes with a new picture immediately. In the conventional film realm, the soonest you can view your results is about 60 seconds after the snap with instant film or up to an hour or more if you use a department store's minilab.

Do you want to save money? Instead of paying around $12 for a roll of film and processing for 24 exposures, you can shoot twice that many pictures on the solid state memory cards that digital cameras use instead of film, and then re-use the card hundreds of times as you take new pictures. You'll save on extra prints and enlargements, too, because you print only the pictures you really want on your home or office inkjet printer.

http://www.muskalipman.com

Are you frustrated because your photos never look exactly as you visualized them? Simple software applications let you zoom in on the exact subject area you want, improve the colors, sharpen blurry images, lighten or darken your pictures, or even add text with a few clicks of the mouse. Even neophytes can easily do magical things with photos that required an expert's skills only a few years ago.

Have you just gotten home from an exciting vacation, attended a memorable wedding, previewed some great new products at a trade show, or captured once-in-a-lifetime sports action? You're probably eager to share your pictures with family, friends, or colleagues. Hook up your digital camera to your computer and send your best shots anywhere, attached to e-mail messages. Or display them on your easy-to-set-up personal Web page. That special person or valued business associate on the other side of the continent can be viewing your latest photographs minutes after you take them.

The special charm of digital cameras is that they are versatile enough to offer something for every photographer. Beginners can enjoy capturing great photos immediately, using automated digital cameras and push-button-easy software on their computer. Serious photo buffs can access optional special features built into most digital cameras to exercise their creative bent, and then manipulate their photos extensively using sophisticated image-editing software. Professional photographers, too, are turning to electronic cameras because of their speed and ability to fine-tune images in the computer. Today, if you take photos, you probably want to take them with a digital camera.

Before we begin looking at what you can do with your images, let's correct some misconceptions about the digital camera and learn about its benefits relative to the film camera. Toward the end of this chapter, you will find practical advice for selecting and buying a digital camera to meet your needs. After this chapter, we'll concentrate on the things that you can do with your images.

Correcting misconceptions about the digital camera

Have you looked at a photograph or a digital image made with a digital camera lately? You probably have but might not have known it. You might still think that digital cameras produce low-quality images and are expensive to buy, bulky to carry, and fragile. In truth, modestly priced digital cameras today rival even high-end film cameras for quality, are often small enough to fit in your pocket, and can easily stand up to the rigors of daily use. Mark Twain is often credited with saying, "It ain't what you don't know that gets you into trouble. It's what you know for sure that just ain't so." (That quote is a good example; Twain was paraphrasing Josh Billings and used somewhat different words!) So let's look at what you know "for sure" about digital cameras and clear up some misconceptions.

Digital pictures are better than you think

Setting aside all the features, capabilities, and cost issues of a digital camera, picture quality is an important reason to use or not to use a digital camera. As camera vendors are now beginning to introduce cameras that are capable of capturing 4–6 million pixels (or megapixels in digi-speak) in the consumer price range, it is safe to say that picture quality is getting to be quite good, often rivaling the results you can get with a conventional film camera. Of course, what is "good" to me might not be "good" to you. If you haven't looked closely at a digital photo lately, you are likely to find that pictures taken with a digital camera are better than you expect.

How good is a print that has been produced from a digital image that was taken with a digital camera? The answer to that question is difficult to demonstrate, but I'll try. First, consider some of the variables that determine picture quality:

- ▶ Picture-taker's photography skills. A poorly focused, badly framed, shaky image will not look good regardless of the type of camera used to produce it.
- ▶ Optical quality of lenses. A poor-quality lens can reduce the sharpness and contrast of an image.
- ▶ Camera's features used to enhance (or degrade) overall picture quality, such as digital zooming versus optical zooming, color balance, or exposure.
- ▶ Quality of the digital camera's image sensors. Some sensors do a better job of capturing detail; others distort the colors, increase contrast, or add unwanted artifacts (digital "dirt") to an image.
- ▶ Pixel resolution (such as 2048 × 1536 versus 1600 × 1200), which is the amount of detail the camera can capture.

http://www.muskalipman.com

- Type of file format (such as TIFF, JPEG, or some proprietary format). Some file formats discard certain image information to make it possible to squeeze more pictures onto a single digital "film" card. Others retain all the information that the camera captures.
- Level and quality of image file compression used. The more an image is squeezed, the lower the quality of the final image.
- Image-editing software used. The way that an image is manipulated in your computer can affect the quality of the finished picture.
- Print size. The larger the final print, the more likely that you'll be able to detect defects in the image.
- Printer type and quality. Some kinds and brands of printers produce sharper, more colorful, and more realistic hard copies.
- Paper quality. Even the type of paper you use to produce a print can affect how good the picture looks. Glossy papers tend to show detail better; matte papers and those that absorb ink can provide muted colors and softer images.

As you can see, many variables affect the ultimate quality of a print. A series of similar variables works for or against getting a high-quality print at a photo-finishing lab as well. If you use a one-hour photo-finishing lab, you are probably aware that you sometimes get great pictures and sometimes get not-so-great pictures. My experience is that many of the better, new digital cameras in the $600 range and up produce digital images that enable you to produce a quality print that is equal to or even better than the prints that you get from a one-hour photo-finishing lab.

For comparison purposes, let's look at two pictures of a log cabin. One was taken with an advanced single-lens reflex (SLR) film camera fitted with a fine 28-105mm f/3.5-4.5 zoom lens, using color print film. This picture was developed at a one-hour lab, and it was scanned with a medium-priced scanner, so our comparison is not perfect. It should give you a good idea of how good the digital camera is, though.

The other picture was taken with a digital camera at 1600×1200 resolution (about 2 megapixels, which is definitely in the medium- or low-resolution range these days). Which picture was taken with the digital camera—the one shown in Figure 1.1 or the one shown in Figure 1.2?

Introducing Digital Cameras – Chapter 1   7

Figure 1.1
Was this picture taken with a digital camera?

Figure 1.2
Or is this the true digital camera photo?

Admittedly, the pictures do look different, but is one necessarily better than the other? With a little work in a good image-editing application, the picture taken with the digital camera, shown in Figure 1.2, could be made to look even better.

Now that you know that Figure 1.2 was taken with a digital camera, you might say that I did not take a very good picture with the film camera. Or for that matter, as the picture-taker, I might claim that the

http://www.muskalipman.com

one-hour lab did not do a very good job of printing the photo—or maybe it was a combination. Still, the fact remains: There are many variables to control, and the digital camera can often take as good a picture as one taken with a good film camera.

Finally, as one last proof of the digital camera's capability to take a good picture, look at Figure 1.3. This picture, taken in a used bookstore with a digital camera, is almost clear enough to enable you to read the titles on the books! The camera was set for fluorescent lighting and automatic flash, and the image was saved using the camera's highest quality file format, but still using only the 2-megapixel setting. If you are not yet convinced that a digital camera is worth using, try one out at a local camera store. For the cost of a print, you can shoot a picture in or near the store and have them print out an 8 × 10-inch print on one of their digital printers. If you buy the camera, the store might not even charge you for the print!

Figure 1.3
This picture was taken with a 2-megapixel digital camera, using the highest quality file format.

The digital camera is not like a film camera

A traditional camera uses film that needs to be chemically processed at a photo lab. ("Instant print" cameras have a miniature chemical photo lab built right into the film cartridge.) A digital camera, on the other hand, converts the photons of light that reach the sensor almost instantaneously and produce a digital file that is stored on a small

Introducing Digital Cameras – Chapter 1   9

magnetic storage medium that is similar to what computers use. Digital cameras enable you to store, erase, and reuse digital image storage media. Figure 1.4 shows one of the more common types of digital image storage media: CompactFlash memory cards. These small memory cards have storage capacities that range up to 512MB or 1GB.

Figure 1.4
CompactFlash memory cards can hold as much as 1GB (a million megabytes) of information.

Although the digital camera does not constantly require new rolls of film, as does a traditional camera, storing the images after they have been downloaded from the camera does require storage space on a hard drive or on removable storage media, such as a Zip disk, or CD-R.

To compose the picture that you want to take, digital cameras typically offer a 1.5- to 2-inch-wide LCD screen, which is similar to a miniature television screen (see Figure 1.5). The LCD can not only be used to compose images, but it can also be used in a textual function mode to change camera settings or as a playback screen.

Figure 1.5
LCD screens allow you to preview images.

http://www.muskalipman.com

Depending on the camera model, a digital camera can have 100 or more different features. These features enable you to do things that are not possible with a film camera, such as adjust the color balance (set for sunny, incandescent, fluorescent, or cloudy conditions), increase brightness (for dark conditions), or even magnify an image electronically for a super-zoom effect.

Whether it's producing a preview image instantly for your review or performing electronic magic on your photos while they're still in the camera, digital cameras can do many things that simply can't be accomplished with a film camera.

You won't use a digital camera like a film camera

Because different kinds of cameras have different capabilities, you'll find yourself using them for different kinds of photographs. For architectural photos, I've utilized massive tripod-mounted view cameras that used flat sheets of film mounted in holders (something like press photographers used in 1940s-era movies). I've worked with roll film cameras that produce a 6 × 7cm (2 1/4 × 2 3/4-inch) negative for weddings, portraits, and model portfolios. When I was a roving photojournalist and sports photographer, I worked exclusively with 35mm cameras. Now when I need a picture in a few minutes for my Web page or to illustrate something for a book or newspaper article, I grab my digital camera. I still own and use all the other cameras in my collection, but I apply each to the kind of photos that they are best suited for.

Odds are that you, too, won't use your digital camera the same way that you have traditionally used your film camera. The real advantage to the digital camera, of course, is that it creates digital images that you can use with a computer. We now live in a "digital world" and need digital images. As an increasing number of people create electronic documents and use the Internet, they will want an easy way to share their digital images without using a scanner to capture them. In many cases, they won't even care whether they have a printed version of the image. If they do want a printed version, there are many ways to get one. Digital cameras might not be an exact replacement for a film camera; in many ways, they're better.

It might (or might not) be cheaper to shoot digital

Is it cheaper to shoot pictures with a digital camera or with a film camera? A good point-and-shoot film camera can cost less than $100. If you buy an $800 digital camera instead, you'll need to shoot a ton of pictures to recoup that extra $700 in film and processing savings.

Justifying a digital camera on a cost basis alone (that is, ignoring the speed, convenience, and "fun" factor) depends on how you use your images and how you compare costs. There are many variables to consider:

- What pixel resolution will you need?
- What level of compression will you use to store images?
- Will you store all the images you shoot or only a few from each series?
- What storage devices do you intend to use: CD-R/RW, DVD, Zip disk, hard drive, tape drive, or another kind of storage device?
- Do you need to purchase a PC, or is printing directly from a camera to a printer good enough?
- How many software applications will you need to purchase and at what cost?
- How many batteries will you use?
- Do you already have an appropriate printer, or will you need to purchase one?
- How many pictures will you print?
- How large will the prints be, and how much ink might they use?
- What kind of printer will you use, and how much do the ink refills cost?
- What kind of paper do you intend to print on, and how expensive is it?
- Will you use an outside service like Shutterfly or an in-store kiosk to print your images, and how much will they cost to be printed? You'll find out more about these options later in this book.

There are more variables than these, but you get the idea, I'm sure.

My guess is that, for some of us, shooting digital images is not likely to be a lot cheaper than shooting with a film-based camera. If you don't take many photos, the economy of digital imaging just won't have much of an impact. For others, though, the joy of taking digital photos might mean that you take many, many more pictures than you would with a film camera. You simply can't afford to burn film at the same rate an enthusiastic digital photographer takes pictures.

Moreover, if you intend to save only the best few pictures from each series and use them only on Web pages and in digital slide shows, you'll find the digital camera to be a real bargain. Conversely, if you are a snapshot photographer and shoot 10 rolls of film while on vacation and you want to have double prints made of each of them, then digital photography is potentially much more expensive for you.

http://www.muskalipman.com

You can't shoot "everything" with a digital camera

The limits of what you can and cannot successfully shoot with your digital camera depend on the cost and capabilities of the camera. The more expensive the camera, the more you will be able to do with it. Digital cameras aren't very good at nighttime photography in most cases because the sensors don't respond well in low-light situations. Many digital cameras don't have zoom settings that lend themselves for long-distance photos. In addition, the lowest-cost digital cameras won't work well for some types of action photographs, such as soccer games, bicycle races, or a skateboard jump, as shown in Figure 1.6, for three reasons:

- ▶ A considerable delay occurs between when you actually push the shutter-release button and when the image is taken, which makes it hard for you to get the picture that you want to take.
- ▶ Many consumer-level digital cameras are not yet able to capture several photos in fast succession because their processor simply isn't able to process all the necessary pixels quickly enough to focus and to store that many pixels.
- ▶ Some digital cameras might make it difficult to specify a fast shutter speed that will freeze the action.

Figure 1.6
Here's a blurry action photo taken with a digital camera.

That doesn't mean that you can't take action photos with an expensive digital camera. It means, simply, that you must plan carefully (perhaps pressing the shutter a second before the "peak" action) to overcome the limitations of your equipment. If you want to take nighttime pictures or long "telephoto" shots, you might want to stick to your film camera, buy a more expensive digital camera, or study some of the workarounds that allow digital cameras to produce these kinds of photos, too.

If a digital camera meets your needs now, don't wait for new technology

When you're buying electronic devices, the natural reaction is to avoid buying until the next new model is out. Such a view delays a purchase for a long time. Unfortunately, most of us have experienced the severe changes in the price/performance curve in a way that can be sorely felt in our wallets. A rather common experience is to buy a new electronic gadget and then see the price significantly drop within a few weeks, as a new model is introduced that not only does more but also costs less than what you just purchased. That is the inevitable result of an innovative industry working hard to meet the increasingly educated needs of prospective buyers who always want more for less. The good news is that if you buy a digital camera that meets your needs today, it should continue to meet those needs for a reasonable period of time, even if there is a newer, better, faster, and cheaper model on the market. Unless you have an unlimited supply of cash, don't plan to always have the most technologically superior digital camera; the technology simply changes too quickly. This is my advice, that is, unless you are exceptionally good at buying and selling at online auctions, such as eBay.com.

My advice is to buy when you can afford to buy and when the technology enables you to do the things that you want to do. Be thankful that we live in a world full of innovative companies that are constantly introducing new products and services. Don't worry about all the new stuff that arrives right after you make a purchase. Shoot your pictures and share and enjoy them; your enjoyment will more than make up for the difference in price and feature disparity.

Reasons why you'll love your digital camera

Digital cameras are fun and useful. There is no question about it. Here are just a few of the many reasons that you will love your digital camera:

- Digital images are instantly available and usable. As soon as you take a picture, the image is ready to be used. This is true even if you decide to take only a single picture; there is no need to wait until you shoot the rest of the roll of film, as you do with a film-based camera. Just shoot and use it.

- You get instant feedback. Using the LCD, you can see the picture that was just taken. You'll know right away whether you got the shot you wanted. If you didn't, you can reshoot until you get the perfect picture. The real benefit is that you will get better pictures.

- Digital images are Internet-ready. You don't have to scan or convert the file into another file format. Most digital cameras allow images to be saved in the JPEG image file format used for the Internet. You shoot the picture, and it's ready to go.

- Your subjects can see how they look. Sometimes, thinking that you took a good picture isn't good enough. Using the LCD, you can immediately show those in the picture how they look. If they aren't happy with the result, take it again. It's guaranteed to be "picture perfect."

- No cost for bad pictures. If you don't like an image, just delete it. It won't cost a penny to store or print.

- Digital images are easy to use. You'll find many ways to use digital images after you find out how easy it is to shoot and download files to your PC. E-mail attachments, newsletters, Christmas letters, greeting cards, and short notes to friends and family, as well as gifts like mugs or t-shirts are just a few of the many ways that you can use your images.

- Digital images are easy to store and manage. Unlike film-based photographs, digital images are easy to store on high-capacity digital media, such as CDs and Zip disks. You won't need shoeboxes, and you won't have the problem of finding a negative for a picture that you want to print; just find the digital image by using convenient software like Adobe Photoshop Album and then print it.

- Digital images are easy to share. You can share them not only through e-mail, but on Web pages using features like the Web Gallery capability built into Adobe Photoshop Elements.

This list could continue, but the message is already clear: The more you use your digital camera, the more you are likely to love it.

What can you do with a digital camera?

Finally, we get to the proverbial million-dollar question: What can you do with a digital camera? That is exactly the question that this book was written to answer. There are so many topics to cover that it will take 10 more chapters to examine the possibilities. For now, though, look at Figure 1.7, which shows many of the ways you can use a digital camera.

Figure 1.7
Here are some things you can do with a digital camera.

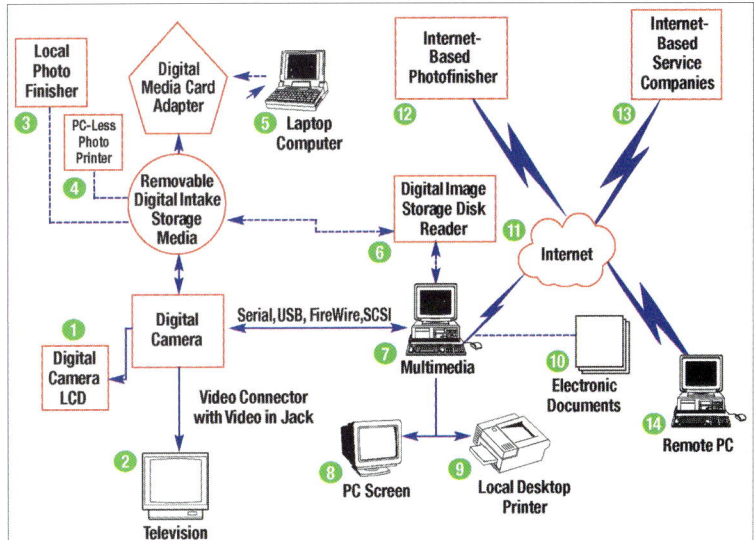

Here is a list of things you can do with a digital camera:

▶ View images as a full-screen image, as a sheet of thumbnails, or as an automatic or manual slide show in the digital camera's LCD.

▶ View images on a television screen as a full-screen image, as a sheet of thumbnails, or as an automatic or manual slide show, by connecting the digital camera to a television or VCR through the VIDEO IN jack.

▶ Get photo-quality prints "on-the-spot" at sizes up to 8 × 10 inches (or larger) by taking your removable digital image storage card (digital film) to a local photofinisher that has an onsite digital file printing service.

- Use a "PC-less environment" photo-printer to select, edit, and print images directly from a digital image storage card. The printer also can be used to save images to a storage medium, such as a Zip drive.

- Use a notebook computer to access images directly from a digital image storage card by using a digital image storage card adapter.

- Directly access digital images from any PC with an inexpensive digital image storage card reader that connects to your computer. The operating system views the card reader as an additional drive, enabling images to be transferred back and forth between the PC and the digital image storage card.

- Use a PC to view or transfer digital images directly with a digital camera by connecting the PC to a digital camera via a cable (serial, SCSI, USB, or FireWire) and using software that the camera vendor supplies.

When your PC can access your digital images, you can do the following:

- Use the PC screen to view the images in slide shows, screensavers, photo albums, and more.

- Print your images with a photo-quality printer on photo-quality paper or on other types of papers, including labels, business cards, fabric transfer papers, folded greeting cards, fine-art papers, and so forth.

- Use images in electronic documents that were created with desktop publishing programs, word processors, spreadsheets, calendars, and more.

- Make images available to everyone on the Internet by posting them to a Web site.

- Upload images to online Internet photofinishers and order photo-quality prints, photo calendars, T-shirts, barbecue aprons, hats, and more.

- Send images via the Internet to service companies to get professionally printed business cards, wedding invitations, letterhead, brochures, and more.

- Share your images with others via the Internet, with chat applications or instant messengers, or share images in online communities or forums.

Figure 1.7 shows the full spectrum of digital camera capabilities. Not all digital cameras will enable you to do everything just listed and shown in Figure 1.7, however.

Selecting and buying the "best" digital camera

As much as I would like to be able to include an entire chapter on comparing and contrasting digital cameras, the time that it takes to write a book, print it, and make it available for purchase is vastly more time than it takes for camera vendors to introduce new products and drop prices on older models. The rapid pace of technology and the speed with which product information can be published on the Internet have made such discussions in books a futile exercise.

Consequently, I cannot make specific make and model recommendations. But don't worry; some fabulous resources are available on the Internet for comparing up-to-date camera specifications and prices. I'll make sure that you leave this chapter knowing how to find all the latest information and advice to make an excellent choice on a digital camera. First, here are a few tips on selecting a digital camera.

One of the peculiar characteristics of our society is that we all want to have "the best." We want the best car, the best digital phone, and the best digital camera. But what really is "the best?" The best for you depends on where you want to go and how quickly; what features you can't live without in your phone; and, in the case of digital cameras, what kinds of photos you want to make. When you begin to look for the best digital camera, the number of features, the range in prices, and the vastly different sizes and shapes available will astound you. With all of these variables, is there really "a best'?

Before you go hunting for a digital camera, you must determine how you intend to use it. To make this determination, first read this book to learn more about what you can do with a digital camera. This will give you a more educated view of what you will want to do with your digital camera after you get it. Then, follow the six easy steps for selecting a digital camera that are provided in the upcoming section.

Things to consider when purchasing a digital camera

Experts who study the psychology of buying have found that most people make an emotional decision rather than a rational decision when making a high-dollar-value purchase. When I bought my digital camera (I'm embarrassed to confess), I did exactly as those experts said I would: I bought mostly on emotion. As you might expect, I searched and read everything I could find on the Internet about digital cameras. I visited a few digital camera forums and asked questions, and I visited the vendor's Web page to read its technical support notes.

http://www.muskalipman.com

Having completed this basic research, I made a list of three camera models that I was going to choose from and then went to a retail store to try them out. I ended up buying the latest Nikon model, not because it had the best features, the sharpest lens, or the most attractive price. The Nikon camera had the edge because I have been using Nikon film cameras for my entire career, have more than 20 Nikon SLRs and 30 Nikon lenses in my collection, and figured Nikon's digital offerings ought to have the same quality and reliability. All my planning was sabotaged by the emotional factor.

However, you won't be choosing your camera with my biases in place. If you want to make a good decision on which digital camera to buy, I suggest following the six easy steps listed next.

Step 1: Decide how much you want to spend

Image quality and digital camera features cost money. The more money you are willing to spend, the more you will get, as you can see in Table 1.1, which is a rough guide only. If you're reading this in 2004 or later, cut the price estimates in half.

Step 2: Decide how large you want to be able to print "photo-quality" prints

Photo-quality means that the image can be printed on an inkjet or similar printer capable of producing photo-like output. The more pixels, the larger and clearer the picture is likely to be. Use Table 1.1

Table 1.1
Digital camera price and image size

Digital camera resolution	Recommended photo-quality print	Approximate digital camera cost	Remarks
1.3MPixels	5 × 7	Under $200	Useful for Web page images
2.0MPixels	8 × 10	Under $400	Great snapshots and small enlargements
4MPixels	11 × 14	Under $600	Excellent for serious photography
6MPixels	16 × 20	$1,000 to $2,000	Approaching pro photo quality
12MPixels	20 × 30	$4,000 and up	Professionals couldn't ask for better

to determine the resolution required to print the size of prints that you want.

Step 3: Find a camera that feels good in your hands and that is well designed

You might not think this is important enough to be number three on a list of six things to consider when buying a digital camera, but it is. Digital cameras can be rather small and lightweight. Using a camera that is uncomfortable to hold can make it hard to hold on to. Several digital cameras that I have used were so hard to hold that it scared me; they were too expensive to drop. Also, take a few pictures to determine whether you can hold the camera level. The shape and size of some cameras makes it hard to shoot pictures that are perfectly horizontal, which might require you to edit each one to straighten it. To straighten an image, you not only lose some pixels, but you also have to store the image again, which can decrease the quality.

Besides considering the shape and size of the camera, you'll also want to make sure that you are comfortable with the camera controls. Often, photo opportunities come and go quickly. If you can't quickly turn on your camera, need to wander through multiple levels of menus to set flash mode, or jump through hoops to make sure that you have the right image resolution and quality settings, you'll miss pictures that you want to take.

Step 4: Learn which features will help you shoot the kinds of pictures that you want to take

Digital cameras can have hundreds of features. Fourteen of the most important standard features that substantially differentiate cameras are listed next. After you decide how you want to use your camera, make sure that your camera has the features that you need to shoot the pictures that you want.

▶ Point-and-shoot (fixed focus) or autofocus. Only the least expensive digital cameras have fixed focus lenses. These are lenses that are set for a particular focus distance that can't be changed. Objects at that distance (which may be six to eight feet from the camera) are sharp, as well as most objects that are a reasonable distance in front of or behind the fixed focus point. Fortunately, digital cameras have a large acceptable focus range (compared to film cameras) because of the way digital lenses are designed. However, autofocus cameras generally produce a better-quality image because they can automatically adjust the zone of sharpness to best suit your subject matter.

- Lens focal length. If you're not a photo buff, you probably think of focal length as the "zoom" setting of your camera. A larger zoom setting (called telephoto) makes your image look larger or closer. A smaller zoom setting (wide angle) makes the subject look smaller and farther away. Focal length determines both the magnification and angle of view that can be taken with a lens. After you get used to the jargon, lens settings are categorized as wide-angle, normal, or telephoto. A zoom lens enables the focal length to change within a specific range.

- Lens speed. Lens speed is how much light the lens can capture, measured using a setting called an f-stop. Think of an f-stop as the denominator of a fraction showing the size of a garden hose: a 1/2-inch diameter garden hose passes more water (actually roughly four times as much) as a 1/4-inch garden hose. So, too, an f2 lens admits four times as much light as an f4 lens. A fast lens (with a larger maximum f-stop) enables you to take a better picture in a lower-light environment than a slower lens (with a smaller maximum f-stop). The speed of the lens also determines how much action-stopping capability your camera can use. A fast lens lets you use a shorter, action-stopping shutter speed.

- Shutter speed. The shorter the shutter speed, the more action a digital camera can freeze. The longer the shutter speed, the better the camera can capture images in dim light. Some digital cameras have brief shutter speeds on one end of the scale and long exposure times (called time exposures after they reach 1 second or longer).

- Exposure controls. The way that a digital camera chooses the shutter speed and f-stop that provides is called its exposure control. Cameras might offer a combination of manual exposure (you make the settings yourself), various kinds of semi-automatic exposure (you choose a shutter speed or f-stop and the camera selects the other setting), and fully automatic exposure. Some cameras have exposure programs that adjust exposure depending on the kind of photos you're taking (action, portrait, and so forth).

- Optical versus digital zoom capabilities. Optical zoom enables you to zoom in on an object by using the lenses. Digital zoom enables zooming through the use of software. Optical zoom provides a far better image than digital zoom.

- Macro capabilities. These enable you to take close-up images.

- Viewfinder and/or LCD. A viewfinder is an optical window that enables you to point the camera. It does not, however, accurately

http://www.muskalipman.com

represent the image that you are taking. In contrast, an LCD is a television-like screen that shows you what your picture will look like.

- Image storage media (CompactFlash, SmartMedia, floppy disk, or other). CompactFlash and SmartMedia are the most common types of storage media and have the most storage capacity. You'll want a camera that uses media that is compatible with other hardware you may own, such as PDAs, laptops, MP3 players, and so forth.

- Type of interface between the PC and digital camera (serial, USB, or FireWire). The interface enables you to hook a digital camera directly to a PC. Serial cables are the slowest by a relatively high factor. Universal serial bus (USB) and FireWire (IEEE-1394) connections are fast and easy to use.

- Image file format, file compression options, and capacity. Digital camera vendors offer a variety of file formats and compression technologies that impact the overall capacity to store images. Different formats also have implications on quality and the capability of the file to be used and viewed by software applications. See Chapter 5, "Getting Images into Shape," for further information.

- Flash capabilities. A built-in flash is useful but not very powerful. If you need more powerful flash capabilities, find out whether you can use the camera with an external flash.

- Capability to add lenses. If you need telephoto or wide-angle capabilities outside the range of your camera, check whether the camera you are considering supports the use of additional lenses. Only the most expensive digital cameras have interchangeable lenses, but many of the less expensive models can use add-on lens attachments that are reasonably priced.

- Capability to output to a television. This is a nice feature that enables you to connect your digital camera directly to a TV screen by using a cable that plugs into the VIDEO IN port in the TV nor VCR. Often, digital cameras that have this feature also offer slide show capabilities.

After you investigate these major features, you're likely to find "surprise" features. Generally, you find out about the surprise features only after you have purchased your camera, shot 100 or so pictures, and finally have decided to sit down to read your user's manual. Such features typically are neither written up in the comparison tables or included in the feature lists on the retail packaging, and you probably won't find a salesperson who would be able to tell you about them.

http://www.muskalipman.com

When I purchased my camera, I was astounded by the number of additional features it had. A small sample of those are as follows:

- Flash settings
- Self-timer
- Film-sensitivity adjustment
- White-balance adjustment
- Continuous-shot mode
- Image adjustment for brightness/contrast
- 1.25 to 2.5 times digital zoom
- Capability to create folders on image disks
- Capability to turn off sound
- Automatic sequencing of image file names
- Printing settings
- Focus settings
- Variable image quality
- Multiple exposure modes
- Three exposure meters
- Three-shot mode
- Best-shot selection
- Choice of black-and-white images
- Adjustable LCD brightness level
- Card format
- LCD slide show capability
- Many more features not listed here

The moral of the story: If you want to know all about the features that a particular model of camera offers, visit a retail store and ask to see the user's manual. Sometimes that is hard to do because vendors assume that you have a PC and provide the user's manual to you on a CD-ROM to be read on a computer.

Step 5: Select a brand and model

As promised earlier in the chapter, this section provides suggestions to help you compare cameras and make a choice of the best camera for your use. One of the most valuable online resources for comparing technical specifications and prices of most models made by the major vendors is the CNET site at **www.cnet.com**.

After you are there, you'll find links that let you shop by categories, prices, and features. There are also links to many of the major online merchants that sell digital cameras, as well as price comparison tools that let you locate the best bargains at the CNET site.

You can find the most up-to-date information and news on products at the manufacturer's site. This is the best place to go for pictures of the cameras, detailed specification sheets, and product brochures, which are frequently available in a format that you can print. The easiest way to get to the various manufacturers' sites is to try typing in the vendor's name in your browser (**www.nikon.com**, **www.canon.com**, and so on) or through a Google search (**www.google.com**).

You can also explore Usenet newsgroups (such as **rec.photo.digital**), forums, and chat rooms on AOL, MSN, or other venues and do some Google searches by using relevant digital camera keywords to find the latest Web sites devoted to these products. Unfortunately, many Web sites are short-lived, so I can't list them here (the last time I tried that in a digital photography book, one-third of the sites were gone by the time the book was published!), but you'll see they are easily located with a quick search.

That just about completes the information that you need to determine what camera you want to buy; now it's time to figure out where to buy it.

Step 6: Decide where to buy your digital camera

Should you buy a digital camera and accessories at your local "brick and mortar" store, or should you buy online? Good question. My short answer is that anyone who is not already an expert in digital photography should probably purchase from a local store. Only if you know exactly what you want, are willing to deal directly with the manufacturer if you have problems, and are desperate to save a few bucks should you consider buying a digital camera online. It's okay to buy things that are more or less commodities, such as software, memory cards, accessories, or even scanners online. However, in my experience, there are some overwhelming advantages to buying from a local retailer. Here's why:

▶ Reviews, online comparisons, and even recommendations from friends don't tell you everything you need to know about the digital camera you intend to buy. You might find a particular camera has the features you need at a price you can afford, but that the particular features you want to use are difficult to access. For example, suppose you shoot many sports pictures and want to be able to choose an action-stopping shutter speed manually. Some digital cameras make you switch to a different mode and then press a menu button and work your way through several layers of menus to select the shutter speed you want to use. Or you might discover that you can't see the full field when looking through the viewfinder wearing glasses. A particular camera might be difficult for left-handers to use. Another might be awkward to use when shooting vertically composed photos. A feature you use daily might be one that a reviewer or your friend never uses. The only way to determine whether a digital camera will suit you is to hold it in your hands and try it out, not look at its picture on a Web page. (Don't even consider tying up your local friendly camera salesperson for hours and then buying your final choice online. That's unethical.)

http://www.muskalipman.com

- ▶ Digital cameras bought online might be "gray market" imports that are not covered by the U.S. vendor's warranty. They might be stripped of cables, memory cards, or other accessories that are supposed to be included. Your online purchase might not save you as much as you think. Buy locally, and you can confirm before you buy that you're getting a camera with a valid guarantee and all the accessories you're paying for.

- ▶ If you're a digital camera neophyte, your local seller can be a priceless source of after-sale advice and training. Your camera store might even offer classes or teach a course at your local community college.

- ▶ The price difference isn't that great, especially for hot cameras that are in demand. I'm looking at a new camera myself right now. I know the exact camera I want and don't need to try it out. I won't be requiring free training. I can buy it online from one of the national chains for $1,999. It's also available on eBay for $1,800–$1,999. My local camera dealer offers it for $1,999, too, but I'd have to pay sales tax. Guess where I'm going to buy this camera? On the day I decide to purchase the camera from my photo store, I can have it in my hands an hour later without waiting for the guys in the brown trucks to bring it to me. I'll save on shipping costs even if I do pay sales tax. And I'll have someone willing to swap my new camera for a replacement if the original proves DOA.

Do you need a PC to use a digital camera?

Silly question, right? The short answer is that you do need a computer to get the most from your digital pictures. You'll want a PC and its software to manipulate your images and use of your computer's hard disk and removable storage to archive your photos. However, there are still lots of things you can do when you temporarily don't have access to a computer.

Many retail stores have standalone digital picture makers like the one shown in Figure 1.8. These accept just about any kind of digital camera media, and they can be used to make prints and enlargements while you wait. An increasing number of stores also have digital picture labs that can make prints from your film cards as easily as they do from rolls of conventional film.

Introducing Digital Cameras – Chapter 1   25

Figure 1.8
The Kodak Picture Maker can make a variety of photo sizes from your digital negatives and prints.

Several vendors sell personal inkjet printers that accept film cards, too. A few printers have infrared links that let you "beam" your pictures directly to the printer without a physical connection. Some have LCD displays that allow you to preview your photos and perform cropping or other manipulations.

Although these specialized devices can work in PC-less environments, what is it that you can't do without a PC? You can't easily upload and share your images on the Internet or via e-mail. However, that, too, is changing rapidly as Kodak and Fuji begin to introduce kiosks to the

http://www.muskalipman.com

market and as photo labs get connected to the Internet. Before long, you will be able to step up to a kiosk and insert your digital image storage card. From there, you can select the images that you want to print and the ones that you want to upload to the Internet to be shared. You will be able to add text, restore color, and copy images from your digital camera's storage media card to a CD-ROM, to mention just a few of the many features offered.

Well then, you might ask, how do you enjoy images from others without a PC? I don't have an answer to that question, and so I still suggest that you own a PC. However, you can bet that there are many companies working hard to solve that problem, as well. I guess the safe answer to the question is that you no longer must have a PC to enjoy using a digital camera, but you can do more with your digital images if you have one.

The next obvious question is this: What kind of PC do you need? Manipulating large image files can be resource intensive, so naturally, the more power you have, the faster you can do what is needed. Since mid-1998, PC prices have dropped dramatically as their performance has increased exponentially.

The following is a suggested computer configuration geared toward using a digital camera:

- ▶ 800MHz or faster microprocessor of the Intel, Athlon, or PowerPC persuasion
- ▶ 128MB or more of RAM (and more if you use a high-end image-editing application, such as Photoshop)
- ▶ 20GB or larger hard drive
- ▶ Graphics card and monitor to support at least 1024 × 768 resolution or higher images with 16.8 million colors
- ▶ CD drive with CD-R and CD-RW burning capabilities
- ▶ At least one USB port (preferably the newer USB 2.0 version) or a FireWire (IEEE-1394) port, both useful features for high-speed connections to a digital camera

Now that you know a little about digital photography and are well on the road to choosing the best camera, it's time to look at what you can do with digital pixel grabbers in Chapter 2, "Learning to Take Better Pictures."

2
Learning to Take Better Pictures

As an avid reader of this book, it is reasonable to assume that you have a digital camera or are planning to buy one. In this age, it's a fair assumption that you also have a computer, various peripherals, and a variety of software. Statistics suggest that you have access to two, three, or more traditional film cameras plus accessories because those who have previously enjoyed conventional photography are most likely the next step and graduate to the digital imaging world. Your total investment, so far, is likely to be in excess of a couple thousand dollars.

You've invested even more in your time spent to learn how to use all this befuddling mass of gear. Most important of all, you've invested your hopes—your desire to produce great-looking pictures you can enjoy and share with others. These are all serious investments; therefore, you should make one small additional expenditure of effort: learn how to take the best pictures possible. Because the chapters following this one concentrate on what you can do with your digital images, we'll devote this chapter to looking at ways to take better pictures as fodder for your creativity.

More specifically, we'll spend some time with the following:

▶ Deciding why you are taking pictures in the first place so that you can work with more focus (so to speak) toward getting the results you want

▶ Working with 10 traditional photography approaches that can spark your imagination

▶ Learning a starter kit of 15 digital imaging techniques that will help you be more creative

▶ Mastering the easy steps you can follow to continue getting better at taking pictures as you gain skills and experience

http://www.muskalipman.com

Why are you taking pictures?

The average beginner, eager amateur, or professional photographer usually has specific reasons that motivate him to take pictures. Perhaps he wants to preserve precious memories for himself and future generations. Many avid snapshooters want to use photography creatively to evoke images they see in their minds. Others need to document events in their profession or simply enjoy making a living taking photographs. If you understand why you are taking pictures in the first place, you can understand what you need to do to improve your results.

When my daughter was three years old, we would spend many of our weekends up in the mountains. We'd sit and watch ants on an anthill for an hour or more. We would throw rocks into the lake or paddle in a small backpacker's inflatable raft, expecting to catch fish—which we never did. I would watch her walk across a stretch of water on a narrow fallen tree trunk, wondering all the time if she were going to fall into the ice-cold water. In the evenings, we would make dinner and then just sit. We'd listen to the outdoor sounds and make up stories before we would climb into the tent for the evening. Those were wonderful and rare hours, which, sadly, vanished too quickly. Luckily, photography has kept those memories alive for all of us in photographs like the one shown in Figure 2.1.

Figure 2.1
This memory is saved with a digitally enhanced photograph.

http://www.muskalipman.com

I also have experienced indescribable joy at watching the expressions of youth soccer players or lacrosse players as they eagerly paw their way through piles of photographs to find themselves in a perfectly captured action shot. I've listened to the lacrosse players argue over which of their digitally edited pictures that I had posted on a Web site were the best ones. Professionally, I have benefited from my skills at creating business proposals, product brochures, slide presentations, and newsletters with digital images that make them compelling business and sales tools. I enjoy displaying my digital artwork on the Internet and getting an endless supply of comments—both good and bad. Many family members and friends make year-round comments about the images that we send out on a Christmas letter each year. Others enjoy photographs that are taken and shared throughout the year. Those are just a few of the reasons I enjoy taking pictures. Why do you take them? What is it that you want to shoot?

Deciding what to shoot

Sometimes the question of what to shoot is an easy one to answer and other times it is not. If you don't know, just think for a moment about your family, friends, or business colleagues. Where can you provide the most benefit or enjoyment? When you answer that question, you'll know what to shoot. Maybe your offspring's grandparents have not seen their grandkids for several months, and you ought to send some pictures to them. Are you working on a new project team that could use a boost in morale? Does your small business need a new visually oriented sales tool—either a print version or an online version? As you read more of this book, you'll begin to see how many possibilities exist to use digital images.

Choosing how you will present and share your images

Okay, you have your camera in hand. It is loaded with an empty digital image storage card. Now what? Stop and think for a minute. Before you begin shooting, decide what it is that you want to shoot. Decide what your final output will be, if you can. Do you need images for a Web page or large prints for a product brochure? Are you going to create a digital slide show or a screensaver? Will your images be used to create a photo album? Will you want to create a panorama? Are the images to be used in a business or school class report? Will your images be printed on a high-resolution printer?

http://www.muskalipman.com

The more aware you are of why you are taking pictures, the more likely you will be to take the pictures that you will need and that will satisfy you. Without having some idea of why you are shooting, you won't be able to choose the right approach, the right images, the right digital camera resolution, or the right compression format. You'll just be shooting to shoot. Sometimes that is okay, too (say, if you're looking to develop the cat-like reflexes of a predatory paparazzo). Other times, you won't obtain the images that you need if you don't know in advance how you are going to use them. Plan—then shoot. You'll be better off because you'll have all the right equipment. Success will follow.

Picture-taking is easy, but getting outstanding pictures takes work

Before we look at some techniques for taking better pictures, let's be realistic about what we can accomplish. Most forms of photography unquestionably involve some element of art. Great art takes hard work, talent, and persistence. Not many people are able to take pictures that are considered works of art, or at least considered sufficiently good enough that buyers will pay money for them. However, almost everyone—with some thought, applied knowledge, and creativity—can create photographs or digital images that will be lifelong valued treasures or that are indispensable business-building tools. You can even take "blah" photos and make them more artistic and useful.

If you've ever taken up a new sport, you might recall the difficulties that you had early on. If it was golf, you probably experienced some painful times learning to drive or putt—I still feel that pain! If you've taken up tennis, it probably was difficult to learn to serve successfully. Even a weight-loss program or piano lessons start with the proverbial "uphill" battle. The fact is that you can learn to take photographs that you will be pleased with—provided that you work at it. Nothing valuable comes easily.

Seeing the "light"

Photography is the art of capturing light. To be considered a photographer (as opposed to a snapshooter), you have to be able to see the light and capture it correctly. To capture light correctly, you need to learn how to control all kinds of variables with each shot. In many cases, your digital camera can do this for you. Your camera can do a good job of choosing the appropriate lens opening, shutter speed, and sensitivity setting (the equivalent of film speed). You might need to chip in and make some decisions yourself as you learn about adding flash and taking control of exposure metering, fine-tuning focus, and choosing lens zoom setting, to name just a few of the more important variables. Some of the new digital cameras have hundreds of functions just to help you capture the light. When you consider all the possible combinations of these variables, you can understand why it is hard to get the perfect picture. It can be done, though—sometimes with luck and sometimes with skill.

Realistically, learning to take the best possible pictures in just a few different types of environments takes years, and sometimes even a lifetime, which is why so many professional photographers specialize, at most, in one or just a few types of photography. They find a niche they enjoy—such as landscapes, portraits, wildlife, sports or action shots, available light, close-up, or underwater photography—and continually hone their skills. They might specialize even further by doing only weddings, shooting building interiors, crafting product shots, or maybe just exploring the world of insects through photography. Creating outstanding work requires a focused, persistent effort, the right equipment, and the right subjects.

Just as most tennis players never play at Wimbledon, even the most avid photographers might never become professional photographers. However, many good tennis players, golfers, and photographers get tremendous joy and value from their respective pursuits. Work hard, and you'll be one of those who gets enjoyment and value from your interest in capturing the light.

Ten traditional picture-taking approaches that always work

Libraries and bookstores have many shelves filled with wonderful books on photography. However, because this book isn't a book about learning how to shoot digital pictures, that subject is best left to those other books. Within the next few pages, however, we'll look at 10 time-honored approaches for taking better pictures. They are invaluable tips that you should know.

http://www.muskalipman.com

Shoot with the best possible light

Generally, if you are shooting pictures outdoors, there are good times and not-so-good times to take pictures. Early morning and late afternoon offer the most dramatic lighting effects. Those times of day not only allow the sun to come in at a low angle, providing the best angle of light to ensure interesting highlights and shadows, but they also can offer exceptionally warm and colorful light, which rarely exists at other times of day. The 20 minutes before sunset and the 20 minutes around sunrise are golden times for taking outstanding photographs. You can see the warm coloring in the faces of the two children shown in Figure 2.2.

The position of the light is important, too. If you shoot with the sun or light source behind the subject they may appear as murky silhouettes. If you shoot with the sun behind you, they may squint from the glare. You should find an alternative with the sun enough to one side that an attractive lighting effect is achieved.

Figure 2.2
Notice the warm "golden glow" of sunset.

Rule of thirds

Symmetry might be comfortable to many, but it generally isn't as interesting as some alternatives. When you shoot a picture, do you frequently aim your camera to center the subject in the middle of the viewfinder? If so, you're probably going to end up with static photos with no apparent movement. Your subjects will appear as if they were framed in a box rather than engaged in real-life activities.

Instead, try taking pictures with the main subject positioned on any one of the intersections of imaginary lines placed about one third of the way from the top, bottom, and sides of the frame, as shown in Figure 2.3. This composition technique is known as the rule of thirds.

Figure 2.3
This picture demonstrates the rule of thirds composition technique.

http://www.muskalipman.com

Vary your camera angles

Taking pictures with your camera at eye-level or five to six feet above ground is common and, consequently, you'll get ordinary or common images because we are used to seeing the world from that vantage point. Try shooting a few pictures with your camera as low to the ground as you can get it—almost at a worm's-eye level. Figure 2.4 shows how effective that viewpoint can be. The new perspective alone adds an interesting, if unfamiliar look to the image. High angles can work, too. The important thing is to provide a viewpoint that is unexpected and interesting.

Figure 2.4
In this picture, a worm's-eye view offers an unusual perspective.

Include an appropriate foreground or background

Although you might want to take a picture of a specific subject, try to include some interesting foreground or background subject matter to help set your main area of interest in the context of its environment. Figure 2.5 shows how the old English hotel adds to the character of the two children. If you look carefully, you'll also notice that a digital filter (a special effect built into image-editing programs) has been applied to the background, which helps bring the children into focus. Learn to look beyond your main subjects and explore their relationship with their surroundings. (And make certain that you don't have unwanted mergers, such as a tree growing out of someone's head!) An interesting environment can make a good picture even better.

http://www.muskalipman.com

Figure 2.5
A background can add character to the subject.

Silhouette a backlit subject

One technique that you might think is difficult to master is the silhouette shot: a photo in which the subject is, typically, all black against a light colored background, as if it were cut out of a black piece of paper. After you know the secret, silhouettes aren't difficult at all. To shoot a silhouette, you need to photograph an object that has a strong light source coming from behind. If you allow your digital camera to expose for the dominant light source, the object that you want to silhouette will become black, or silhouetted, as shown in Figure 2.6.

Figure 2.6
This palm tree picture is taken as a silhouette.

http://www.muskalipman.com

Bright subject on black background

This technique is the opposite of the preceding technique. Instead of shooting a backlit subject and making the object in front turn into a black silhouette, you make the subject bright and colorful and the background completely black, as shown in Figure 2.7. Obviously, you need the light source in front of the subject instead of behind it. You'll find that images like this will look exceptionally good displayed on a computer screen in a slide show, screensaver, or as wallpaper. Such photos are also great for applications where you want to include text, as light-colored text will really pop from the background.

Figure 2.7
Note the dramatic effect created by a black background.

Create frames around your subjects

When placed around a picture displayed on the wall, a frame can create a setting for an image that captures the eye and helps concentrate interest on the subject. You can use frames within your photographs, too. Often, you will have the option of stepping behind a few tree branches or to the side of a building to add a frame to your subject. Alternatively, you can shoot an image that has a frame around

http://www.muskalipman.com

it, or you can shoot a picture of a frame and digitally include it in another image, as shown in Figure 2.8. Besides framing the image, this technique adds depth to your image.

Figure 2.8
A framed subject can be more interesting than an unframed one.

Crop or shoot for "partial images"

One mistake beginners often make is to stand too far away from their subject, usually so they can "get the whole thing in" or to avoid "chopping off heads." You do not have to shoot your entire subject to make an interesting image. Often, you can compose a picture that includes only a small portion of the subject, and the picture will be more interesting than if you had shot the entire subject. In Figure 2.9, the decision was made to fill the entire picture with just part of a cat's face. The effect is powerful—you almost feel like you are face-to-face with the bright-eyed fur ball! You can just about see the reflection of your face in her eyes and feel her whiskers.

http://www.muskalipman.com

Figure 2.9
Cropping can create interesting images.

Use partial focus to increase the emphasis on part of your image

Depth of field is the area of the picture that is in sharpest focus. This is another valuable technique, made more challenging by the fact that, with digital cameras, so much of the image is constantly in focus. Compared to an image that is created with a conventional film camera, an image at the same magnification produced with a digital camera will have much more depth of field.

However, after you become aware of how much depth of field is available in any particular situation, you can use that knowledge to add emphasis to some parts of your image. Concentrate the sharp-focus area on your dominant subject and allow everything else to become blurry, as in the picture of a crab on the beach in Figure 2.10. You might have seen the holes that these crabs make, but rarely will you see the crabs because when they see you with those big eyes, down the hole they go. This particular crab had his picture taken with about a four-inch depth of field. The two inches in front of him and the two inches behind him are in focus. Everything else is blurred, which helps bring him into sharp focus and makes him the center of attention.

NOTE: WHY DIGITAL CAMERAS HAVE MORE DEPTH OF FIELD

You don't need to understand focal lengths and other jargon to understand this semi-techie explanation. Simply put, the sensors of a digital camera are typically much smaller than the film area in a conventional camera, so a lens with a shorter focal length is needed to paint an image on that area. (Take my word for this.) A "normal" lens on a 35mm camera might have a focal length of about two inches (50mm), whereas a lens providing the same magnification on a digital camera might have a focal length of only one-quarter of an inch (7.5mm). Shorter focal length lenses provide more depth of field, so the typical digital camera will have a large area of sharp focus, even with the high magnifications of telephoto zoom settings (which normally have shallow depth of field with 35mm cameras).

Figure 2.10
There's a four-inch depth of field around this crab.

Look for strong geometry

One way to create an interesting picture is to shoot subjects that offer strong lines or shapes. The water lily image in Figure 2.11 is interesting not only because of the flower but also because of the geometric shape of the flower and the circular pads surrounding the flower. The diagonal lines of the petals lead our eyes from one part of the photo to another, constantly giving our gaze fresh things to look at. You can use curving lines, shapes of diminishing sizes, repeating

http://www.muskalipman.com

lines, and other geometrical relationships to add movement and interest to your photographs.

Figure 2.11
Strong geometry attracts attention.

These 10 techniques are some of the more basic techniques for taking better pictures, although they don't even begin to touch on the knowledge base that is available for learning how to take pictures. I know these techniques will help you for as long as you take pictures—either with a traditional film camera or a digital camera. Now let's look at some techniques for taking better pictures when they will be used in the new world of digital photography.

A "starter set" of 15 digital imaging techniques

When you move into the world of digital editing, you're entering a new realm of possibilities. Your power to control size, shape, color, light, and almost every aspect of any part of any image will enable you to do dazzling things. This is especially true if you learn to shoot images specifically for digital editing and then begin combining images. Therefore, to take advantage of the many features of the endless supply of new digital imaging software and hardware, you need to begin thinking differently about how to take photos. How do you think differently? The easiest way is to learn the following 15 techniques and then begin inventing your own.

Shoot interesting objects for their own sake

When I first started digitally editing images, I was thrilled to see what could be done. I could place any kind of object in an image, then scale it, alter perspective, and manipulate colors and lighting to match that of the scene that it was being placed in. One object can be placed in front of or behind another object. Objects can be removed as well as inserted. They can be duplicated, blended, transformed, and manipulated in an endless number of ways. After a few of these sessions, I became aware of the importance of shooting objects for the objects themselves.

After you learn how much effort it can take to remove an object from one image to place it in another image, you'll start thinking about ways to diminish that effort as much as possible. Chapter 6, "Performing Digital Imaging Magic," covers masking for those of you who want to get into object creation. Upon reading that chapter, you'll know how to shoot objects—just for the objects themselves.

You'll also learn to pay close attention to light sources and the resulting highlights and shadows. For example, if the light is coming from the left and it leaves a shadow on the right of one object, and another object has a shadow on the left, you'll have a lot of work to do to remove one shadow and create another one to make the image look correct. Complex objects often make correcting shadows and highlights difficult, if not impossible. The solution to this problem is to shoot with the correct lighting.

I keep a separate file directory just for objects. In it are butterflies, seagulls, people, cats, turtles, mushrooms, moons, boats, flowers— even LEGO models. Figure 2.12 shows the results of combining a North Carolina turtle (the Loch Ness monster), a South Carolina seagull, and an old wooden boat from Portugal into an image off the coast of Scotland. You might call this an international image.

Figure 2.12
You can insert objects from all over the world.

Shoot poses

Several years ago, I watched as my kids jumped up and down on a trampoline. At the time, I noticed how cool they looked just as they reached the highest point in each jump. For just an instant in time, they were suspended in air and looked as though they were floating. I quickly fetched my camera and took two photographs of them jumping, as shown in Figure 2.13. Several years later, I was able to remove the floating kids, find a moon object from my object collection, and create the magical image shown in Figure 2.14.

Figure 2.13
Here are my kids jumping on a trampoline.

http://www.muskalipman.com

Figure 2.14
This one shows an inline flight at dusk with the seagulls.

The second technique, then, is to shoot people while they are posing in the right way. Think about the angle you'll want later. Perspective is an important and sometimes difficult thing to show correctly. Our eyes are good at spotting image fraud if the perspective is not correct.

Shoot backgrounds just as a background

Deep inside a cavern, I found a most amazing place, which is shown in Figure 2.15. The colors were incredibly rich and the shapes were out of this world. I took a few long exposures of several seconds (called time exposures), knowing that someday I would want the images just for the backgrounds they might provide. Then one evening, with a few moments to spare, I created the even stranger world shown in Figure 2.16. On a more serious note, look for backgrounds that are more ordinary and take pictures just to be used as background images at a later time. After a few years of shooting such pictures, you'll find that your collection of backgrounds is quite valuable as you learn to combine them with images from other pictures. They also make great desktop wallpaper as well as backgrounds for Web pages and print documents.

http://www.muskalipman.com

Figure 2.15
The unusual world of stalactites and stalagmites makes for a great background.

Figure 2.16
This strange world is made even stranger with a few odd subjects added.

Shoot to create fantasy

Shoot images that you know will be fun to use. Figure 2.17 is a low-angle view of a few lily pads. I'm not sure what I'm going to do with this image yet, but I took the picture simply because I know that, someday, I'll have the inspiration to do something cool with it. When I took the picture, I could imagine a few cats lying in the sun on several of the lily pads. Because my object collection has many sports objects, I might even create a practice area for lacrosse or soccer players on each pad. The point is that you have to use your imagination and think differently to create unique and creative images.

Figure 2.17
Here's a lily pad land waiting for someone or something.

Shoot just for color

This might seem like an odd technique at first. Why would you want to shoot a picture just for the colors in the picture? It turns out that some digital-editing applications enable you to create a color palette based solely upon the colors contained in an image. If you take a picture that has outstanding colors, such as the rich brown colors of a decaying log shown in the inset in Figure 2.18, you can then use it as a palette for another image such as the soccer player that has been transformed into a graphic for a T-shirt.

http://www.muskalipman.com

Figure 2.18
This image was colored by using colors from the inset image.

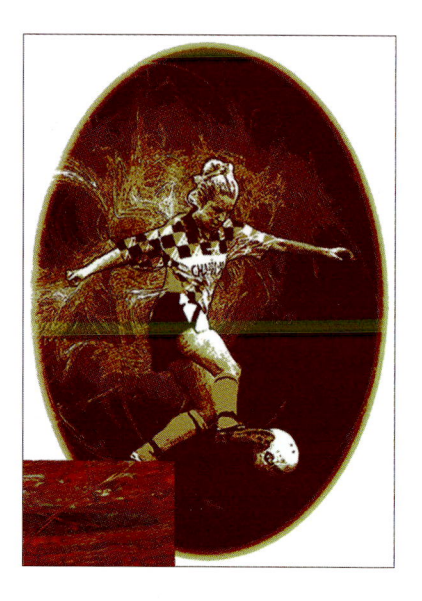

Shoot sequences of images

After you see a series of photographs that has been taken in sequence for a digital slide show, you'll love this technique. By reducing the image size, you also can use the right kind of image series as animation on a Web site. A fun sequence you might want to try is to shoot a whole series of pictures of a person's face while they talk, laugh, and even make faces. Played back as a slide show with an appropriate slide transition and speed, the series can be very lifelike— almost as if you were there with that person.

If you want to shoot pictures of an old home that you have lived in for years, you could shoot a series of pictures as you walk up to the front door from the street. You could pause at the door, walk in, and take more pictures as you walk about the house. When you create the slide show, you could add sound files that add a doorbell sound, kids running around the house, or other sounds that make you feel like you are there.

Standing on the sidelines of a final state-wide, year-end soccer match a few years ago, I watched in complete suspense as the ultimate winner was to be decided on the last of 10 penalty kicks. Methodically, I took a picture of each penalty kick and later created a slide show. Now, anyone watching that slide show can relive that winning event—one kick at a time! It is even more exciting for me, because my daughter was the keeper that made the stop! Yes, good pictures help you brag more convincingly!

Shoot panoramas

One of the real limitations of traditional film photography (and of most cameras and lenses) is that it does not represent life as we see it. We have peripheral vision of nearly 180 degrees, which can make our surroundings incredibly beautiful. How many times have you just sat on the beach with your toes in the sand and looked out over the sea at the spectacular view? Maybe you've looked at a snow-capped mountain range in amazement at the beauty of the wide expanse of mountains along the horizon. To record those views, you shoot a few photographs that represent a very narrow slice of the world that you see with your eyes. When you get the photographs back showing only the partial scene, you wonder why you wasted the film. I have surely done that more times than I'd like to admit.

Shoot images for a photomontage

A photomontage is a composite picture made by combining two or more separate images. This technique can result in wonderful images, but it is a complex technique that requires one of the more advanced digital-editing applications and sufficient memory and processing speed to manage multiple files. Figure 2.19 is a photomontage showing that a good soccer goalie can be in more than one place at the same time. A true "no-goal" goalie!

Figure 2.19
This photomontage shows five images of the same goalie catching a ball.

Shoot for specific effects

Most of the time, we do all that we can do simply to shoot pictures that are in focus and as sharp as possible. However, a sharply focused image that has edges is not necessarily a good image for a soft, no-edge watercolor image that will be printed on fine-art watercolor paper. You can digitally edit the image to blur it, but an image that is intentionally taken out of focus (see Figure 2.20) can produce a nice effect, as shown in Figure 2.21.

Figure 2.20
Here's a soft focus image of a cat.

Figure 2.21
A watercolor filter has been applied to the image shown in Figure 2.20.

Shoot personality

Not too long ago, school children were required to have a stern look on their faces when they had their school pictures taken. Sadly, right about the time they were allowed to smile and look normal, portrait galleries popped up all over the country and began shooting "canned" portraits. Sure, they allowed their subjects to smile, but they all looked the same and showed no character. When you shoot pictures of people, shoot them in a natural environment, and let their personalities and characters show through. When you look at the kid in Figure 2.22, there is no question that she has character! Capturing character will make you a favorite photographer to all of your subjects.

Figure 2.22
Here's a cool kid with lots of character.

Shoot to create Web page images

Keep your eyes open for interesting things that can be used as images on a Web page. Web pages need backgrounds, buttons, images, and textures. It is surprisingly easy to take pictures that can be turned into fast-loading artwork for Web pages—especially if you use a digital camera. Figure 2.23 shows a photograph taken of a real art gallery door in Charleston, South Carolina.

http://www.muskalipman.com

Figure 2.23
This is a real art gallery door in Charleston, South Carolina.

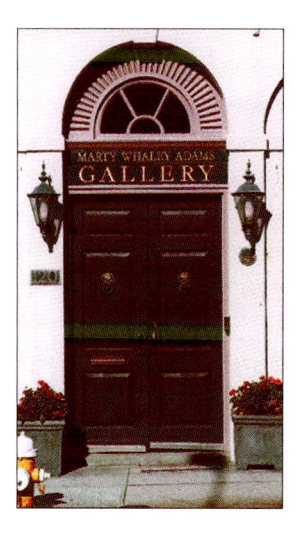

Figure 2.24
Here's the door after being digitally edited for an online digital art gallery.

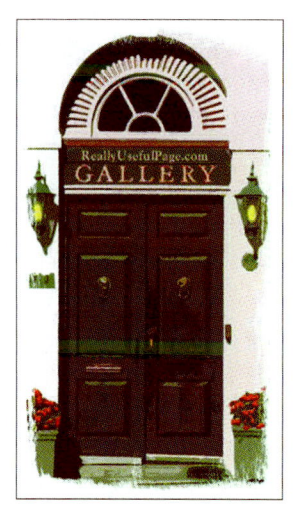

Shoot knowing that you can fix it

Often, a shot that you want to take might be obstructed by a telephone pole and lines, a billboard, or some other object that ruins the scene. Or maybe the picture is perfect, except that you are there at the wrong time of day and the lighting is bad. You cannot fix everything that is bad, but good digital-editing software, knowledge of what can be done, and some skill can fix quite a lot. As an example, you can see how the image of downtown Chapel Hill shown in Figure 2.25 was fixed and turned into the fine-art image shown in Figure 2.26. You can learn how this "fixing up" was done in Chapter 5, "Getting Images into Shape."

Figure 2.25
This is not a very good picture. It needs lots of fixing up.

Figure 2.26
Here's Figure 2.25 fixed up and turned into fine art.

Shoot for varying photo proportions

Have you found that the 8 × 10-inch ratio of height to width sometimes just doesn't suit a particular image? Once again, the magic of working with digital images and the fact that you have control over the printing process enables you to print the image using any proportions (called aspect ratio) that you choose. Figure 2.27 shows how a single 4 × 6-inch photograph taken with a normal lens can be cropped, enlarged, and enhanced to create a panoramic view.

http://www.muskalipman.com

Likewise, you can create an equally tall and narrow image of a few white-barked birch trees basking in bright sunlight. Have it your way. You now have a choice.

Figure 2.27
Here's an Iowa farm in full panoramic view.

Shoot for intrigue, conflict, mystery, action, or . . .

What makes a novel or movie good? You're right. It's intrigue or conflict. The same concept can apply to your images if you want. Figure 2.28 shows an ordinary hole in the base of a tree trunk. When I first saw the black hole, I was intrigued as to what might be in it. As you look at it, what is looking at you? Can you tell? Besides adding intrigue, you can add conflict, mystery, action, or all kinds of other feelings by using a variety of digital-imaging tools and techniques.

Figure 2.28
What is looking at you?

Shoot for a dramatic effect

I have always liked high-contrast images, which are images in which the dark shades and light shades are distinct, but there are few intermediate shades between. Sometimes, high-contrast images might even be primarily black and white, which is particularly dramatic. Yet getting good images with that classic black background can be challenging. Figure 2.29 shows a cat face with a black background that helps to make this cat look unusually fierce.

Figure 2.29
This cat has a dramatic look.

You are now familiar with a "starter set" of 15 digital-imaging techniques. This set is by no means exhaustive. It is not unique to me or to you. It is just a starter set to help you begin to think differently about how you take pictures so that you can ultimately create wonderful digital images that you will be pleased with. Practice using these techniques and even create your own, and you'll be destined to have success!

Ways to improve your picture-taking skills

We've now covered 25 techniques to help you take more creative and better pictures. Learning these techniques unquestionably will help you, but there are more "pieces to the puzzle" than just learning those techniques. Here are a few more things that will help you take better pictures as you gain experience.

http://www.muskalipman.com

Know thyself and thy equipment

Whether you shoot with a digital camera or a film-based camera, it will have user-controlled features that have been designed to help you take better pictures. Many of the more expensive and feature-rich cameras can offer hundreds of features. Read your camera manuals, and then read them again. Then, periodically reread them until you understand how you can use your camera to capture all of those moments and scenes that you want to capture. There simply is no substitute for knowing all about your equipment. Understanding your gear will help you not only use every bit of functionality that is built in, but it will also enable you to access those features quickly when you need to. For example, what's the use of knowing that your camera can enhance its zoom capabilities with an electronic magnification feature when you don't know how to put that capability to work when you really need it?

Know your digital camera settings

In conventional photography, one of the most important factors in getting the right image for your needs is to understand the characteristics of your film. All film is not created equal, and all film is not appropriate in all shooting conditions. In the digital realm, you need to know what image resolution, file format, and compression setting to choose to give you the best compromise between sharpness and image size. Really huge images are sharper, but they take longer to store on your camera's media and reduce the number of shots you can take with a digital "film" card.

Some digital cameras enable you to make adjustments for lighting conditions, such as when it is sunny or cloudy or when you are shooting in a room with incandescent or fluorescent lighting. If you use the wrong setting, you might not be able to correct the image. Some digital cameras also have exposure compensation settings and other settings that can dramatically improve (or degrade if improperly used) your images. Learn about these settings and use them to your advantage.

Nothing is worse than thinking that you got the perfect shot of something and later finding that it was stored in a blurry high-compression format and at a mediocre 640 × 480 resolution setting. Know your digital camera settings!

Visit art galleries and digital photography Web sites

If you are truly serious about developing an eye for art or photography, then you need to spend time looking at the works of great artists and photographers. Evaluating the work of others can help you become a better photographer.

When you read interviews with popular bands, one of the first questions asked is "Who are your influences?" Even the most famous and original bands all had influences, regardless of genre. The Rolling Stones took their name from a Muddy Waters song, and young rapper Bow Wow says his moniker is an homage to Snoop Dogg. Photographers have influences, too. You can learn from the masters and incorporate the best ideas you see creatively in your own work.

The best place to learn about the masters is at art galleries or museums, where you can look at the originals in full living color (or, in the case of black-and-white masters like Ansel Adams, in glorious monochrome). When you do visit such a place, look at each piece that you like and ask yourself: "Why do I like this piece? What makes it a good piece?" The more you do this, the more you'll develop your own personal view on creating fine-art works with your camera and your digital-editing tools.

Shoot over and over until you get it right

Practice makes perfect. I'll bet you've heard that one before. The real advantage of a digital camera is that you can shoot repeatedly—with no additional cost. When a specific image is important to me, I usually take 5, 10, or more images with different settings and light conditions just to get the perfect one. Unfortunately, with film-based cameras, we don't enjoy that luxury without the expense of film, processing, and printing.

Create for, and share with, others

The single most important thing that you can do to learn more about how to take great pictures is to enjoy taking them. If you develop a passion for taking the pictures and digitally editing them, your work will improve rapidly. You can take that idea one step further by creating and sharing your images with others. The more others enjoy your images, the more you're likely to enjoy creating them. If you have a neighbor who is greatly attached to a dog or a cat, try creating a frameable, fine-art-like image of their pet. Create a photomontage of the members of a youth orchestra for the conductor. Send a continuous supply of digital images to friends or family members of those things that interest them. Document the work done on a new project for the benefit of the team members. Doing these kind of things will create joy for everyone, including you—and that is what life is all about.

The next chapter, "Turning Photographs into Digital Images," is for those of you who shoot pictures with a film-based camera and want to convert them to a digital format. It is a "must read" chapter if you want to enjoy all the benefits of the rest of the book. If you shoot with a digital camera only, then feel free to skip Chapter 3.

3
Turning Photographs into Digital Images

Your digital photos don't have to start out in digital form. A treasure trove of potential digital gems hides in those shoeboxes of still photos you've accumulated over the years. In addition, pictures you take today using a conventional film camera can be converted easily to digital form. This chapter will show you how to transform still photos into great digital files that you can manipulate by using the techniques described in the rest of this book. The good news is that the options available for turning your pictures into digital images are more numerous and cost less than ever before. In this chapter, we'll look at the following five approaches:

- ▶ Using a flatbed or film scanner to create digital images
- ▶ Using the digitization services of a local one-hour photo lab
- ▶ Visiting a local photo-processing retailer and using a photo kiosk to scan your photos or negatives
- ▶ Using the digitization services of a mail-order photofinisher
- ▶ Using the services of a custom photo lab to get the files that you want

The basics of digital image files

I'm going to avoid the hyper-techie "bits and bytes" kind of descriptions throughout most of this book. However, you need to know certain digital image file fundamentals. If you already know about color depth, image resolution, file compression, and other related terms and concepts, skip this section if you'd like. If you do not know these concepts, you ought to read this section; it covers most of what is considered to be fundamental and essential content for even beginning digital image users. If you are not technically oriented, don't worry; we're just going to cover seven terms and concepts.

Image and print quality are based on a number of interrelated factors, including, but not limited to, image size, resolution, color depth, file type, and level of file compression. Some of the more important terms that will help you understand these factors are defined next.

Pixels and resolution

Pixels and resolution can be a confusing concept for anyone who doesn't normally have to think about such things. Your computer display deals with two different kinds of resolution, both of which involve pixels (short for picture element). A pixel is the smallest unit used to display an image on a computer screen. The two kinds of resolution are these:

▶ Display resolution. This is the resolution that is used to show your image on the screen, such as 640 × 480, 800 × 600, or 1024 × 768 pixels. The higher the resolution, the smaller a particular object will appear on the screen relative to the other objects. For example, at 640 × 480 resolution, a window that measures 320 × 240 pixels will occupy a full one-quarter of the screen. Increase the display resolution to 1024 × 768, and that same window will now occupy only 10 percent of the image area, as you can see in Figure 3.1. Because the monitor screen size hasn't changed, the window will appear to be smaller at the higher resolution. So, higher resolutions allow you to display more things on the screen at once.

Figure 3.1
The two images represent views of a 320 × 240-pixel image on a 17-inch monitor at 96 pixels per inch. At the upper right, the monitor's resolution has been set to 1024 × 768 pixels. At the lower left, the resolution has been set to 640 × 480 pixels.

http://www.muskalipman.com

▶ Monitor resolution. This is the amount of actual information that can be displayed per inch of screen width. Most PC monitors can display between 72 and 120ppi (pixels per inch)—usually 72 or 96ppi. You can tell Windows what monitor resolution to use, depending on the size of your monitor. With 14- and 15-inch monitors, the resolution is usually set to about 72ppi. Larger 17- and 19-inch monitors might be used at a resolution of 96 or 120ppi.

Surprisingly, many PC users are not aware of the fact that they can change the resolution settings of their monitors. If you are going to be working with digital images, you should learn how to change settings when needed. Sometimes you will want to use a higher resolution so that you can see all of, or at least more of, an image. For example, if you have an 800 × 600-pixel image, such as the one of the chameleon shown in Figure 3.2, you cannot see the bottom one-third of the image when your display resolution is set at 800 × 600 pixels. When you change the display resolution to 1024 × 768, you can see the entire image, although the image (and text) will be smaller, as shown in Figure 3.3.

Figure 3.2
Here's an 800 × 600-pixel image displayed in a browser that is maximized on an 800 × 600 desktop.

http://www.muskalipman.com

Figure 3.3
This 800 × 600-pixel image is displayed in a browser that is maximized on a 1024 × 768 desktop.

To change the display resolution setting, right-click on the Dekstop and then click Properties. Click the Settings tab, and you will see the Display Properties dialog box, as shown in Figure 3.4. To set the display resolution, simply click and move the Screen area (Screen resolution in Windows XP) slider on the Settings tab. To the left of the screen area slider is another important setting control—Colors, which is the color depth setting. (In Windows XP, this is the Color quality setting, and it's on the right.) You might notice that when you select a higher resolution, the color depth is sometimes automatically reduced. If this happens, your video card might not have enough memory for some of the higher resolutions and color depth settings. This is seldom a problem with newer computers because even "basic" video cards now come with 16 to 32MB of memory, enough for full-color displays at fairly high resolutions.

Figure 3.4
You use the Windows Display Properties dialog box to change the display resolution.

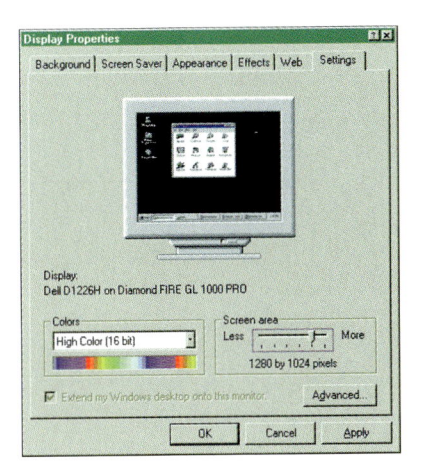

When you're surfing the Internet, especially on image-intensive pages, you might have noticed the notes that recommend the page be viewed with a 16K or 24-bit color setting; the Display Properties dialog box is where you go to change that setting. Setting your monitor to the appropriate setting enables you to view images optimally, and it minimizes having to scroll up and down or left and right to view an entire image.

Dots per inch (dpi)

Dots per inch is a simple term that tends to be confused with image size. Dots per inch is an important characteristic of output devices like printers. If you have a photo-quality inkjet printer, you might know that it prints at 1200dpi or higher. This means that for each square inch of print, 1200 times 1200, or 1,440,000, dots are in each square inch. Why do we care? We care because, up to a certain point, more dots per inch will make a better-looking image. Gradations will be smoother, with no banding, and they will look more like a continuous tone image than one composed of fewer dots.

Image color depth or number of color bits

Image color depth, or number of color bits, refers to the number of bits (a technical term meaning a single digit) used to describe the smallest unit in a display (a pixel), a printer (a dot), or a scanner (a sample). (Note: You'll sometimes see the term dpi used to express scanner resolution, even by people who should know better. However, scanners don't really work with dots any more than monitors do.)

http://www.muskalipman.com

The more bits you have to describe each unit (pixel, dot, or sample), the more colors you will be able to display. Obviously, being able to display more colors will improve the quality of the image. The total number of available bits needs to be divided among the red, green, and blue color channels, which are the primary colors of light used to create the images you see on your display. So, for example, a 24-bit image is represented by 8 bits of red, 8 bits of green, and 8 bits of blue (8 + 8 + 8). Likewise, 30-bit images have 10 + 10 + 10 bits, and 36-bit images have 12 + 12 + 12 bits.

The complicating factor is that nearly all imaging software works with up to 24-bit images only. You might, therefore, wonder why it is important to have a scanner that can scan more than 24 bits of information. Scanner vendors claim that this technique, called over-sampling, enables scanners to provide more details in the shadows than you would get with a lower-bit scan. If you are interested in an especially high-quality scan, look for a 30- to 48-bit scanner. Many of the scanners in the $100 to $200 price range now offer 36-bit to 48-bit scanning capabilities.

> **NOTE: THE NAKED TRUTH ABOUT COLOR DEPTH**
> You can't always tell how well a scanner will reproduce details in the highlights and shadows based on the scanner's claimed bit depth. Vendors tend to exaggerate, and some information is always lost due to electronic noise in the signal. As a result, a high-quality 36-bit scanner will probably provide a better image than a lower-quality 48-bit scanner at the same resolution. Your best bet is to read online reviews or test the scanner yourself before purchasing.

Image size

Image size is usually expressed in terms of inches or pixels. Generally, when we speak of images that are to be output on paper, we use inches. When we speak of digital image sizes as displayed on a monitor screen, we refer to their sizes in terms of pixels. For example, the Web page shown in Figure 3.2 displays an 800 × 600-pixel image that takes up the entire screen when the monitor is set at 800 × 600 pixels.

An important point concerning image size is that every time the resolution is doubled, the resulting file size of the image quadruples. A 4 × 6-inch photograph scanned at 300 spi (samples per inch) results in a 6.48MB file. The same photograph scanned at 600 spi will consume four times that amount, or 25.92MB. To compute image file size, simply multiply the image width in pixels by the height in pixels and then multiply by a factor of three—one for each of the three color channels (red, green, and blue). In case you are wondering, an 8 × 10-inch photograph printed at 300dpi consumes 21.6MB, and the same image at 600dpi requires 86.4MB! This important mathematical relationship will affect just about everything you do with digital images, including storing, transporting, editing, printing, and scanning. Keep in mind that using a high resolution printer to print an image scanned at low resolution won't improve the appearance of the image.

Image compression

Image compression is used to reduce image file size so that the image file will consume less space and can be transported (e-mailed or downloaded from the Internet) more quickly. All compression does is represent the long string of numbers that make up a file with a shorter string that consumes less space. For example, if an 800 × 600-pixel image had two horizontal lines containing the same shade of blue, instead of using 4,800 bytes to store that information, a compression algorithm might instead use just 4 bytes. Some kinds of compression algorithms, such as the algorithm used by the TIFF or PCX file formats (called lossless in techie jargon), provide absolutely no loss in image quality during the squeezing/unsqueezing process. Others, such as GIF and JPEG, are called lossy compression schemes, and provide even smaller file sizes by discarding some information as the file is compressed. The type of compression used by the GIF file format, for example, reduces the number of colors in a full-color image from 16.8 million to no more than 256 different colors. GIF is usually not a very good choice for photographs.

JPEG, on the other hand, retains most of the colors in an image but discards some of the image detail. JPEG works well with photographs as long as you are willing to make a tradeoff between image file size and image quality. JPEG is the most common compression technique because it provides the most compact images for full-color photographs. Therefore, it is the most widely used method of compression for such images on the Internet.

Figures 3.5 and 3.6 show the same image with and without JPEG compression. The 800 × 1066-pixel image shown in Figure 3.5 is a compressed JPEG format file and is a mere 50K—or about 2 percent of the 2.5MB uncompressed BMP file shown in Figure 3.6. The compressed image in Figure 3.5 shows how using compression can degrade image quality.

Figure 3.5
This 50K image is saved as a compressed JPEG file.

Figure 3.6
This 2.5MB image is saved as an uncompressed BMP file.

You now should have a good understanding of how color depth (number of digits to describe each display unit), image size (width and height of image), dpi (number of dots per inch), and image compression all contribute to or degrade the overall quality of an image. The moral of the story: Bigger files contain more image information, and they look better both in printed form and on a computer screen. The downside: Bigger files also consume more space and are more difficult and time-consuming to transport.

Just to make sure that you understand the material just covered, try answering the questions in the next section. You will often be faced with problems like this one when you start turning your photographs into digital images and printing them.

Using a scanner to acquire digital images

In many ways, a scanner is similar to a camera, but instead of taking pictures by using natural light to expose film, the scanner's light bar exposes the image to solid state sensors. The sensor array captures the image as light bounces off the original (or passes through the original when scanning a negative or slide), and the scanner converts it to digital information.

There are more reasons than ever to have a scanner of your own:

- ▶ Scanners are becoming less expensive, with acceptable models available for less than $100.
- ▶ Each new generation of scanner can scan more quickly and produce a better scan.
- ▶ The number of ways to use digital images is increasing rapidly.
- ▶ Having your own scanner makes getting digital images easy and convenient when you need them.

If you don't own a scanner, this section will help you decide whether you should get one, how to select it, where to buy it, and what you can do with it after you get it.

Should you buy a scanner?

Deciding whether or not to buy a scanner is easy. Owning your own scanner can be convenient. When you need a digital file made from a photograph, simply scan the photo, and you have a digital image. You don't need to take film or prints to a photo lab to have the work done.

http://www.muskalipman.com

You also have control over the quality of the scan and the size and resolution of each scan.

If convenience alone does not compel you to buy a scanner, consider the costs of paying for the use of a scanning service. How many images will you need to scan in a year? Scanning services are most cost effective when you have scans made at the same time that you have your film developed and prints made. The cost to scan a roll of film ranges from $8 to $25, depending on the service that you use and the resolution that you require. Assuming a cost of $12 per roll for scanning, having 12 rolls of film scanned costs about the same as a $150 scanner.

Another good reason to buy a scanner is if you want to scan things other than photographs, such as books or other three-dimensional objects that aren't very thick. Most new scanners take up much less desk space than the older scanners. They connect more easily, and with the benefits of a universal serial bus (USB) connection and Plug and Play, scanners are easy to install and use. If you need scanned images, you really ought to consider buying a scanner.

Six easy steps for buying the right scanner for your needs

Now comes the fun part. You've decided that you want a scanner, and now you have to decide on a specific manufacturer and model. The following six steps will help you get the right scanner for your needs.

Step 1: Decide how much you want to spend

Like color printers, digital cameras, and other electronics, scanners vary dramatically in terms of features, capabilities, and price. Your challenge: Find one that suits your needs and fits your budget. Although some scanners cost well over $2,500 (all the way up to about $40,000 or more), many home scanners are available at just about any price point between $80 and $1,000.

For the majority of people wanting to use a scanner, some of the newer scanners in the $150 to $500 price range, like the one shown in Figure 3.7, are sufficient. They produce good scans, and they definitely create more than adequate images. If you want a true professional-quality scanner, you'll need to spend $500 or more for a flatbed scanner and $1,000 or more for a film scanner.

Figure 3.7
Excellent flatbed scanners are available in the $150–$500 price range.

Step 2: Determine which type of scanner you want

What do you intend to scan? Besides being able to scan photographs, you can scan other flat "things," such as book pages, artwork, newspaper or magazine clippings, and more. Some scanners even make good images from things such as leaves, pressed flowers, jewelry, or other small 3D objects. If you shoot slide film, you might want to be able to scan slides or even negatives. After you decide exactly what you want to scan, you can decide which kind of scanner to buy.

The following are the three kinds of scanners:

▶ Flatbed scanners. Scan flat, printed materials such as photographs and printed pages

▶ Film scanners. Scan film (photographic negatives), slides, and transparencies

▶ Combination scanners. Scan film and slides, as well as flat, printed materials

If you need to scan film, make sure you get a scanner that enables you to scan film in the format that you need to have scanned. Some film scanners scan just 35mm film or slides, whereas others also scan APS film or wide format, such as the 120 or 220 roll film that professionals use. If you've spent years shooting slide film, as many photographers

http://www.muskalipman.com

have, you will most likely want to get a scanner that can scan slides or one that at least has an optional slide adapter that you can purchase.

Until recently, combination scanners did not do a very good job with slides or film. Now, several scanners, such as the Epson scanner I use, produce reasonably good film and slide scans in addition to high-quality scans of reflective originals. However, if you want the best scans from film or slides, you need to get a film scanner.

Step 3: Consider features that impact image quality

Although many factors affect the quality of a scanned image, three of the most important factors are optical resolution, color depth, and dynamic range.

Optical resolution

Optical resolution of scanners varies from around 600spi up to over 4,000spi for some of the better film scanners. Consider scanners with at least 600spi or higher. Also, make sure that you are looking at the optical resolution rating and not the interpolated dpi rating, which is achieved with software. Although scanning photographs rarely requires more than 300spi resolution, you can benefit from higher resolutions when scanning nonphotographic material, such as stamps or engravings.

Color depth

Color depth was covered earlier in this chapter. A 24-bit scanner (if you can still find one) might be adequate for your needs; however, a 30-bit scanner is generally better, and a 36-bit or 48-bit scanner can be better yet. Although color depth is an important determinant of image quality, often, the more important factor is the quality of the scanner. Some expensive 24-bit scanners produce a better-quality scan than an inexpensive 36-bit scanner. As usual, you get what you pay for.

Dynamic range

Dynamic range is a measurement of the breadth of the tonal range that a scanner can capture. This is one of the most important values for film scanners and professional scanners. Most consumer-level scanners do not emphasize their dynamic range rating values. If you want image quality, look for a dynamic range above 3.2; preferably, find a scanner within your budget that has a 3.4 or even 3.6 or higher density rating. Keep in mind that these numbers are not absolute descriptors of the quality the scanner can produce. Vendors tend to exaggerate their products' dynamic range.

Step 4: Other things to consider

Depending on what you intend to scan and how you intend to use your scanner, you might want to consider these other factors.

Scan speed or time

Scan speed is the amount of time that it takes to scan a single page at a specific resolution. If you plan to scan many images or large images, scan speed might be important to you. Scan speeds vary greatly from scanner to scanner.

Interface

The choice of interface (the connection between your scanner and your PC) is not such an important issue as it once was. Only a few years ago, you had to choose between parallel (printer) port interfaces, SCSI, and several varieties of serial interface. Today, virtually all scanners use either USB 1.1 (or its newer incarnation USB 2.0) or FireWire (IEEE-1394). Some scanners include both. Macintosh owners will probably opt for a scanner with the FireWire connection; PC users can use either.

Scanner software

Scanner software varies greatly among different manufacturers. The first thing to ascertain is whether your scanner's software is compatible with your operating system. Windows XP supports some scanners automatically, although even if XP does work with your scanner without any extra software, you'll often find your scanner vendor's software is more advanced and flexible. On the Mac side, some scanners still aren't supported under OS X; to use them, you'd need to start up in Classic mode. If that's a pain for you (and it probably would be), you'd probably prefer to buy a scanner that does work under OS X.

If scan speed or image quality is especially important to you, it will be worthwhile for you to look closely at the scanner's software. Some software enables you to scan an image with a single button click, whereas other packages force you to look at an image preview after the image has been scanned and then wait again while the final scan is made. Likewise, some scanners offer software that gives you lots of control over your scan to optimize the resulting image, whereas others offer little control. In the latter case, you have to manually adjust your images with image-editing software.

http://www.muskalipman.com

Bundled applications

More often than not, scanners come with a bundle of software applications. Sometimes, these applications are "lite" versions or are one version older than the most current version. In other cases, you get terrific software that makes the bundle a "good deal." Some of the more common bundled applications include optical character recognition (OCR) software, document management applications, and various painting or digital image-editing applications.

Special features

Many scanners offer special features that might be valuable to you. For example, many Nikon scanners enable batch scans and come with proprietary software that automatically removes dust and scratches. Some scanners come with automatic document feeders or transparency adapters, whereas other scanners do not offer such features or offer them only as add-on components that must be purchased separately.

Step 5: Selecting a brand and model

After you decide what you want to scan and decide on the type of scanner and features that you need, you must then select a specific brand and model. As explained in Chapter 1, "Introducing Digital Cameras," attempting to provide detailed and specific information on electronic products such as scanners isn't worthwhile because these products change much more quickly than a book can be written and printed. However, there are many excellent online resources with all the up-to-date information and pricing that you could possibly need.

I strongly recommend that you first visit one of the Web sites, such as CNET (**www.cnet.com**), which reviews scanners. Not only can you search for scanners by manufacturer, merchant, computer type, interface, and price, but you can also read product reviews and articles on how to buy scanners. It is a "must-visit" site for anyone who is considering purchasing a scanner.

After you explore the Web and have a few ideas about which scanners might be right for you, you should visit the Web sites of each of those scanners' manufacturers to learn more about their products.

Step 6: Buying a scanner

After you know what kind of scanner you want, you have many buying choices. Scanners are one product that it is usually safe to buy online. You probably don't need to put a scanner through the exhaustive in-person testing I recommend before buying a digital camera. If you want to buy from a local store, try one of the national retail chains, such as CompUSA, Office Depot, Best Buy, or Office Max.

If you decide to buy online, I again recommend using CNET because it enables you to compare the prices for a specific product at many online merchants. CNET makes your online shopping about as easy as it can be. If you are interested in a high-end scanner, you might want to visit **www.publishingperfection.com**.

Using Kodak digitization services

Kodak products and services enjoy widespread use in the traditional film market. Kodak has positioned itself nearly as well in the new world of digital photography. It offers a wide range of products and services to help you share your images digitally. Many of these offerings are available from more than 40,000 retailers plus a rapidly growing number of Internet-based companies.

Besides its Kodak Picture Center Online (formerly PhotoNet Online) service, Kodak provides equipment and supplies to a variety of companies that enable those companies to offer four different disk-based services: Kodak Picture Disk, Kodak Picture CD, Kodak Photo CD, and Kodak Pro Photo CD. Further details on each of these offerings are provided next.

Kodak Picture Center Online Services

If, for one reason or another, you are not interested in getting your images back on a CD or floppy disk and you'd prefer to receive the digital files made from your photographs online, try the Kodak Picture Center Online service. You simply drop off your unprocessed 35mm or APS film to any of the 40,000 retailers or mail-order photofinishers in the U.S. and ask for Picture Center Online service.

When your film is processed, the photo lab will scan your images and upload them to the Internet, where you can access them. You, friends, or family can view your pictures individually or in slideshow form, order prints and enlargements, or create picture gifts such as calendars, greeting cards, or "picture pages" that combine several photos on one page. You can even crop your pictures, lighten or darken them, or remove red-eye glare, all automatically while you're online.

Kodak Picture Disk

The Kodak Picture Disk service is the entry-level digitization service. Digital images are created and written to a 3 1/2-inch floppy disk, which can store up to 28 images. Acceptable film formats include 35mm and APS. APS processing can take up to a week, whereas

Picture Disks for 35mm film can be done in one hour or up to two to three days, depending on where you get your film processed.

The image files are delivered in JPEG format at a 400 × 600-pixel resolution. This makes the images good for using on Web pages or for displaying on a computer monitor. Because of the small file size, you will not be able to print prints that are particularly good unless they are small.

> **NOTE**
>
> A novice to digital photography who did not have a PC, a scanner, or any digital-image editing software wanted to try using digital images. After shooting a roll of film at a company party, he dropped it off at his regular local photo lab for processing. He requested that they print prints and create a Kodak Picture Disk. Using the 400 × 600-pixel JPEG images that came on the floppy disk, he was able to upload them directly from his PC at work to an Internet-based, photo-sharing site so that he could share the photos with his co-workers. After receiving many positive comments about his images, he made plans to buy a PC and a scanner for home use.

Kodak Picture CD

Picture CD is the consumer-level offering for 35mm and APS film. It takes about three days for processing (using your local photofinisher), and the files are returned on a CD. When you get your prints and negatives back, you also get an index print, along with a CD that contains digital versions of each of your pictures. All of the images are 1024 × 1536 pixels and are compressed in the JPEG file format. A file-conversion program and viewing software are included on each disc. Each CD contains images from only a single roll of film.

A roll of 36 pictures will take about 13.5MB, with each file ranging in size from 275K to 550K for a 1024 × 1536-pixel image when stored in the JPEG file format. Using a 300dpi printer, the optimal print size is 3.4 × 5.1 inches. Many of the advanced printers that photo-processing labs use print an exceptionally good print using only 200dpi. This enables them to print near-photographic quality prints for up to a 5 × 7-inch print.

If you don't have a scanner and want digital images, using Kodak Picture CD services is an excellent way to get good scans done inexpensively. Most services that offer the Kodak Picture CD require you to have prints printed when you order a Picture CD.

NOTE

A schoolteacher wanted to get digital images made of her students' science projects. After taking pictures of each science project with a film camera, she dropped off the film at a local photo lab and ordered a Kodak Picture CD. She was then able to use the digital images for school reports, for her annual class report, and for the students. She saved the Picture CD so that she could show the projects to students in her classes in subsequent years.

Kodak Photo CD

The Photo CD is the professional version of the Picture CD. Pictures are stored by using a special proprietary image file format developed by Kodak that stores data at five different levels of resolution. This format enables you to get images from a single PCD (.pcd extension) file at resolutions of 2048 × 3072, 1024 × 1536, 512 × 768, 256 × 384, and 128 × 192. When you open a PCD file with an application that accepts PCD file formats, you will see a dialog box like the one shown in Figure 3.8, which enables you to choose the resolution that you need.

Figure 3.8
You must select an image resolution when you open a PCD digital image file.

http://www.muskalipman.com

Kodak Photo CDs can take up to a week or more for processing. Acceptable film formats include 35mm and APS, as well as slide film. Using Photo CDs is a handy way to store and manage your digital images. Each Photo CD is placed in a standard CD music case with a cover that displays small thumbnail images of each image on the CD.

A roll of 36 pictures in the Kodak PCD format requires 145MB, and the file size typically varies between 3.5MB and 5MB. Seven rolls of 36-exposure film stored in the PCD format consumes about 1GB of storage space. Although this seems like a lot, it would take even more space if the files were stored in almost any reasonably uncompressed format.

It is also possible to have your already-developed negatives or slides transferred to a Photo CD. There are some variations in service, depending on the service provider. Not all will do Photo CDs from already-developed film. Prices can vary between $.50 per picture to $4 per picture. You will need software that supports images on a Kodak Photo CD, such as Paint Shop Pro, Adobe Photoshop Elements, Microsoft Picture It!, Photoshop, ThumbsPlus, or one of the many other applications that support the PCD file format.

Kodak Pro Photo CD

The Pro Photo CD is similar to the Photo CD except that it adds an optional sixth level of resolution: an enormous 4096 × 6144-pixel image. Acceptable film formats include 120/220 film, 4 × 5-inch film, as well as 35mm. Depending on the film format and the images, the CDs can hold up to 100 images. The Pro Photo CD is also a rewritable CD, so you can continue to add images to the CD until it is full.

With four choices of Kodak digitization services, which one is best for you? Table 3.1 will help you answer that question. After you decide how you are going to use your images, you can select the right service.

Table 3.1
Kodak digital image CD image sizes

Image size			Print size at 200 dpi in inches		Print size at 300 dpi in inches	
Pixel height	Pixel width	File size	Height	Width	Height	Width
128	192	72K	0.6	0.96	0.4	0.64
256	384	288K	1.3	1.92	0.8	1.28
512	768	1.1MB	2.6	3.84	1.7	2.56
1024	1536	4.5MB	5.1	7.68	3.4	5.12
2048	3072	18MB	10.2	15.36	6.8	10.24
4096*	6144	75MB	20.48	30.72	13.65333	20.48

* Available only on Kodak Pro Photo CD Master

Getting digital images from a local photo lab

In the previous section, you learned about five Kodak services that you can use to turn your photographs into digital images. These Kodak services and other services that are similar to them are available at most camera stores and at thousands of mass merchants, such as drug stores, supermarkets, and discount stores. Using these services is easy. Just drop off your film, fill out the film-processing envelope, and place a check in the appropriate box to order the digital images that you want.

If you intend to use these services frequently, you might want to check prices and offerings from several different companies; the scan quality, price, turnaround time, and service can differ substantially. Chapter 11, "Turning Digital Images into Prints," offers more information on many of the companies that offer these services. You can also learn more about them by visiting any of these sites:

▶ www.kodak.com
▶ www.ritzpix.com

Using a photo kiosk to get digital images

If you don't have your own scanner and you need to make just one or a few scans from existing prints or negatives (as opposed to a fully undeveloped roll of film), then one of the photo kiosks might be the most cost-effective way to get what you need. Kiosks are self-serve photo labs that you can operate. You will typically find these kiosks in camera stores. (Figure 1.8 in Chapter 1 shows a Kodak Picture Maker kiosk.) Another excellent photo kiosk is the Fuji Pictrography kiosk, shown in Figure 3.9. Many of Ritz Camera's retail stores have Fuji Pictrography kiosks.

Figure 3.9
Fuji's Pictrography photo kiosk enables you to scan, print, and upload images to the Internet.

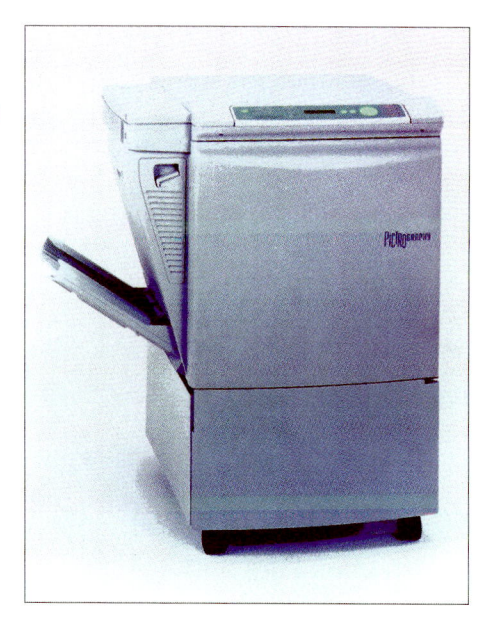

Although the plan is to have all of the photo kiosks be capable of scanning an image and writing it to a variety of media, including CDs, floppies, and, in some cases, Zip drives, not all of them currently have such capabilities.

In the long-term, kiosks will become a key part of digital photo networks that tie many retail stores into photo labs and the Internet. When you get an image scanned, you will have the option of writing it to removable storage media, printing it, or uploading it to the Internet. Images that are uploaded to the Internet can be shared, and online prints and photo gifts can be ordered. Eventually, anyone who has the correct access code can view your images and print copies at networked kiosks.

To find a Kodak Picture Maker near you, visit **www.kodak.com**, click the Service & Support button, and then select Where to Find Kodak Products and Services. Then select Picture Maker and fill in your city, state, or ZIP code to get a list of Picture Makers near you. Fifteen thousand Picture Makers are installed worldwide, so you are likely to find one not too far away.

Using mail-order photofinishers

Besides using the services of local photo labs, you can use the services offered by mail-order photofinishers. You can request mail-in envelopes for your film from a mail-order lab by visiting any of the following sites:

- **www.agfanet.com**
- **www.clubphoto.com**
- **www.filmworks.com**
- **www.ezprints.com**
- **www.mysticcolorlab.com**
- **www.yorkphoto.com**

Using a mail-order service can save you the aggravation of dropping off and picking up your film at a local photo lab. Simply put your film in a preaddressed, stamped or postage-paid envelope and put it in your mailbox.

> **NOTE**
> When traveling in Europe for two months, a retired couple used mail-in envelopes to have their film processed, scanned, and uploaded to the Internet. Doing this eliminated the possibility that they would lose their film while traveling, and it enabled them to view the images online while they traveled. Their children and grandchildren also were able to view the places that they visited while they were away.

http://www.muskalipman.com

Getting scans from custom photo labs

Occasionally, you might need a particularly good or large scan. In this case, you should look for a local custom photo lab that you can visit in person and discuss your requirements. Custom photo labs are used to meeting the higher expectations of professionals. Additionally, they generally have high-end scanners and software that enable them to create superior image files.

> **NOTE**
> An aspiring artist wanted to turn a picture she had taken into an 11 × 14-inch print to hang on the wall of her living room. The picture was taken on slide film, so she took it to a nearby custom photo lab to have it scanned. Using a high-end scanner, the photo lab was able to scan the slide at 3,600 dpi, which resulted in a 45MB image. The 3226 × 4849-pixel image was perfect for making an 11 × 14-inch print on her 300dpi color inkjet printer. After some digital-image editing, she was able to produce an image that she was proud to display on her wall.

At this point, you should have a good idea as to how you can turn your photographs into digital images. Before your image collection grows too large, you should learn how to manage and store your digital images, which is the topic of the next chapter.

4

Managing and Storing Images

One of the unsung advantages of working with digital images is just how easy they are to store, manage, and retrieve, especially when compared to traditional photographs. How do you store your pictures? Are they in shoeboxes or plastic containers stuffed in the bottom of a closet or pushed under a bed? Are they in unorganized drawers? Are your photographs, like those of my family, dumped into a steamer-trunk sized chest in roughly chronological order, ready for a family archaeologist to dig down through the various strata? Are you the one-in-a-million photo archivist who catalogs pictures in any meaningful way, or does the order change each time you rifle through them? If you want a few specific photographs and their negatives, can you find them?

Odds are good that you take pictures and then store them without taking time to add a date or subject title to the envelopes or to file them in any organized way. If you're over 30, you might have class photos of friends you attended school with for a dozen years, and you can't identify half of them by name. This lack of organization makes sharing pictures difficult, time-consuming, and frustrating.

Digital images, in contrast, are potentially much easier to store and manage than traditional pictures. You can fit thousands of digital images on a stack of CDs less than an inch thick. If the CDs are carefully labeled with their content and you use one of the many image management/cataloging programs, you can store your images efficiently and compactly, browse through them visually using handy thumbnail views, or search a database of keywords that you've used to describe your pictures. Figure 4.1 shows Adobe's new Photoshop Album application, one of the best of the latest crop of image-management programs.

http://www.MUSKALIPMAN.com

Figure 4.1
Photoshop Album is a great application for managing and organizing digital image files.

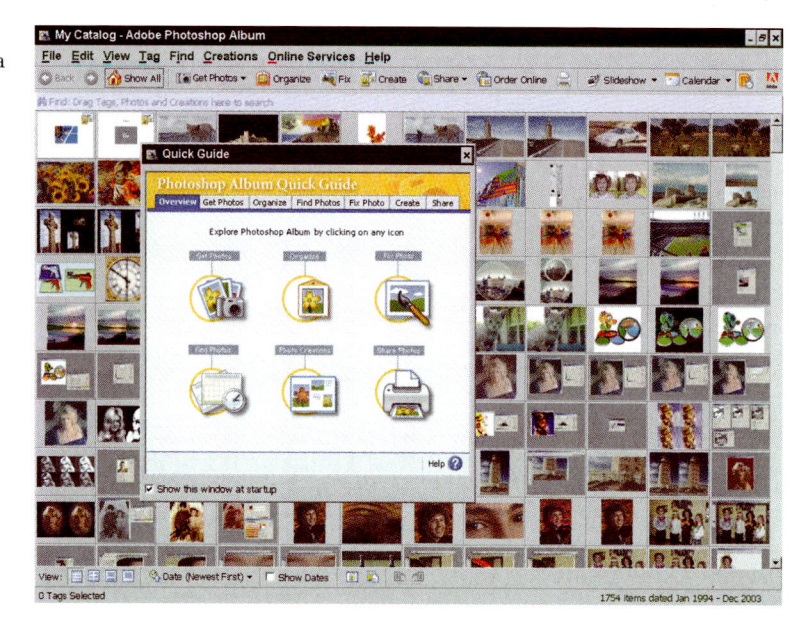

However, not everyone who works with digital images will realize the organizational potential of computerized image management. If you're sloppy, having an unorganized digital image collection is just as easy as compiling an unorganized traditional picture collection. It might even be easier. Digital image assemblages can grow quickly; it doesn't cost much to take the pictures, so you might have far more pictures than you imagine. Although you can delete your bad shots, the fact that retaining them costs you nothing but a bit of space on your storage media can tempt you to keep clunkers that really deserve to be shuttled to the bit-bin. If you are not careful, you'll also end up with multiple copies of the same images scattered across your system and various kinds of removable media. Every time you modify an image, it makes sense to save the changed version under a new file name, just in case you want to go back to the original. The result? You end up with multiple files with names like MiamiBeach01.jpg, MiamiBeach01a.jpg, MiamiBeach01b.jpg, and so forth. You might not be able to find the images that you want when you want them—at least not without a lot of work.

Another reality is that you can't keep your pictures on your hard disk forever. Ultimately, you'll have to take time to organize your images and transfer them to removable storage media because you'll run out of hard disk space. The longer you wait, the more time it will take to

http://www.muskalipman.com

organize and save your images. When you finally do save them to removable media, you'll need to do it in an organized fashion; otherwise, you'll just add to the mess when trying to free up some hard drive space.

In this chapter, you'll learn how you can set up a storage system that will work for you. You will look at software that makes it a pleasure to work with your digital image collection. With a good filing system and the right software tools, you'll be able to store, organize, and manage your digital images so that you can find the images that you need when you need them. In the end, you'll get more enjoyment and value from your digital image collection.

How much storage will you need?

Within the first month of buying my most recent digital camera, I took 1,500 pictures—the equivalent of 63 rolls of 24-exposure film. I know this because my digital camera consecutively numbers each photo with names like DSCN3245.jpg, and so forth. During that time, I was also learning how to use the camera and the many features it offered, so I didn't expect to shoot that much in the future. I was wrong. After I learned to use the features, I found many more things I wanted to photograph, and I wasn't constrained by the cost factor as I was with conventional film.

The total cost for all of those images was about 30 cents, the cost of the three CD-Rs I bought in bulk for about a dime each. That is in sharp contrast to roughly the $800 that it would have cost for 63 rolls of film, processing, and printing. The point of this story is that digital an images can be so inexpensive to take that you might end up with lots of images. Finding one image out of thousands that you might take over a few years can become as difficult as finding a negative and image in your traditional film collection—unless you have some method to your madness.

By now, you probably are thinking that you are going to have to buy several new hard drives and a truckload of CDs to store your images. Before you begin considering ways to store images, get a better idea of how much storage space you will need. To estimate storage requirements, you need to make a few assumptions. First, you need to decide on the probable image resolution and level of file compression that you will use.

http://www.muskalipman.com

I'm going to make a few calculations based on a 4-megapixel image, which is an image resolution, in the case of one popular camera, approximating 1704 × 2272 pixels. A 4-megapixel image equates to about 12MB before you start squeezing it down with compression. Fortunately, digital cameras can provide excellent quality images using minimal compression (and highest quality), so you can expect your 4-megapixel image to consume about 1.5MB of space on your camera's memory card or, when transferred, your computer's hard disk.

To make a rough estimate of your storage requirements, you will have to make a guess as to how many images you will take in a year. It's not unusual to shoot three to five times as many digital pictures as you would film pictures. After you have made an educated guess, multiply the number of digital pictures per year by 1.5MB to determine the total storage requirement.

Counting only the images taken for personal use, on average a typical user can easily snap off 300 images a month (only about three and a half 128MB memory cards), or about 5.5GB of storage a year. That might not sound like a lot of storage space in an era of cheap 80–120GB hard drives, but I've found that each image you store on your hard disk soon multiplies into three or four different copies, probably stored at lower compression levels to preserve quality as you edit them, so your 5.5GB of "original" snapshots can easily grow to 30–40GB of working files.

Fortunately, not all those images have to remain on your hard drive. You can move many of them to other storage media, such as CD-R/RW discs. You can store an entire year's worth of images on eight CD-Rs, which should total no more than $3.00 at non-sale prices, or a lot less than a dollar if you do like I do and take advantage of manufacturer sales and rebates to buy a whole spindle of 50 CDs for $5.00 to $10.00.

You now should have a good idea about how much storage you'll need for the images that you'll create with a digital camera; but what if you don't use a digital camera and instead scan your photographs with a scanner? Every 4 × 6-inch photo that you scan at 200 dpi and save as a TIFF file will occupy about 2.5MB of disk space; an 8 × 10-inch photo will account for 6.5MB of storage. If you scan your old collection of 4 × 6-inch photos at a leisurely rate of 33 a month, you'll need to add another gigabyte of storage space to your requirements.

To get the total disc space requirement for a three-year period, you need to add the space required for the initial images you took with a digital camera and then add space requirements for the converted digital camera images and scanned images. If you frequently use a digital camera and scanner and often digitally edit your images, you'll find that you need to store and manage thousands of images across several dozen CDs and a hard drive—that is roughly the magnitude of your storage requirements.

What do you want to be able to do?

In an ideal world, all of our digital images would be online at the same time (that is, locally accessible to your computer. Online had that particular meaning before the Internet became so prevalent.) Each image would be cataloged by date, subject, image size, type of camera used, file type, and a few other chosen characteristics. Using thumbnails, the images could be grouped by subject, client, book, or project. However, the reality is that all the images are not likely to be online, and categorizing every image might be more work than it's worth. The trick is finding the optimal balance between the effort required to properly store and manage your images and the benefit you get from having them properly stored.

What do you want to be able to do with your images? Will you need to access every one of them by multiple keywords, such as subject and date? Do you want to be able to print contact sheets or upload HTML-based image catalog pages to the Internet? Do you need to catalog images on lots of removable media? Is it important to you to be able to group images together for various projects and share them with other team members? Or, do you simply need to find a few images every now and then and are happy to browse a few CDs to find them?

Recognizing the wide range of user requirements for storing digital images, this chapter does the following:

▶ Provides tips for storing and managing image-file collections of any size

▶ Shows how to use Windows Explorer as an image-management tool

▶ Presents a few simple, powerful, and inexpensive utilities that make it easier to manage digital images

http://www.muskalipman.com

- Provides overviews of several powerful consumer-level digital-image editing and project applications with image-management capabilities
- Shows the capabilities of advanced image-management tools

Upon completion of this chapter, you'll be able to select the appropriate tools to do what you want to do, effectively and efficiently.

Tips for storing and managing image files

No matter what your requirements are and no matter how many images you need to store and manage, you must have a plan—or even several plans. You might choose to have one plan for digital image files made with a digital camera, another plan for scanned images, a third plan for images that you have digitally edited, and a few other plans for the various projects that you are working on. The following six tips will help you save time, minimize the chances of losing valuable digital images, and enable you to enjoy and share your work more fully.

Create an organized folder/directory system

One of the most important and easy steps that you can take to keep your digital images organized and safe is to create and maintain an organized system of directories (or folders) on your hard disk. As your digital image collection grows, you'll find that it's not hard to delete the wrong directory of files or to misfile an image and not be able to find it. You can also end up duplicating files that consume lots of space if you are not aware that other copies exist. Finding duplicates and deleting them after you have added new files to the same directories can be time-consuming.

Take advantage of the long file name feature built into Windows and Mac OS. Use descriptive folder and image names that clearly remind you of their contents, such as cats, wedding, horseshow03, chap06-image magic, or soccer06-08-03. When you create a second set of images that can be deleted after you use them, add tmp to the folder name so that you know all the images can be deleted. For example, you might copy 20 images from multiple folders for use in a calendar. Each of these copied images can be placed in a directory called monthly images tmp, indicating that after the calendar is complete, you can delete the entire folder.

Make and follow a plan for digital camera images

Images that you take with a digital camera can create cataloging problems that are unique to digital cameras. Some cameras sequentially number each image until you download them to your computer. Then the counter is set back to 1 and the numbering starts all over again. This means that you have to keep each set of images in a separate directory. Alternatively, you can renumber each image so that the file names are unique and can thus be safely stored in the same file folder.

Fortunately, newer digital cameras don't follow this scheme. They remember internally the last number applied and start with the next consecutive number each time you begin a new session, whether or not you have changed film cards or moved the files in the interim. Another nice feature offered by some digital cameras is that they time and date stamp each image automatically. Providing that you use the right software, you will be able to find images by time and date.

Copy images to removable storage media

Over the past five years, the reliability of most hard drives might make you think that your hard drive will last forever—but they often don't. If you have valuable images, make sure that you are writing them to some kind of removable storage media. Remember: The more images that you save exclusively on your hard drive, the bigger your loss will be if you have a failure. On a frequent basis, copy all of your digital images to removable storage media.

Save original digital camera images

When you first start shooting with a digital camera, you might have a tendency to delete images that aren't up to your visual standards in order to save space. If you have the capability to store them, my suggestion is to keep all of your images. As you learn more about what you can do with these images, you'll find that it can be useful to have a soft, out-of-focus image or an image that is too light or too dark. It costs little to store digital images, so consider keeping them unless they are really bad. Chapter 5, "Getting Images into Shape," shows how you can turn some poor-quality prints into rather astounding images.

In many ways, your original digital files are like the negatives for traditional film. The original images contain the best information and the most information possible about the image that you took. Any time that you run filters and digitally enhance an image, it might look

http://www.muskalipman.com

better, but you are altering and decreasing the original image in one or many ways.

If you store original digital camera images and you edit them, you'll have to store them again. If you store the image in a lossy compressed format such as that used by the JPEG file format, you'll decrease the quality of the image in a manner that is similar to the decreased quality of a photocopy of a copy. Each successive generation loses a bit more of the original image. It's better to store in a nonlossy format such as those used by TIFF, PSD (Photoshop's native file format), or PCX file formats.

If you're using Windows, my recommendation is to use the Windows capability to mark all your original digital camera images as read-only files; treat them as valuable negatives and keep them safe and in their original condition. To set a file attribute to read-only, right-click on the file name in Windows Explorer. You can Ctrl+click to select more than one file if you want. Then select Properties, and on the General tab, click on Read-Only. After you have set a file's attribute to read-only, you will not be able to edit and save the file under the same name without again changing the read-only attribute. You can, however, save a read-only file under a different name.

Consider implementing a backup plan

If you spend many hours digitally editing images, you might want to consider keeping the images in a separate directory that is set up to be automatically backed up weekly or even daily. In the case of a drive failure, you could save yourself many hours of unnecessary work. Most versions of Windows come with a simple, yet useful, backup utility called Microsoft Backup (see Figure 4.2). If this system utility is installed, you can launch it by selecting Start, Programs, Accessories, System Tools, Backup. If this utility isn't installed, you can install it from the Windows Setup tab in the Add/Remove Programs application, located in the Control Panel.

If you're using Windows XP Home Edition, you'll find that Backup is not installed by default, nor is it even listed as an option in the Add/Remove Programs control panel. You'll have to install it manually. Simply insert the Windows XP Home Edition CD-ROM in your CD drive and navigate to the folder \VALUEADD\MSFT\NTBACKUP. Then double-click the NTbackup.msi file to install it.

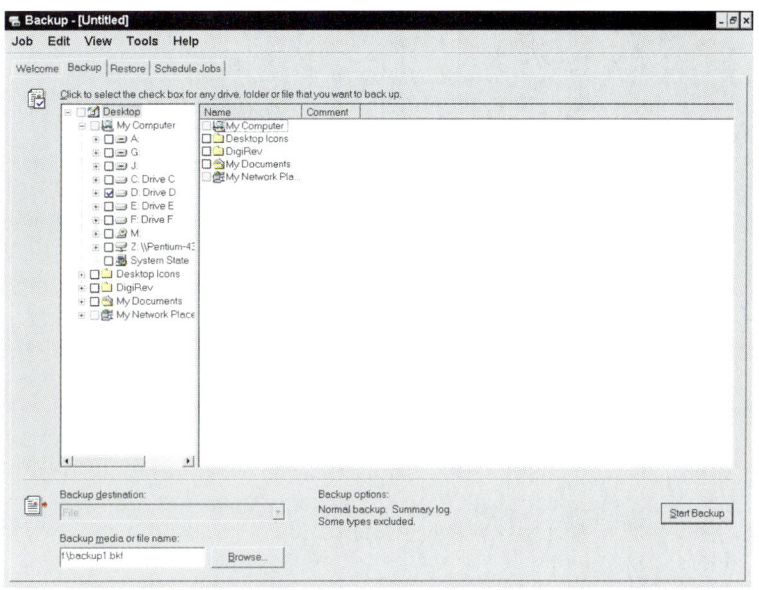

Figure 4.2
It's easy to use Microsoft Backup to back up digital images.

You can also set up Microsoft Backup as a scheduled task by using another system tool called Scheduled Tasks; it, too, can be found on the System Tools menu, or, in the case of some versions of Windows, in the same dialog box that includes Backup. This is a good way to make sure that your backups are done routinely. You might want to schedule backups when you are not using your PC; backups can dramatically decrease the performance of your system if you're trying to make a backup and work on something else at the same time.

Although I back up my hard disks regularly, I'm happier with a semi-automated system that backs up every single data file that has changed six times a day. Backing up these files six times a day is probably closer to underkill than overkill, in my opinion, but it has worked for me for many years. Here's how my system works:

▶ Files are backed up to removable media with plenty of space to hold large image files. I installed hot-swappable hard disk racks in two of my computers so that I can slide a hard disk (contained in a special tray) out of one computer and slide it into the other computer at any time (see Figure 4.3). I have half a dozen trays, which I've filled with older hard disks that I can no longer permanently install in a computer because of their (by today's standards) limited capacity (30 to 60GB). I keep one of these drives installed in my main computer at all times, and my files

Figure 4.3
Removable hot-swappable hard disks make a great daily backup destination.

are backed up to it. If my main computer's primary hard drive fails, or even if the entire computer crashes, I can remove the backup hard drive and slip it into my backup computer and have instant access to the files. You can use other removable media, such as Zip disks, if you like.

▶ I created a tiny text file called a batch file of instructions that Windows can run at my command and back up the files I want to protect to the location I specify. The batch file looks like this:

```
@echo off
echo Copying document files...
xcopy c:\*.doc /s /m j:\ /y
echo Copying Tif files...
xcopy c:\*.tif /s /m j:\backup\image /y
echo Copying Pcx files...
xcopy c:\*.pcx /s /m j:\backup\image /y
echo Copying Psd files...
xcopy c:\*.psd /s /m j:\backup\image /y
```

If you've never worked with batch file instructions before, my little file might look confusing. The echo command tells Windows to display a message on my screen informing me of what's going on. Each of the other lines looks something like this:

```
xcopy c:\*.tif /s /m j:\backup\image /y
```

http://www.muskalipman.com

The previous line simply instructs Windows to copy all the TIF files it can find on drive C:\ to my removable hard disk folder, drive J:\backup\image. The switches /s, /m, and /y tell Windows to search in all the folders underneath C:\ (/s), to copy only the files that have been modified since the last time they were backed up (/m), and to go ahead and overwrite any files that already exist on the destination hard drive (/y).

Similar instruction lines are used to copy all my .doc, .pcx, and .psd files. Other lines in the file (not shown) back up my browser bookmarks, Quicken data files, and a few other important bits of data that change frequently. I use the Windows Scheduler to run this batch file of commands every day at 12:00, 4:00, and 8:00 a.m. and 12:00, 4:00, and 8:00 p.m.

You might find my system to be overkill. Some people back up their files only once a week (or even less often) to a writable or rewritable CD. That's fine if you don't mind the risk of losing an entire week's work (or more). But after you've spent three or four hours working on some images, and then you have to repeat the entire three or four hours of effort, I think you'll find that more frequent backups are well worth the almost negligible effort they take.

NOTE

A retired couple spent a considerable amount of time over a four-month period creating a digital photo album for their children and grandchildren. They used digital images from a digital camera and selected images from CD-ROMs that were created by photo processing services and from scanned photographs. To get the best possible images, the majority of images had to be digitally edited. To protect their work, they used an automatic backup utility to copy all of the edited images to two CD-RWs. One was for the first and third week of each month, and the other was for the second and fourth week of each month. The backups were automatically done at midnight. Fortunately, they did not suffer from a hard drive failure, but on two separate occasions, they did accidentally manage to erase an entire directory of edited images. Because of their backup plan, they did not have to re-edit any images; they just copied the images that they had deleted from their backup files!.

Create extra copies of some images on an organized basis

Although extra copies of images can increase your storage requirements, there are good reasons why you'll want to make them. When you begin working on a project that requires the use of valuable images, think about creating a new directory or folder and making temporary copies of those images you need. This will prevent you

http://www.muskalipman.com

from destroying the original image, should you mistakenly save an edited image over one of the copied, original images. It's also wise to create an extra directory full of copied images when you use batch-processing capabilities. This will, for example, prevent you from accidentally converting an entire directory of high-resolution images into reduced-size JPEG files for a Web page. You might not think that you could make these mistakes, but they really do happen—I've made them myself!

Image management with Windows

Before you consider purchasing image-management software, first look at what you can do with the tools and features that are available with the Windows operating system in all its Windows 98/Me/XP/2000 incarnations.

Using Windows Explorer

Windows Explorer is the main operating system-level tool for managing folders and files. If you don't already know how to use it, you really ought to learn everything you can about it. It will enable you to move, add, copy, delete, and rename files or folders on your system. You can also set file attributes for archiving purposes or protect the files by setting them to be read-only files. From Explorer, you can select an image or images and send them to a mail recipient, to the Windows Desktop, or to another application such as Microsoft Word. Explorer also enables you to drag and drop files and folders onto other applications. Explorer is a powerful tool that accomplishes tasks quickly, but it can also do a tremendous amount of damage if you don't know how to use it and you use it incorrectly.

Now I'm going to show you something that you might not know about Windows Explorer (the following steps are not needed for Windows XP):

1. Right-click a folder in Explorer that contains graphic files, and then click Properties on the shortcut menu.
2. Select the General tab of the Properties dialog box. At the bottom of the tab, click the box to the left of Enable Thumbnail View to put a checkmark in it.
3. Click the OK button. Strangely, you now need to close Explorer or press F5 to update the folder.
4. Reopen Explorer and select the same folder.
5. Select the View menu and then click Thumbnails.

Managing and Storing Images – Chapter 4   91

Under Windows XP, all you have to do is choose View, Thumbnails in either the Explorer or My Computer views.

You now have an Explorer window with thumbnails, as shown in Figure 4.4. What a great way to view a folder with images, right? Well, almost. Explorer suffers from a limited set of file types (BMP and JPEG) that it can preview. It is so limited, in fact, that you might find it isn't worth using at all.

Figure 4.4
You can use Windows Explorer to display thumbnail images.

If you want to find a file or folder, your operating system can help you. Under Windows XP, press F3 to produce the Find Files and Folders dialog box. With earlier versions of windows, you can use the Explorer's Find File or Folder feature—provided that you know something about the name of the file or folder. To find a file, select Tools, Find, Files or Folders, and fill in the fields (see Figure 4.5). You can find a file either by looking for a specific name or file type or searching by date. Windows Explorer is an essential part of the Windows Desktop, and it has made us comfortable with the familiar directory tree view shown in the left pane in Figure 4.5; learn to use it well.

Figure 4.5
You can locate a file with the Find feature in Explorer.

http://www.muskalipman.com

Using image-management utilities

After you see how easy it is to work with directories full of images by using thumbnails, you'll rarely want to do without them. Windows Explorer showed you how useful these thumbnails can be, but you really need to see thumbnails of all images types. It would be nice if we could also see other multimedia file types (such as WAV or MIDI) and video files (such as AVI or MOV). Fortunately, our wish is well within the range of possibility.

Midnight Blue Software's SuperJPG

If a picture is worth a thousand words, a directory of thumbnails is worth millions of words. That's my thought, anyway. If you want to view nearly instantaneous thumbnails of your images, SuperJPG is a good tool to use (see Figure 4.6). This high-performance utility creates a small thumbnail image file for each file in each directory that you want to view with thumbnails. It then saves thumbnails for all the files in a directory as a single file in that directory. After you view a directory, the thumbnails open quickly because they need to be created only once. SuperJPG also enables you to select and view images in a slide show fashion.

Figure 4.6
You can use SuperJPG to view images in a folder.

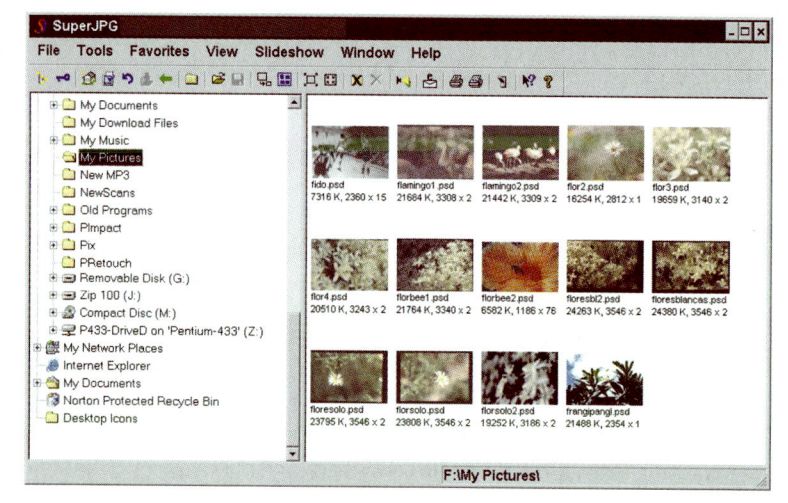

http://www.muskalipman.com

Paint Shop Pro

If you use or are considering using Paint Shop Pro, you are in luck. It offers a superb directory-browsing feature that you can access from Explorer or from the File menu in Paint Shop Pro (see Figure 4.7). Notice the cool status line in the lower-right corner of the window, which displays the exact pixel dimensions and number of colors of the currently selected thumbnail.

Figure 4.7
Paint Shop Pro has a directory browser.

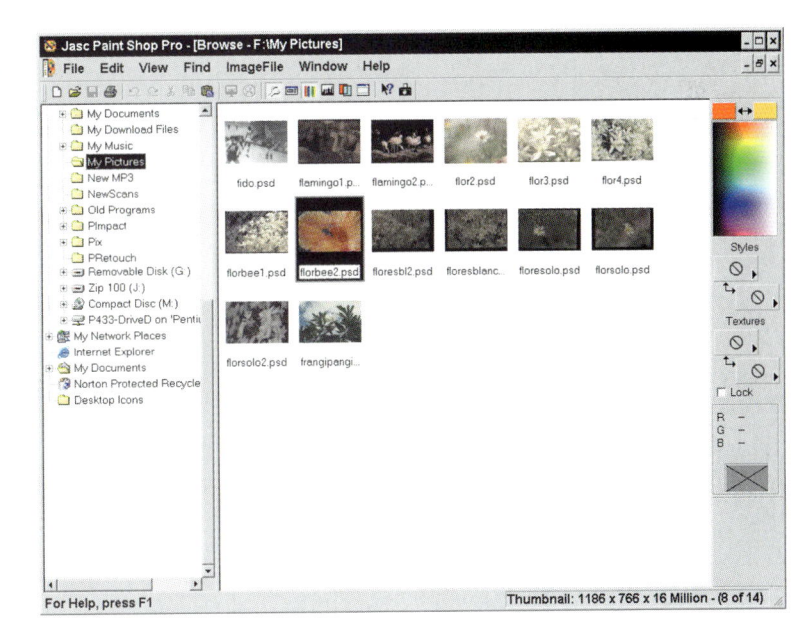

Using consumer-level image editors and project applications

For years, the software industry forced users to be application-centric rather than task-centric. Recently, some terrific products have been introduced that work the way that you want to work instead of making you work the way the applications make you work. These new products tightly integrate all the functionality into a single interface that enables you to go about your tasks as you want.

http://www.muskalipman.com

Roxio's PhotoSuite

One of the most exceptionally well-designed products in any software category I've seen in the past few years is Roxio's PhotoSuite, which it calls the "PC & Internet Photography Power Pack," which it is. PhotoSuite tightly integrates file management with image-editing and project-creation tools. This logical interface makes it easy to get your work done by selecting from the seven workflow steps shown at the top of the interface (see Figure 4.8). You can move between Get, Prepare, Compose, Organize, Share, Print, and Browse with a click of your mouse button. Each time you change steps, all the information, help, and controls that you might need in each step appear on the left side of the screen, as shown in the Prepare step in Figure 4.9.

Figure 4.8
You can organize images easily with PhotoSuite.

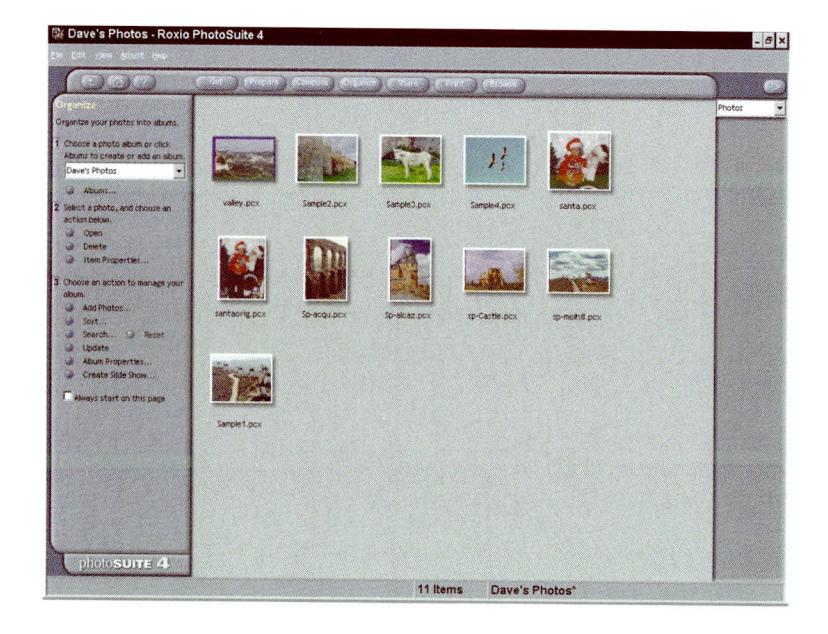

Figure 4.9
You can prepare (edit) an image with PhotoSuite.

Adobe Photoshop Elements

Photoshop Elements is probably the best compromise for those who need a fast, easy-to-use image editor but aren't ready for the steep learning curve of the professional-level product Photoshop. Elements is built on the same foundation as Photoshop and shares many of its menus and features. However, Elements is designed to be much easier to learn than Photoshop. It brims over with helpful wizards, hints, and an onscreen How-To guide that shows you exactly what steps to follow to perform various tasks, such as fix an exposure or remove a color cast.

Elements' File Browser, shown in Figure 4.10, is pretty cool, too, giving you thumbnails of images as well as information about each selected file.

http://www.muskalipman.com

Figure 4.10
Adobe Photoshop Elements has the tools you need to view your images and enhance them with editing techniques.

Although these products offer image-management capabilities complete with thumbnails and the capability to add and use keywords for selection, they are not intended to be used as image-management applications for thousands of images on multiple volumes and removable media. Rather, these products are designed to enable you to complete projects easily by building portfolios of images that you are considering using for specific projects. They also can be used to manage a few directories of files quite effectively.

These consumer-level products might meet all of your image-management requirements. If not, consider using one of the more advanced image-management applications discussed in the next section. They offer many more features and capabilities, and most of them are built on powerful databases that enable tremendous flexibility and speed that are absent from the consumer-level products.

NOTE

A parent took pictures of youth soccer players both on and off the field during the season. He used a film-based camera for most of the action shots and a digital camera for the rest of the pictures. When pictures from the film-based camera were processed, he had his local photofinisher scan them and provide them to him on CD-ROM without regular prints. Using image-management software, he was able to view each photo and enter jersey numbers into a keyword field in an image for any players who were prominent in the picture. At the end of the season, he created a CD-ROM with two slide shows for each of the players. The first show was about the whole team and key events as well as a variety of shots of all the players. The second slide show displayed slides of that specific player only. These CD-ROM shows were easy to create because the parent could do a simple search on the image database by player number and then create a slide show with a simple drag-and-drop operation to the slide show software. Using digital images exclusively and inexpensive CD-ROMs, he was able to provide these shows for little cost.

Using advanced image-management applications

So far in this chapter, you have looked at using Windows Explorer, several inexpensive browsing utilities, and consumer-level image-editing applications to store and manage images. This section introduces you to some more powerful image-management applications that have been designed solely for managing large digital file collections.

Advanced image-management applications to consider

Although each of these applications has been designed differently conceptually, each does the same thing: Each application enables you to create one or more databases that contain a thumbnail image of the digital file types that you select. With each thumbnail, you can optionally store other kinds of information, such as keywords, a description, or other custom fields. Most of these products are built around sophisticated database engines that offer speed and the capability to manage large numbers of images.

If you intend to efficiently manage a large digital image collection, consider using one of the products described next.

http://www.muskalipman.com

Cerious Software Inc.'s ThumbsPlus

Up front, I must tell you that I've never worked for Cerious Software, nor do I know anyone who works there. Okay, I'm in a defensive mode because you might feel that my praise for this product is too great—until you try it. The fact is, ThumbsPlus is one fantastic program. I have used it in many versions and over many, many years; it just gets better and better. I don't know how I could have even begun to manage all the images that I looked at, created, and used in this book without using nearly all the capabilities in ThumbsPlus. For my purposes, it is the perfect application. Okay, enough praise. What can you do with it?

The ThumbsPlus interface looks and works just like Windows Explorer, making it an easy tool to use from the moment that you install it. The left side has a window that shows your system in the familiar tree style, as shown in Figure 4.11. The right side enables you to view thumbnail images of any graphics file in the directory; in fact, ThumbsPlus supports more than 70 file formats. You can navigate through the folders by clicking them to expand or contract them. The third window at the bottom left of the screen is the Task window, which shows when tasks are running, such as the scanning of a folder or volume or a batch-processing task. You can run most of these and other tasks in the background while you continue to use ThumbsPlus's other features.

Figure 4.11
Cerious Software Inc.'s ThumbsPlus shows thumbnails of files in a directory.

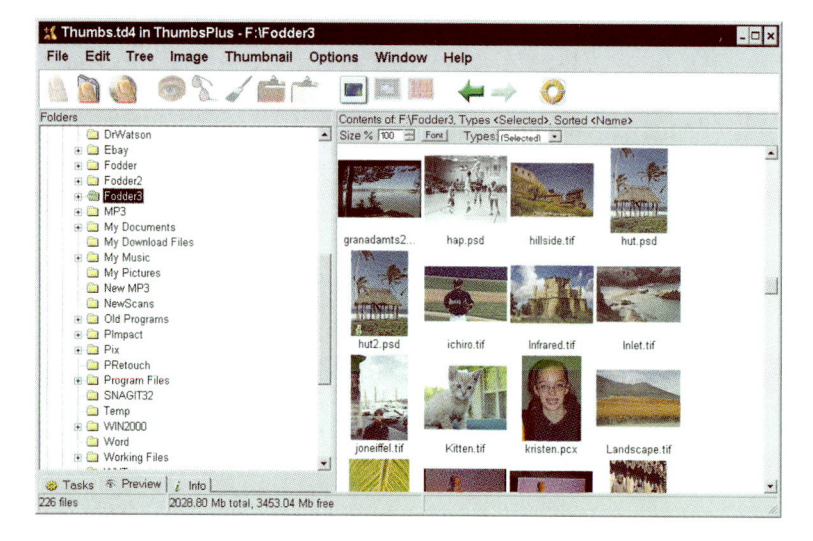

If you have a tendency to scatter image files that you need and use all over your hard drives—which is not unreasonable or uncommon—you can have ThumbsPlus scan your entire system. It will color-code any folders that contain images, enabling you to rapidly browse through all the images on your system.

One of ThumbsPlus's most valuable features is its capability to manage offline CD-ROMs. As you click each directory, the appropriate thumbnails are shown, thus enabling you to search for images without having to insert each CD-ROM. After you find the image or images that you want, you can insert the CD-ROM and get access to the images. This is a real time-saver.

ThumbsPlus's Automatic File Rename feature enables you to automatically rename files in a directory according to the scheme that you choose. This is an excellent tool for renumbering files you created with a digital camera. ThumbsPlus offers many other useful features, including the capability to find similar images, perform a thorough search, run batch processing, create watermarks, build Web pages, create contact sheets, and print catalogs. It also includes a reasonable set of digital image-editing tools. I like this application—a lot!

Extensis Portfolio

Available in versions for both Macintosh OS and Windows, Extensis Portfolio is another exceedingly capable, industrial-strength tool. It is designed for use in workgroups to manage digital media files, including presentations, movies, sound files, and some other common files, such as Microsoft Word documents. Although you certainly can use Portfolio to successfully manage digital media files as a single user, its real strengths and unique features are most apparent when used in a networked environment by multiple people.

In a workgroup setting, catalog administrators can control what each user can do with the images in the catalog. Members of workgroups can simultaneously search, view, and use images from catalogs whose source files are located on one or many network servers, shared volumes, CD-ROMs, or removable drives. Users can even access the Portfolio Server remotely by using a network connection. If you work in a group and need to share files between different group members, this might be the best application for you.

Unlike most image-management applications that work with directory trees, Portfolio's interface has been designed to facilitate working with images by using keywords. Figure 4.12 shows the keyword palette on the left side. How do you use keywords? To manage the chapters in

http://www.muskalipman.com

this book, for example, you could assign chapter numbers to each image. If you want to view, copy, edit, or move images in a specific chapter, you could do so simply by clicking the appropriate chapter keyword. Alternatively, you could use the powerful keyword search facility. This search facility enables you to find all pictures of flamingos, cats, mushrooms, soccer players, or any other topic across all chapters or across just a few chapters—or whatever else you might want.

Figure 4.12
You can search for images by keywords when you're using Extensis Portfolio.

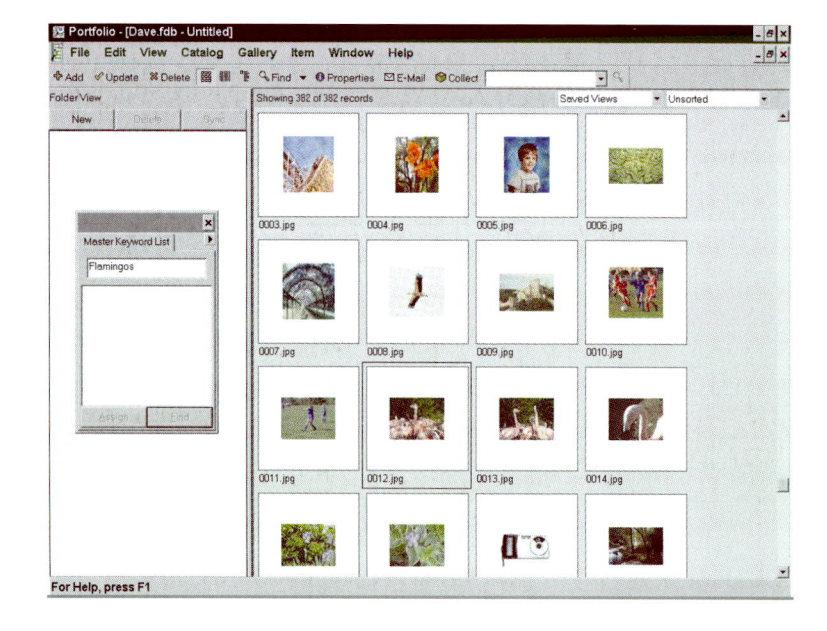

Adobe Photoshop Album

Photoshop Album, introduced in February 2003, is Adobe's solution to the problem of finding, fixing, and sharing all your digital photos and images. Photoshop Album has more in common with Extensis Portfolio (which uses keywords to organize your photos) than with ThumbsPlus (which works with your directory trees). Album uses a tagging system to organize and find your images.

As it gathers images from your hard drive, Album organizes them by date. Then, when you want to look for a particular photo, you can use Timeline and Calendar views to find all the photos taken on a particular day and month. You can further tag images to make it easy to locate favorite people, places, events, or other categories, as shown in Figure 4.13.

Figure 4.13
The tags palette at the left side of the screen lets you designate particular images as belonging in any category you choose.

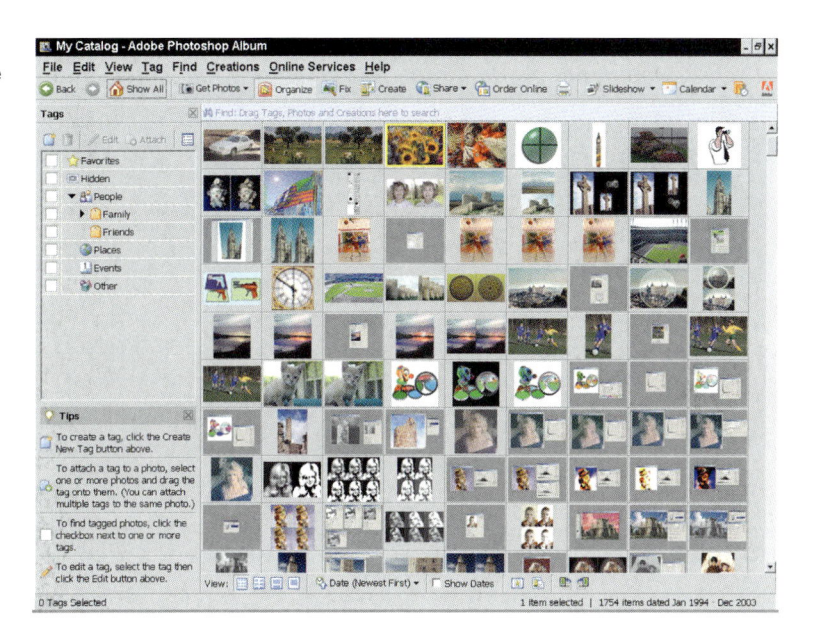

Although Album has tools to fix common problems—such as red-eye or errors in color, contrast, or brightness—it also integrates smoothly with Photoshop Elements when you need to make more advanced corrections. Album also has a backup feature that allows you to store your images on CD or DVD (that is, if you have a compatible burner).

Perhaps the most striking feature of Photoshop Album is the ability to create slide shows in Adobe PDF format, readable by anyone with Adobe Acrobat Reader software. You can include captions, video clips, and background music in your slide shows. It's also possible to order prints, calendars, and other products from online service providers without leaving the Album application.

Ulead's PhotoImpact Album

This is another outstanding cataloging tool, furnished with the PhotoImpact image-editing suite. Indeed, I've been using an older version of PhotoImpact Album (Version 3.02) for more than five years to manage my collection of several hundred thousand images. Later versions removed a couple minor features that I learned to depend on for handling zillions of images, or I would have upgraded long ago. However, for most people, PhotoImpact Album's latest incarnation is easier to use and is a great choice when you don't have quite as many photos to manage as I do. Besides its image-management capability, PhotoImpact is also a good digital image editor, especially for Web graphics.

http://www.muskalipman.com

Other useful things that you can do

Some of the applications discussed in this chapter have other features that might be especially important to you. Several of these features are described in this section.

Create a gallery

The capability to create a gallery is a useful way to select a group of images from multiple locations for different projects and to manage them effectively while avoiding having multiple copies of the same image stored in multiple places. For example, when writing this book, I was able to store all the images used in the book in chapter folders. If I then decide to offer a sampling of the images on a Web site, I can create a gallery for images from two or more chapters. By copying the thumbnails into a gallery, I will always be using the same original images, yet I can see all the images chosen for the Web site in its own gallery (or folder).

Export to HTML

The capability to automatically export thumbnails and images to the Internet can be a valuable feature. Although most image-management applications enable images to be exported as Web pages, some enable more control over the look of the pages than others. Figure 4.14 shows one of many possible Web pages that you can create with ThumbsPlus by using the Webpage Wizard.

Figure 4.14
This Web page was created with ThumbsPlus.

Find duplicates

Finding duplicates is a useful feature that is not available in all image-management applications. If you have a tendency to end up with many copies of the same image scattered about your hard drives and removable media, this feature can help you save disk space. If you have Norton Utilities, you can use the Duplicate File Processing feature in the Space Wizard to accomplish the same task.

Generate slide shows

Another good way to view images in a folder is with a slide show, as described earlier in the section on Photoshop Album. This is a particularly useful feature if you use a digital camera because it's a fun and practical way to view your images in slide show fashion. You can also select just the images that you want to show instead of all files in a folder by clicking the desired thumbnails.

If you have or intend to have a large collection of digital images to store and manage, the tools discussed in this chapter will become some of the more useful and valuable tools you can have. Not only will they take the tedium out of managing your images, but they also can dramatically save you time and help you to safely store your digital assets.

Saving images to removable media

Even if you have lots of available capacity on your PC's hard drive, you'll want to make sure all of your images are backed up or stored on some kind of removable storage media. The questions you must answer are what media to use and how to go about copying all of those images.

Choosing removable storage media

Remember record albums on vinyl? Remember 8-track or cassette tapes? Heck, do you remember any music format prior to MP3s?

What's the point of this stroll down memory lane? As you begin storing your digital images, which will in time become a valuable visual record of your past, make sure that you store them on the most lasting storage media that you can find. By lasting, I mean both in terms of media that will last for a long time and in terms of the technology that you use to store them—and that you will need to play them back. A quick review of the brief history of the PC recalls the moves from 8-inch floppies to $5^1/_4$-inch floppies to $3^1/_2$-inch floppies to CDs and now DVDs and a variety of other media, such as Zip, Jaz,

Clik, DAT tape, and others. All of these different media serve (or served) a purpose; however, most of them are not going to be around for as long as you are likely to need them for image storage and playback. Clik and Jaz, for example, are not seen much anymore, although I still have a Jaz drive I use on an older computer.

My educated guess is that CD technology will be one of the more lasting storage media types that we will see for some time. That's because even the next-generation product, DVDs, is backwardly compatible with existing CD technology. So, as long as DVDs remain popular (and the technology is truly in its infancy), CDs will remain readable on virtually any PC or Mac. DVDs, as the newest thing, should be around even longer.

My suggestion, then, is that if your digital-image collection is valuable to you and will be for many years, you should store your images on CDs or DVDs. At present, CD technology might be your least expensive option, and it's still possible to wait another year or two before moving to DVD. Right now, a single CD can hold up to 700MB of images, which is a considerable number of images. If you are thinking about any other type of storage media, ask yourself whether such a playback device will be available to enable you to access and view your stored images and multimedia files in 5 or even 10 or more years.

Writing image files to CDs

To write files to CDs, you need a CD burner that enables you to write data to a CD as well as read it. Most PCs come equipped with a CD drive; many are also furnished with a CD burner. When using a CD burner, you have a choice of two different kinds of writable CDs—each of which has advantages and disadvantages. CD-Recordable (CD-R) discs enable you to record files on them once and only once. CD-Rewritable (CD-RW) discs, on the other hand, can be written to many times. CD-RWs can function exactly like a regular hard drive or floppy drive, if you use special packet writing software that makes your CD look like just another drive to your PC.

You can use several products to write files to CDs. There are two basic methods of writing files. Most use an Explorer-like window to select files that you want to write to a CD and then have them written in one session. Alternatively, you can set up a CD to function just like a new drive on your PC. This method enables you to write and delete files to the CD as you choose. Both Windows XP and Mac OS X now include CD burning features built-in, so you may want to try them out before moving up to a more fully-featured third-party application.

Tips for storing images on CDs

After you begin writing digital image files to a CD, you might want to consider following one or more of the following tips. These tips will not only minimize the chances of your losing images, but they also make it easier and more enjoyable to use and view your images from CDs.

Save thumbnail images in each folder for quick browsing

To enable quick browsing of CD-ROM directories with thumbnails, consider using a utility such as Midnight Blue Software's SuperJPG. If you write thumbnails to each directory when you write the files to the CD-ROM, you will not need to wait for thumbnails to be created each time you access the folders. This tip can save a considerable amount of time, especially when you have large image files, full CDs, or a slow CD-ROM drive.

Use a combination of CD-RW and CD-R to save images

As your digital image collection grows in size, you might find that your images are most easily found and used when they are categorized into subjects like birds, landscapes, seascapes, family, or other appropriate categories. Then when you need a bird, for example, you can load the CD with a bird directory and choose from all of the bird images.

The problem with this approach is that it takes a long time to get enough images to make a whole directory of birds, frogs, landscapes, seascapes, or whatever categories you choose. One solution to this problem is to use a combination of CD-RWs and CD-Rs. Initially, use the more expensive CD-RWs to collect images. After you have filled several CD-RWs with images, you can then organize all the images into certain categories and write them to a CD-R disc for permanent storage. These stock albums sorted by subject can become exceedingly useful for years.

Make more than one copy of each image

A CD can hold more than 900 700KB images (like those from a 2-megapixel digital camera). If you filled your CDs and something happened to one of them, you would lose all 900 images. Obviously, one way to help prevent this from happening is to make one or more copies of your images on additional CDs. If you have a CD burner plus an additional CD drive, you can copy one CD onto a second CD.

Alternatively, you can duplicate 50 percent of the images on one disc onto the next disc that you write. For illustration purposes, assume that you sequentially number your directories; directories 101 through 130 contain about 900MB of images. On the first CD, you would copy 600MB of images from directories 101 to 120. Next, copy directories

111 to 130 to a second CD. Directories 121 to 140 would be copied to a third CD, and so on. This approach minimizes the number of images that you need to leave on your hard drive, and it enables you to have two copies of each of your images—one on each of two CDs. Using this approach, you won't need to have two CD drives to successfully make copies of your files.

Make multiple copies of your "best images"

Each time you write a collection of images to a CD, make a new directory on your hard drive for the best images from that image collection. Then, on each successive CD, add several of these "best of volume" directories to the new CDs. This strategy not only protects your best images by having multiple copies of them on different CDs, but it also makes it easier for you to access these images. Using an image-management application that creates thumbnail images, you can easily browse through a large collection and create a "best of volume" collection.

Label each disc with a unique label and write it on the face of the disc

Before you write images to a new CD, make sure that you label the disc with a unique disc label using your CD writing software. Unique labels enable you to catalog offline CDs in an image-management application. Without these labels, you won't be able to differentiate one CD from another, so you won't be able to store the thumbnails as an offline image collection.

Using photofinishing services

One of the easiest ways to get your images written to a CD is to use one of the many digital image-processing services offered by a wide variety of photo labs. Many of these services not only provide you with a CD with your images, but they also provide a paper-based color printout showing each image on the CD, as well as software with thumbnails that enable you to browse all the images easily and quickly.

Some of the more expensive services, such as the KODAK Photo CD service, provide multiple resolutions of each of your images. To learn more about these services, see Chapter 3, "Turning Photographs into Digital Images."

This chapter concludes Part I, "Starting with a Few Good Digital Images," in which you learned about digital cameras, how to take better pictures, ways to convert photos into digital images, and how to manage and store images. Part II, "Transforming Ordinary Images into Extraordinary Ones," begins with a chapter on how to get your images into shape.

Part II
Transforming Ordinary Images into Extraordinary Ones

5	Getting Images into Shape	109
6	Performing Digital Imaging Magic	129
7	Filtering for Special Effects	153

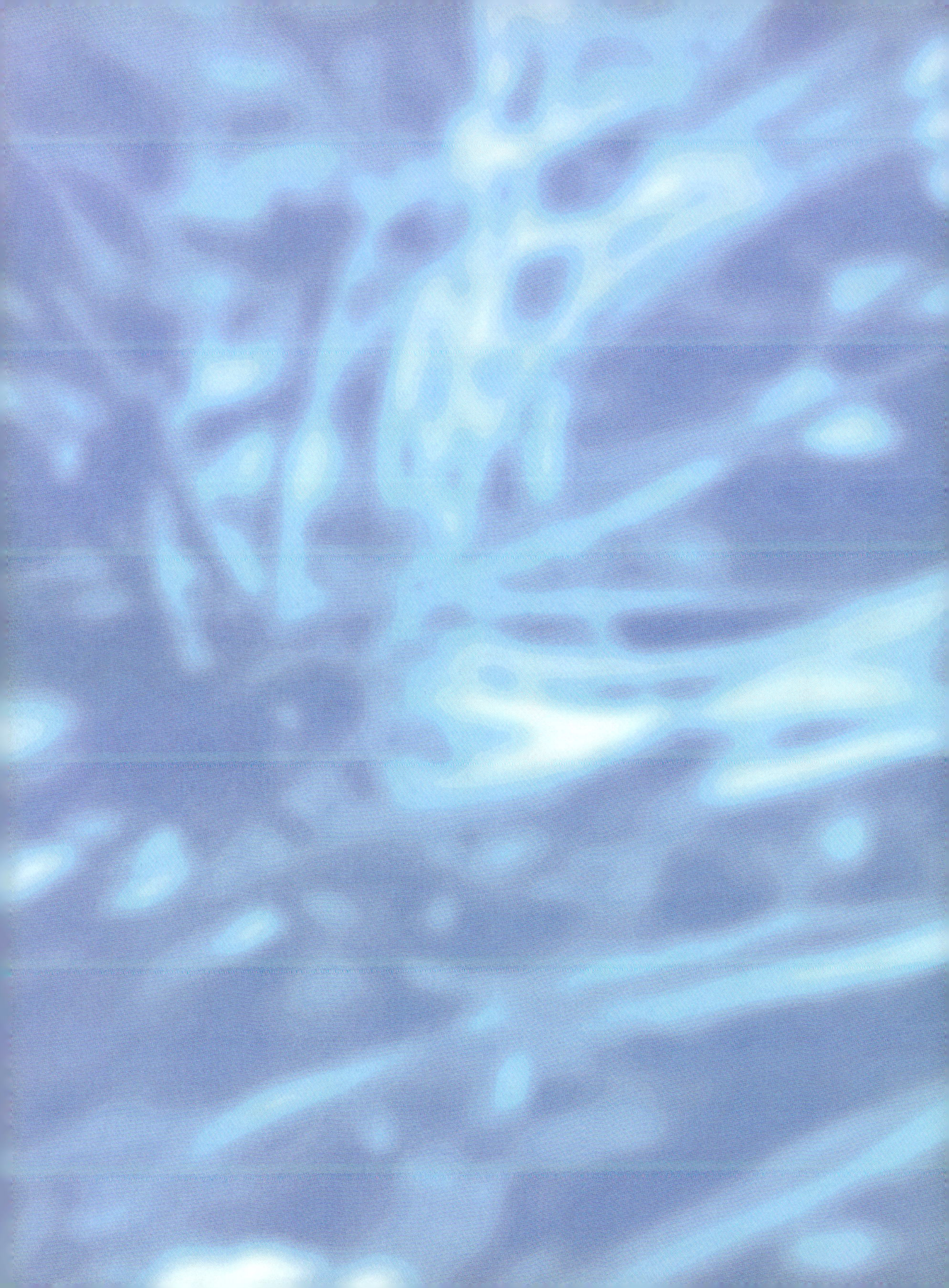

5
Getting Images into Shape

Practice makes perfect. However, the moment you enter the world of digital imaging, you will soon realize that the "perfect" picture is a relative term. After you've taken a great picture, your goal will be to take a better one the next time. And, as you gain experience, you'll see that a perfect picture has to be perfect for its intended use, too. A digital image that makes a perfect print on a color inkjet printer will not make a perfect image for a Web page, nor will it make a perfect image for use as an attachment to e-mail. So exactly what is the perfect image? Besides showing the perfect subject that is well composed, our elusive "perfect" picture ought to do the following:

- ▶ Be free from dust, scratches, tears, wrinkles, stains, smears, or other defects (if the image was scanned).
- ▶ Look good. That is, it should have a wide tonal range, the colors should be correct, and the image should be sharp, if that was the intent.
- ▶ Be the right size, both in terms of the aspect ratio (that is, horizontal or vertical orientation) and the physical size, which can be expressed in inches, pixels (or dots per inch), or a combination of the two.
- ▶ Be saved in an appropriate file format so that it can be viewed or used in the intended applications.
- ▶ Be saved in a file that is the right size. If the image is to be downloaded from a Web site, it might require file compression, which involves a trade-off between image size and image quality so that an optimal size must be chosen.

In summary, we will consider a digital image to be in shape when it looks its best and the file is the right size and in an appropriate format. When considering all of these variables, you can understand why this chapter is titled "Getting Images into Shape." The tools that you use to do this work all loosely fall into the category of digital image editors. Not only are there a tremendous number of these tools, but they also vary in their capabilities and in the quality of the results that they produce. The purpose of this chapter is two-fold:

- ▶ To give you an idea of the kinds of tools that are available and how they can help you get your images into shape
- ▶ To help you find one or several tools that will suit your purposes

Correcting imperfect images

To learn about digital image editors, we'll walk through the process of getting three sample images into shape. The three images we will work on are quite different in both their subject matter and in their original form.

The first image shown in Figure 5.1 is of downtown Chapel Hill, North Carolina. It was taken with a digital camera while waiting for the streetlights to change. The light level was low enough to require a tripod, but one was not used. The image was taken out-of-level; that is, the imaginary horizon is not parallel with the top and bottom of the frame. The picture is underexposed, and it is hard to see much of the detail in the buildings. Sadly, a few of the more dominant features of the image include the traffic lights and the wires that hold them up. We'll refer to this poorly taken picture as the "Chapel Hill" image.

Figure 5.1
Here's a poorly taken picture of downtown Chapel Hill.

The second image, shown in Figure 5.2, was made by scanning a 6 × 6-inch photograph that was taken with a medium-format camera in typical English weather with heavy, gray, overcast lighting. We will refer to this image as the "castle" image. The intent is to turn this image into a high-quality image that will make an 8 × 8-inch print on photo-quality paper. If we are successful, it'll turn out to look like a professionally taken photograph that we will be pleased to frame and hang on a wall. We want to see more detail in the shadows of the castle wall, more of the bright green colors in the plants, and the golden yellow glow of sunset that existed when this picture was taken.

Figure 5.2
Here's a "not-quite-right" print of Warwick Castle in England.

Our final picture is of a beloved grandmother taken in 1924. Figure 5.3 shows the classic, old-time, hand-printed, hand-signed, sepia-colored print. Besides a few spots and crinkles, the 5 × 7-inch print is in relatively good shape, with the exception of a horrible tear near her forehead. Because this was a special lady, we want to make a fine-art print of this image on high-quality art paper if we can repair and improve the image. Because we have a 5 × 7-inch print, we'll plan to scan it and then make an 8 × 10-inch print so that it will fit in a standard frame. You still aren't sure what we are going to do with that tear near her forehead, are you?

Figure 5.3
Here's a damaged picture of a grandmother, taken in 1924.

Before we get started on the images, we need to select a tool to do the work. Just as all photofinishers are not created equal, nor are all digital image editors created equal. For years, Adobe's Photoshop has been, and still remains, the ultimate digital image-editing application. Photoshop is such an exceptional product that it can command a price approaching $600. If you want the best digital image editor and the best results, this application is the one to get.

In the same league as Photoshop are Corel Photo-Paint, procreate Painter, and Jasc Software Paint Shop Pro, all of which sell for several hundred dollars less than Photoshop while offering many of the same features in addition to some unique ones.

TIP

For years, Jasc Software's Paint Shop Pro has stood out as one—if not the very best—of the shareware products in the software industry. Paint Shop Pro has become a powerful image editor (it also includes Animation Shop) that compares well with many of the capabilities offered by Photoshop, Photo-Paint, and Painter, and it is much easier to use. Even more significantly, many of the Photoshop plug-in vendors are now making sure that their add-on filters work with Paint Shop Pro because it dramatically lowers the cost of using their products by about $500. Paint Shop Pro is available as a shrink-wrapped product at major retail stores and most Internet and catalog retailers. It is an excellent product and a great value for digital camera owners.

http://www.muskalipman.com

An even lower-priced group of editors includes MGI Software's PhotoSuite, Adobe Photoshop Elements, and Ulead Systems PhotoImpact. Any of these tools enables you to do a great job on all three images we are about to work on and most of the images that you will work with in the future.

The common characteristic of all of these packages is that they are professional tools that enable you to make many modifications to your digital images—if you know how to use them. These editors aren't necessarily easy applications to learn to use, but after you learn how to use them, you'll be able to get excellent results from your images.

For each of the three imaging examples, I will refer to generic tool features that are typically available in all of the applications in the first group and in some of the second group mentioned so far. If I use a unique feature or filter to perform an action, I will tell you what application I used to do it. For those of you who are curious, I happen to be a Photoshop addict and use it on practically every image that I work on. However, I use many other tools when they offer something unique or can produce a better result than Photoshop. The following steps show general techniques only to let you know what can be done, rather than the step-by-step instructions you would need to carry out the task.

Fixing an image taken with a digital camera

Let's start on the Chapel Hill image first:

1. First we need to straighten the photo by correcting the tilt. Most image editors have a Rotate command. In Photoshop, you can use Image, Rotate Canvas, Arbitrary, and rotate the image counterclockwise about 2.5 degrees. Now the horizon is level, and the steeple no longer leans like the famed Leaning Tower of Pisa.

2. Using a constrained aspect ratio of 10 × 8 (this is the ratio of width to height of our intended final print), select the part of the picture that you want to appear in the final image, as shown in Figure 5.4. In Photoshop, you would do this by selecting the Rectangular Marquee tool, choosing the Fixed Aspect Ratio style in the Options bar, and then entering 10 in the Width box and 8 in the Height box. Then crop the image and save the file in an uncompressed format, such as TIFF.

http://www.muskalipman.com

Figure 5.4
Here we select a region of the straightened image for the final print.

3. To add some depth to the image, we need to adjust the highlights and shadows. We'll do this with the Curves tool, found in most image editors. Photoshop's version is shown in Figure 5.5. The Curves dialog box enables you to adjust the tonal range of an image with great precision. In this case, we will brighten the face of the building so that we can see more detail. We also want the street to be a bit lighter gray than it is.

Figure 5.5
Here we're adding tonal range with the Curves tool.

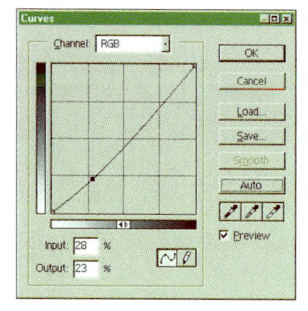

4. Next, we must get rid of the streetlights and wires. To do this, we use a simple tool called the Rubber Stamp or Clone tool found in most image editors. This tool is like a clone brush, which allows you to paint one part of an image onto another part. In other

http://www.muskalipman.com

words, you simply copy sky over the streetlights and wires. When you get to the buildings, you copy bricks over the top of the streetlights and wires that you want to remove. You can see this being done in Figure 5.6.

Figure 5.6
Here we're removing the ugly streetlights and wires with the Rubber Stamp tool.

5. Because the sky is overly light and void of much character, we'll select it with the Magic Wand tool (a selection tool that grabs all adjacent pixels of a similar color and brightness as the pixel you click) and then use the Curves tool again to add tonal range to the sky.
6. Create a poster-like look with an edge-enhancing filter in your image editor. I used Photoshop's Poster Edges filter.

We have a nearly perfect image—one that would print on photo-quality paper on a good inkjet printer in a way that would rival a one-hour photo lab print. That wasn't so hard, was it? Now we need to transform this image into something more artsy. That is the subject of Chapter 7, "Filtering for Special Effects," so for now we are just going to apply a filter, the result of which will look like Figure 5.7. The whole process so far has taken less than 10 minutes, with the printing taking another 5 minutes. Already we have a fine-art print on watercolor paper that is suitable for framing!

http://www.muskalipman.com

Figure 5.7
Here's the completed image with the Poster Edges filter applied.

Fixing a scanned image

Okay, that's one photo fixed. Now, let's start on the castle image. This image was shot in the golden glow of sunset; therefore, it has a warm glow that we need to be careful to bring back into our final image along with additional detail in the castle wall.

1. To see more detail in the castle wall, we need to adjust the image so that it shows a wider tonal range in the shadow areas. All image editors have a control to adjust the brightness and contrast of an image. To do this automatically in Photoshop, select Image, Adjustments, Auto Levels. Suddenly it's possible to see the texture of the castle walls, window details, and even more of the plants.

2. To put the warm golden glow of the sunset back into the image, use the image editor's color correction tools. In Photoshop, select Image, Adjustments, Color Balance, and move the red/cyan, blue/yellow, or green/magenta sliders to add some yellow to produce the golden glow, as shown in Figure 5.8.

http://www.MUSKALIPMAN.com

Figure 5.8
The Color Balance slider can put the golden color of sunset back into the image.

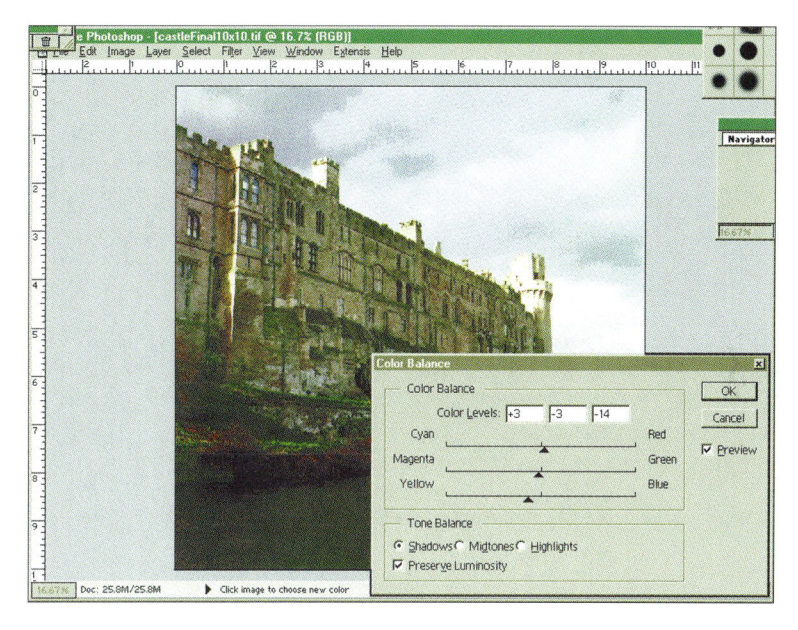

3. Finally, we'll strengthen the definition of the edges by selecting Filter, Sharpen, Sharpen Edges, which results in the final image shown in Figure 5.9.

Figure 5.9
Here's the final corrected castle image—better but not great!

http://www.muskalipman.com

At this point, we can see the detail in the castle wall that we wanted, and we've returned some of the golden glow from the sunset that we had hoped to get. What do you think of the image now? There is no question that it is better than it was—but it is surely not going to be one of my favorite images. Our lesson here is this: Not all images can be turned into good images. Our initial objective of turning this into a print that is good enough to frame and hang on a wall is not likely to be met, especially because we had to double the size of the image. There is a limit to the magic that you can perform with a digital image editor. If you want a really good image, you need to begin with a really good photograph or digital image.

Fixing a damaged photograph

Now let's see how we can grow some hair back on Grandma's head. Believe it or not, this will be the easiest of the three images to fix.

1. First, let's get rid of that awful tear in the photograph surface. Use the magnifier to enlarge the area of the tear, as shown in Figure 5.10. Then, using the Rubber Stamp tool, select a part of the image that matches the area that needs to be filled in. Carefully copy one part of the image over the tear until most of the tear is gone, leaving a part of it where we need to put hair. While we are at it, let's cover up all the other spots and imperfections on the image in both the light and dark areas until no flaws remain. We'll also replace a few dark spots on her dress with part of the clean dress.

Figure 5.10
You can fix the tear in the photo with the Rubber Stamp tool.

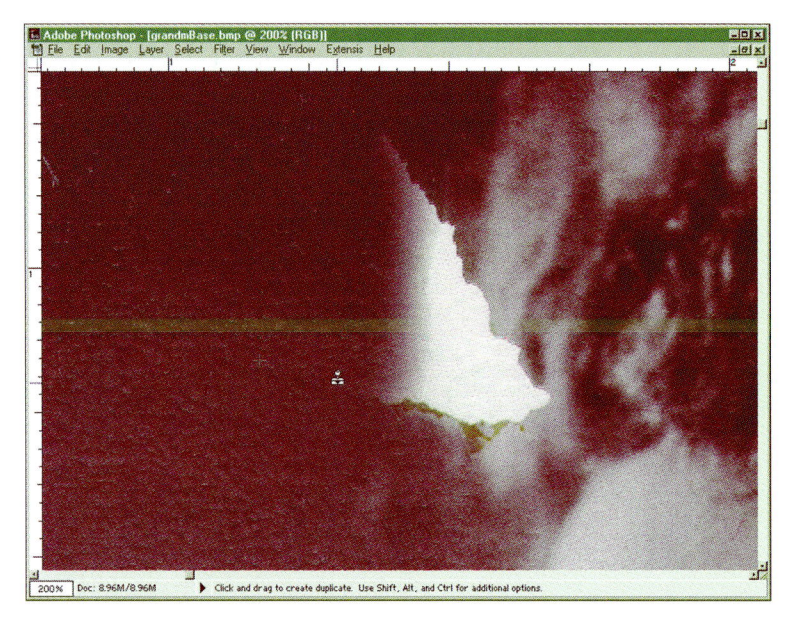

Getting Images into Shape – Chapter 5   **119**

2. Next, let's put some hair back where it needs to be. Once again, we'll use the Rubber Stamp tool. In this instance, select part of Grandma's hair that looks like it could work where the tear was. Copy and mix the hair with the Rubber Stamp tool until her hair looks like it did in 1924 (see Figure 5.11). Looks better than her beautician could have done, don't you think?

Figure 5.11
The hair replacement is complete.

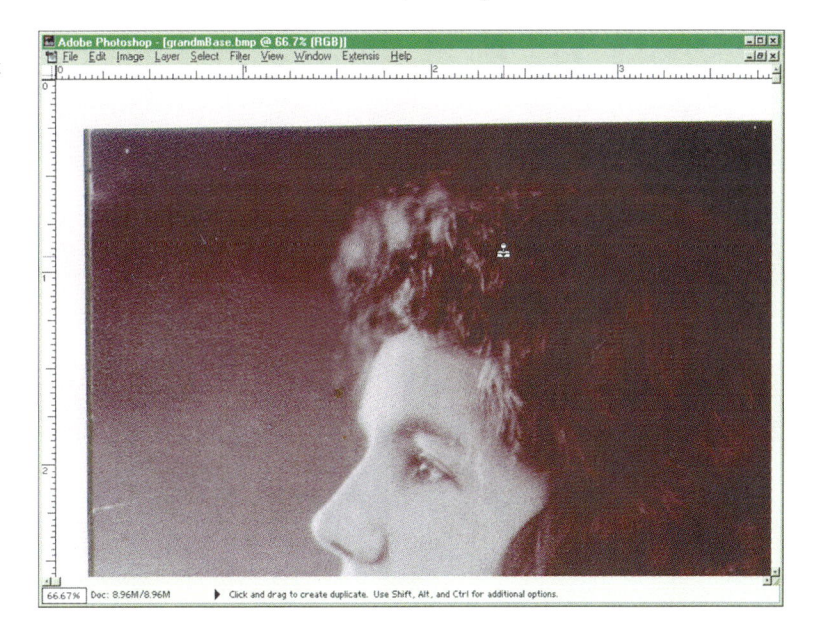

3. Now we need to clean up the edges by selecting an area within the photograph that is rectangular and then copying that selected part onto a new white image that is a half-inch wider and taller so that we have a quarter-inch border all around, as shown in Figure 5.12. As one final detail, select the border with the Magic Wand tool and then use the Eye Dropper tool (or whatever tool your image editor uses to sample a color in the image for use as the foreground "painting" color) to select an almost-white color to use as a fill for the border. The pure-white border is too bright.

http://www.muskalipman.com

Figure 5.12
The grandmother image has been restored.

4. As an optional step, you can elect to give Grandma a little warmer color by applying a preset duotone color scheme, available with most image editors, like the one shown in Figure 5.13. (In Photoshop, you must be using a grayscale image. Then choose Image, Mode, Duotone, click the Load button, and choose one of the many preset duotone presets that Photoshop provides.) I printed this image on a piece of Digital Art Supplies' canvas paper. It looks wonderful framed.

Figure 5.13
Here's the result of applying a preset duotone color scheme.

http://www.muskalipman.com

At this point, you are probably becoming a believer in the awesome capabilities of digital image-editing software to make an image look better. You have also learned how important it is to have a good image to start with. Now, if you recall, at the beginning of this chapter we agreed that an image is not "in shape" until it both looks good and the digital file is the right size and in an appropriate format. To get the file into shape, we have to know how the image is going to be used, which in turn determines the file format, file size, image resolution, and other characteristics. We'll cover all of that in the next section.

Selecting the proper file characteristics

Why do we care so much about getting digital files into shape if the image looks good on our computer screen? That is a good question, and it is worthy of a complete answer. Honestly, in many cases, you won't care, but in other cases, you'll care a whole lot!

Suppose that you have selected 20 digital images that you took with a digital camera. You want to use those images to create a PC screen-based slide show. The reason for the show and the importance of the images compels you to try to make this the best show possible. Knowing that you are going to be presenting on a high-resolution (1280 × 1024 pixels or greater) projection device, you might want to use carefully edited, uncompressed images at the full 1280 × 1024 image resolution. This means that the JPEG files that your digital camera created must be converted, and you will need to edit each image to make it perfect.

Now suppose that you want to e-mail that same slide show. Those huge, high-resolution images will overload almost anyone's e-mail. Even if the recipient has a broadband connection rather than dial-up, he might use a mailbox that limits the size of the e-mails he receives. Therefore, you'll have to reduce the images and possibly convert them to a file type that allows the file size to be reduced via a compression technique. How about taking those same images and putting them on a Web page? You can begin to understand why it can be so important to get your images into optimal shape for their intended purposes.

To get your image files into shape, you might need to complete one or more of the following steps:

▶ If the image is to be digitally edited, you should first save it to a lossless file format, such as that used by the TIFF file format.

http://www.muskalipman.com

- Straighten the image if it needs it, or rotate the image if it is in the wrong orientation.
- Crop the image if it needs it.
- You might need to change the bit depth, either to reduce the file size (by using fewer colors) or to increase the quality of the picture (show more colors). Bit depth relates to the number of allowable colors. The most common bit depths are 8-bit, 16-bit, and 24-bit images, which allow 256, 65,536, and 16.7 million colors, respectively.
- Depending on what you are going to do to the image and how you will use it, you might need to set the image size (in inches or pixels) and change the resolution or dpi.
- After you have completed the editing, you need to save the image to the appropriate file format. If it is to be a compressed file format, you need to adjust the level of compression for optimal viewing quality and file size.

So far in this section, you've learned about the kinds of things that you might need to do to get your image files into shape. Now we'll look at how you might actually go about doing these things. Before spending money for more software, look carefully at the software you currently own to see whether it can do what you need to do. Most graphics applications enable you to convert file types simply by using either File, Save As or File, Export. This makes saving a JPEG file as a TIF (or vice versa) easy.

Changing bit depth is equally easy. Just look for a menu item that says something like Bit Depth or Image Mode and make the changes. If you are changing from a lossless format to a lossy format, you'll want to be able to see the relationship between file size and image quality.

Using software to automate image correction

We've covered how you can use a digital image editor to fix an imperfect image. We've also looked at how to resize a digital image file and save it to a different file format. In each of these cases, we've done all of the work manually, in a step-by-step fashion—visually checking and refining adjustments in each step. This process not only requires a good digital image editor and the skill to use it, but it also takes time—often more time than we want to spend.

When your image collection grows and you begin to use your images more frequently, you might find yourself with numerous images that you'd like to get into shape for a specific purpose. In the next two sections, we'll look at two different approaches for getting your work done easily and quickly. The first approach involves using software with presets, and the second approach has to do with automatically processing an entire group of digital images.

> **NOTE**
>
> A homebuilder needed to provide a progress report to the future home-owners, who lived overseas. Using an expensive digital camera, he took 20 images of the work done on the house and landscape. Some of the images were not as good as the homebuilder had hoped. Using an image editor, he was able to dramatically improve the quality of the images, as well as reduce their file size and change their file format to make them quicker to send via e-mail. The corrected images were sharper, with more tonal range, and the color was improved—all of which made his work look better.

If you'd like to have advanced capabilities but you don't want to buy Photoshop or another "Photoshop plug-in compatible" application, consider Auto F/X Corporation's AutoEye, which works with Photoshop as a plug-in or as a standalone product.

AutoEye examines and then automatically enhances digital images, providing full-spectrum color correction, increased color vibrancy, contrast and sharpness, and rebuilt detail. AutoEye enables you to work in one of two modes. In the manual mode, you can select from presets and then manually fine-tune those adjustments, as shown in Figure 5.14. Alternatively, you can drag-and-drop a few files from your desktop onto the AutoEye icon and have the preselected preset enhancement be automatically applied to the images in batch-fashion. AutoEye is an excellent product to use to enhance digital images taken with a digital camera. Just be mindful that even with a product like AutoEye, you can make the images look only so good. Digital cameras that store images in a lossy format create images that will have some loss of detail that can't be fully restored. AutoEye will help make most of your images look better, more often than not with little effort.

Figure 5.14
Here's Auto F/X Corporation's AutoEye digital image enhancement screen.

> **NOTE**
> After making a three-week tour of Europe, a retired couple wanted to share some of the images from their trip with friends and family. After signing up for free photo space in a picture-sharing community, they needed 30 JPEG images to put on the site. After the couple selected and scanned 30 photographs, they used a simple image editor to enhance and convert the images so that they looked good and would download from the Internet quickly. They then sent an e-mail to friends and family inviting them to view the images.

Batch processing

In the prior two sections, we looked at a number of applications that enable you to quickly enhance your images and save them in an appropriate file—one image at a time. In this section, we'll look at how you can use Photoshop and PhotoImpact to batch process selected images automatically.

http://www.muskalipman.com

For example purposes, let's assume that we have a directory of 40 images that were taken with a digital camera at a 1600 × 1200 resolution, and we want to put the images on a Web page. We want to reduce all of the images to fit within a 640 × 640 pixel space, and we want to digitally enhance each image before saving all images as optimized JPEG files in a separate directory. If you had to do this to each of the 40 images manually, you would surely go crazy—at least, I would.

With Photoshop, it is nearly as easy to perform the necessary steps on 40 images as it is on a single image. From the Action dialog box shown in Figure 5.15, you click on the palette menu button (the triangular arrow) and select New Action. Then type in the name of your action. Actions are macros, which means they record all of the steps that you take until you turn the recording off. After our action has been set up and the record facility is turned on, we perform all the necessary steps to complete the first image. Then we turn off the Action recorder.

Figure 5.15
Here we're using Photoshop's Action recording capability.

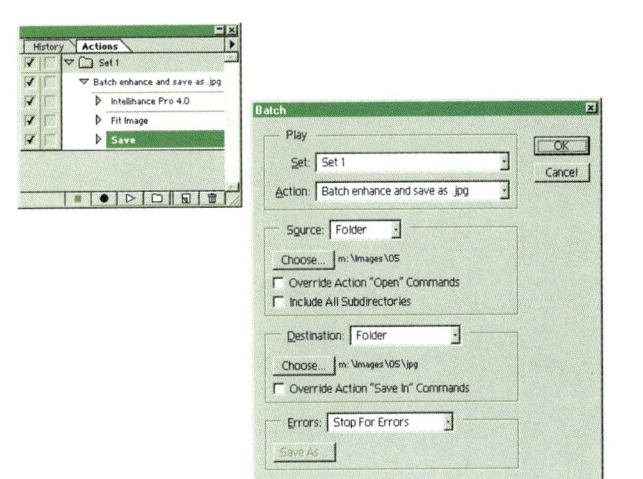

To run our new action against the other 39 images, select File, Automate, Batch to get the Batch dialog box. In this dialog box, you select the action that you want to use, the Source folder containing the original images, and the Destination folder where you want the enhanced images to be saved. To start the automatic processing, you click on the OK button, and the software does the work for you—quickly and error free!

If you work in a production environment or if you need to process large numbers of digital images, there is no equal to the batch-processing capabilities found in Photoshop. Not only can you apply all of the actions that are found in Photoshop, but you can also apply any of the actions that might be available with plug-ins.

One other application (that costs hundreds of dollars less than Photoshop) that can help you do more with your images in less time is Ulead's PhotoImpact. To accomplish our task of enhancing and converting 40 images for a Web page with PhotoImpact, we would have to run the PhotoImpact Batch Manager, as shown in the menu in Figure 5.16, three times—once for each step. For example, to reduce each image to fit within a 640 × 640 pixel space, we could use the Batch Manager to apply the Format, Image Size command. Likewise, we would have to again run the Batch Manager for the Format, Auto-Process command to enhance the image. Again, we would need to run a batch process to convert the images to an optimal JPEG compression level. For the conversion step, we would use the Batch Convert dialog box that is shown in Figure 5.17. Unlike the Batch Manager, which can perform actions only on files that are open in the workspace, Batch Convert enables you to select both a source folder and a destination folder. You can also select from a variety of JPEG compression presets or define your own.

Figure 5.16
This shows PhotoImpact's Batch Manager.

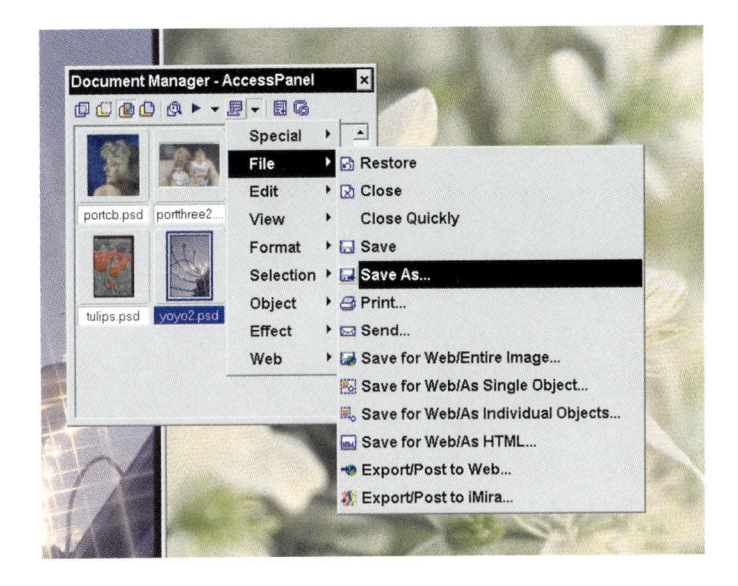

Figure 5.17
We can use PhotoImpact's Batch Convert to convert a directory of images to JPEG images.

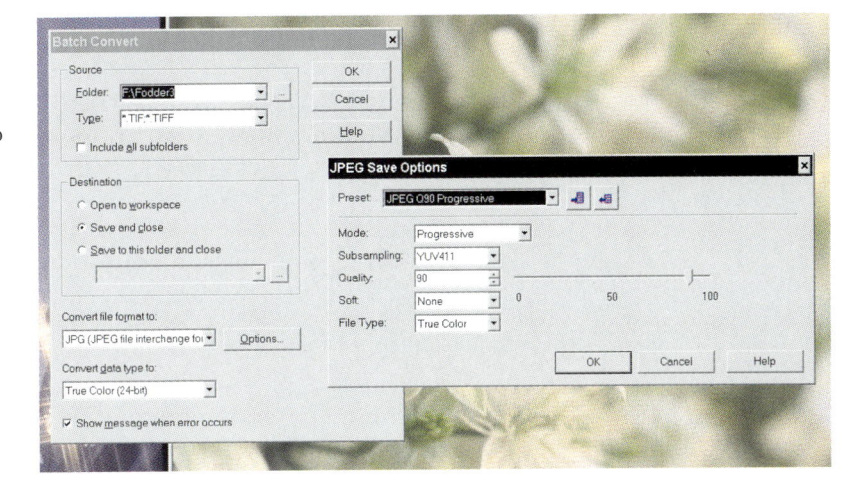

Until you find yourself needing to perform repetitive steps on many digital images, you might not see the value in the batch-processing capabilities discussed in this section. However, when you are faced with such a task, you will want Photoshop, PhotoImpact, or some software that can do the work for you error free.

http://www.muskalipman.com

> **NOTE**
>
> A photographer who wants to post 60 digital images to a Web site needs to convert high-quality scans of his photographs into good "Web-quality" digital images. To accomplish the work, he needs to reduce file size, change image resolution, change bit depth, resize images, and convert the images to the JPEG format with the best balance between file size and image quality for each individual image. To avoid making this a tedious and time-consuming job, the photographer uses the action-recording feature in Photoshop while he completes the first image. Then, with the batch-processing feature, he runs the macro against the selected directory of images and has the work all done automatically. The finished images are written to a second directory. The whole process took just a few minutes instead of hours, and with no errors.

Now that your images (both the actual image as well as the image file) are in shape, you are ready to continue transforming your ordinary images into extraordinary ones. In Chapter 6, "Performing Digital Imaging Magic," you'll learn about many other ways to change your images from ordinary ones to extraordinary ones.

http://www.muskalipman.com

6
Performing Digital Imaging Magic

Welcome to the chapter on performing digital imaging magic. In this chapter, you will not learn how to pull a rabbit out of a hat, but you will learn how you can create a digital image of yourself pulling a rabbit out of a hat. Alternatively, you might want to show yourself pulling an elephant out of a hat, or maybe you want an image of a rabbit pulling you out of a hat! If that is not magic enough, then just wait. We'll also create three images that will leave you thinking that your imagination is the only limit to how you can transform digital images.

Just as a magician must learn the secrets of the trade, you must learn the secrets of digital imaging. To digitally edit an image, you must first have a digital image editor of one kind or another. Many software applications offer digital editing capabilities. Each one has strengths and limitations. Depending on your skill level and your intended use, one application might be better for you than another. The goal, then, is to determine which product is best for you. To help you make this determination, we'll do three things in this chapter:

▶ Briefly look at four categories of digital image-editing tools

▶ Learn eight of the more basic, yet powerful, digital image-editing techniques, which will give you an excellent idea of what you can do to an image

▶ Complete all the necessary hands-on work to create three different images with three different image editors

http://www.muskalipman.com

After you finish this chapter, you should not only have significant insight into the magic of digital imaging, but you should also have a better idea of which application or applications will be most appropriate for your use. Most important, though, you'll learn what you can do to digitally transform your digital images.

Choosing a digital image editor

First, what is a digital image editor? Simply defined, it is a software application that enables you to edit a digital image on a pixel-by-pixel basis to enhance, alter, or transform it into the image that you want it to be. The number and kinds of things that you can do to an image, as you will see, are virtually endless. Most of this digital transformation occurs as a byproduct of running complex mathematical algorithms on the digital image.

One of the major differences between various applications for digitally manipulating images is the amount of control, or lack of control, they provide to the user. To some degree, the more control provided to the user, the more difficult the application can be to learn how to use. The corollary: Applications that provide less control are generally easier to learn how to use, but they are less capable of doing as much as those that provide more control. Thus, the tradeoff you must consider is the classic case of ease-of-use versus more powerful capabilities.

Let's look at a few image editors. The following list should not be considered to be a complete list of competitive products, nor should it be viewed as a product evaluation or review. Rather, it is a list of applications widely recognized to perform well and produce excellent results. The purpose of the list is to show the kinds of products that you can purchase and the wide range of features that these products offer. We'll review applications in the following four categories:

▶ Category I: Professional-level digital image editors

▶ Category II: Advanced consumer or business-use digital editors

▶ Category III: Consumer-level digital imaging applications

▶ Category IV: Professional-level plug-ins

Professional-level digital image editors

If you intend to become a master of illusion and create digital masterpieces, you need powerful tools as well as expertise. The three products in this first group offer you as much power as you will find in any product. These are the "best of the best."

Adobe Photoshop

Photoshop is unquestionably the professional image editor's choice. It is the best of all the image editors in terms of breadth and depth of features. If you can't do it in Photoshop, it can't be done. Photoshop is also the most expensive and the most difficult image editor to learn how to use. Adobe assumes that Photoshop's users are professionals and, therefore, offers few presets for instant success. Expect both a steep learning curve and the best possible results from this product.

Corel Photo-Paint

Photo-Paint is a powerful image-editing and painting application. It also comes with a media asset management tool, textures, thousands of photos and clipart images, digital watermarking, morphing software, and more. Besides getting all of these extra goodies, Photo-Paint also offers a feature-rich editor, with many presets that enable you to get good results—quickly.

procreate Painter

Painter, which has changed ownership many times in the past few years (from Fractal Design, to MetaCreations, to Corel, to the Corel spin-off company known by its lowercase designation procreate), is known for its capability to faithfully capture the subtleties of an artist's brush strokes and translate them to print or the Web. Painter's Natural-Media digital technology faithfully re-creates traditional artists' mediums in unlimited quantities, such as oils and acrylics, airbrushes, colored pencils, chalk, charcoals, crayons, and felt pens, combined with hundreds of papers, patterns, and textures. In addition, Painter offers most of the capabilities found in Adobe Photoshop, as well as other techniques Photoshop doesn't offer. For those who have a fine-art background, Painter will both amaze and please you unlike almost any other digital tool on the market. For some of the painting features, a digital tablet is desirable.

http://www.muskalipman.com

You might now wonder which of these three editors is right for you. If you have a limited budget, you might want to consider buying Photo-Paint or Painter because Photoshop has a price around $600. Photo-Paint can be purchased for less than $300 and Painter for about $400. If you are artistically inclined, Painter is an excellent choice. Photo-Paint is a good mix of the two products. If cost is not a consideration, then get more than just one, as many professionals do. You'll find that most graphic artists own both Photoshop and Painter.

Advanced consumer or business-use digital editors

This category of tools offers a mixture of the power of the more professional tools and the ease-of-use of the consumer tools. Each of these products offers strong Internet capabilities as well as standard digital image-editing features. With a moderate amount of skill, you can achieve excellent results with little effort and in a short amount of time.

Jasc Paint Shop Pro

Arguably one of the best values in terms of features for the money, Paint Shop Pro is a complete solution for creating Web graphics and enhancing digital images. It also comes with an excellent animation tool and a good image browser. This is a good choice for almost any digital image-editing task, especially if the images will eventually be used on a Web page.

Ulead Systems PhotoImpact

PhotoImpact is far more than an image editor. It offers one of the most useful image album tools, Web graphics tools that are considered by some to be the best, and an extensive range of image-editing capabilities. Web designers and business users will find PhotoImpact's vast number of presets useful for getting projects completed speedily.

Consumer-level digital imaging applications

All three of the products in this category are both fun and simple to use. The strength of this product group is that users do not have to understand fundamental image-editing concepts. They just have to be able to follow logical steps and select the results that they want from automatically generated previews or presets.

Adobe Photoshop Elements

Photoshop Elements is Adobe's dynamite replacement for its older Photoshop "lite" consumer applications, including Adobe Photo Deluxe. Built on the same underpinnings as Photoshop, Elements has a lot of power, and it is much easier to use. You can do most of what you can do with Photoshop, and you will find some exclusive features, such as red-eye repair, not found in Adobe's flagship program.

Roxio PhotoSuite, Platinum Edition

A wide range of powerful features is accessible from an exceptionally clean interface with PhotoSuite. PhotoSuite makes it easy to get, prepare, compose, organize, share, and print photos. In addition, this editor offers image management, digital image stitching, and PhotoTapestry features, as well as the capability to create Web pages complete with thumbnails that contain links to full-size images.

Ulead Photo Express

What a bargain! (The price keeps changing, but it's always way under $40 for this program.) You get an image cataloging tool, a calendar maker, a Web studio, more than 500 project templates, interactive 360-degree or wide-angle panorama capabilities, a photo assistant, and more than 6,000 graphic elements for your projects. A great interface makes this an excellent product that is easy to use.

Professional-level plug-ins

A plug-in is an application that has been designed to work seamlessly with a host application, such as Adobe Photoshop. Although most of the plug-ins have been designed to work with Photoshop, an increasing number of them also work with MetaCreations' Painter, Corel's Photo-Paint, and Jasc's Paint Shop Pro. There is also a trend to make these plug-ins work as stand-alone applications (in other words, without the help of an application such as Photoshop). If you are buying a plug-in, make sure that you understand what other applications (and specific versions) you might need to make them work properly.

Extensis PhotoFrame

This product enables you to interactively design border and edge effects in a multitude of combinations. A full-screen preview enables you to create great frames and excellent edges.

http://www.muskalipman.com

Extensis Intellihance Pro

Intellihance is a plug-in that is dedicated to image enhancement and color correction. With both automatic and manual controls, this product makes it as easy as possible to make your images look their best. It even offers special presets for digital cameras. You can fine-tune and compare different settings for fast, professional results by viewing up to 25 setting combinations or multi-pane previews simultaneously (see Figure 6.1). If you can't fix an image with this plug-in, it can't be fixed.

Figure 6.1
Multipane preview mode allows you to compare image enhancements in Intellihance Pro.

Extensis Mask Pro

Mask Pro enables you to remove with precision and ease almost any object from its background by using the Magic Brush, Magic Wand, Magic Pen, and Magic Fill tools (see Figure 6.2). Not only does this plug-in save an enormous amount of time, but it also produces cutout objects that will blend seamlessly into new backgrounds as if they were taken with the background picture. If you frequently need to cut out objects and you use Photoshop, you must have this tool.

Figure 6.2
You can use Extensis Mask Pro to remove a butterfly from its background.

Right Hemisphere's Deep Paint

Although you can use Deep Paint as a stand-alone product, it was designed to complement Photoshop by adding artistic tools to Photoshop's powerful editing tools. This tool creates distinctive work that is unlike work created by any other software, with the possible exception of procreate Painter. The Artistic Cloning feature enables you to transform digital images into rich oil paintings, delicate charcoals, or any one of many other media types. If you have artistic skills and a graphics tablet, you'll love this product.

Auto F/X Dreamsuite

This plug-in includes a variety of texture and painting effects you can apply with a great deal of precision, with full control over lighting, colors, and other parameters.

Auto F/X AutoEye

This plug-in was designed to enhance and improve digital images. Significantly, you can also use it as a stand-alone product. Batch processing and drag-and-drop file launching capabilities make this an excellent product for production workflow.

Auto F/X Photo/Graphic Edges

Like AutoEye, this application works as a plug-in and as a stand-alone application. It creates awesome edge effects for images of any type. Multiple edge portfolios are available that contain thousands of edge effects. If you want edges on your images and you want the greatest control possible over your edge effects, this is the tool to use (see Figure 6.3).

Figure 6.3
Use Auto F/X Photo/Graphic Edges 4.0 to create an edge effect.

Alien Skin Software's Eye Candy

Eye Candy is one of the leading special effects plug-ins, with 21 special effects, including Fire, Smoke, Antimatter, Chrome, Carve, Cutout, Drop Shadow, and Bevel filters.

Alien Skin Software's Xenofex

Xenofex offers 16 time-saving special effects filters for print, Web, or multimedia projects. This tool helps you create lightning, clouds, and stains. Other unique effects include Stamper, Constellation, Crumple, Origami, Rounded Rectangle, and Shower Door.

Alien Skin Image Doctor

This package of tools helps you repair scratches, clone backgrounds over unwanted objects, and remove spots from your images.

Alien Skin Splat

Splat is a useful plug-in that creates borders, frames, fancy edges, fills, and patchwork effects.

procreate KPT Effects

The grandaddy of all Photoshop plug-in effects, the original Kai's Power Tools (now called KPT Effects) is a collection of plug-in applications that includes a host of clever tools. If you are the creative type and want to do something different with your images, then get KPT Effects.

Xaos Tools' Total Xaos

This includes a bundle of three designer plug-ins: Paint Alchemy, TypeCaster, and Terrazzo. Paint Alchemy transforms images into fine art, with more than 100 preset paint effects, such as Colored Pencil, Impressionist, or Pastel. TypeCaster turns ordinary type into broadcast-quality 3D titles. Terrazzo creates symmetrical tiled backgrounds.

A digital imaging techniques sampler

The previous section provided a quick overview of a wide selection of software products that offer a diverse range of features and capabilities for editing digital images. Now we'll get much more specific about what you can do with these products. In this section, you'll look at eight basic digital image-editing techniques and how they can be performed with Photoshop. Although these techniques are demonstrated with Photoshop, please understand that any one of the other editors in Category I will produce equally good results—and always for less money. Applications in Category II and III will enable you to do some of these techniques with varying degrees of success, ranging from equally good to not possible. That is okay, though; we don't want everyone to be an equally magnificent digital imaging master, do we?

To demonstrate seven of the eight techniques, we'll use three images taken with a digital camera and combine them into a single image. For the background image, we'll use an image of two daylilies. This image has already been digitally enhanced to look like a fine-art print. We will also use two images of butterflies that were taken with a digital camera—but in different states! The intent is to combine these images in an interesting and unusual way.

http://www.muskalipman.com

Selecting parts of an image

Our first technique, one of the most important, is to be able to select a specific object or area in an image. Without being able to accurately select those things that we want to select, our magic would be severely limited.

To select an area, you must first select a tool. Photoshop offers the Marquee, Lasso, Polygon Lasso, and Magnetic Lasso tools, to name a few of its available selection tools. After you select a tool—in this case, I used the Magic Lasso tool—just drag the tool around the area that you want to select. If your settings are correct, the selection marquee (the line around the part of the image that you want to select) should snap onto the object that you want to select. It can be that easy, or it might take many adjustments and multiple tries. In Figure 6.4, the selection marquee shows that we have successfully selected the butterfly.

Figure 6.4
You can use the Magnetic Lasso tool to select the butterfly.

With Photoshop, you can also select by color or color range, invert selections, or use the Magic Wand. You can use the Pen tool and select by drawing a freehand or straight line, or you can use any one of many other methods. With a little skill and practice, you can select practically anything that you want to select with the exact level of precision necessary to meet your needs.

Adding objects to an image

Now comes the fun part. Using the previous technique, we selected the butterfly in our first image. Before we open the background image consisting of two daylilies, we first need to copy the selection by choosing Edit, Copy. Now we can open the daylily image and select

Edit, Paste. The butterfly is copied onto the daylily image. That was so cool, let's do it again—four more times. Drag the objects to their new positions, and now we have two daylilies and five butterflies in the same image, as shown in Figure 6.5.

Figure 6.5
The daylily image now has five added butterflies.

Transforming parts of images

Some of you might have been impressed with the results of the previous three techniques, whereas others of you might have said, "That's cool, but the butterflies all look the same." Therefore, we'll now learn how to transform things. Our image has two fundamental problems: The butterflies all look identical, and they are all the same distance from us—that is, they are in the same plane. Nearly anyone can see this, and we must be concerned about our audience screaming out, "Image fraud!" and forever ruining our careers as practicing image editors.

The solution is easy, as each butterfly is on its own separate layer. Select one of the butterflies, select Edit, Transform, Scale, and scale the butterfly to look as if it is flying at a distance further away from us than the first butterfly. Then click another butterfly, select Edit,

Transform, Rotate (see Figure 6.6), and rotate that butterfly until you are happy with it. Besides scaling and rotating, you also can use the Skew, Distort, and Perspective features to arrange your butterflies to look like they are part of the original image.

Figure 6.6
Here's the transformation of the added butterflies.

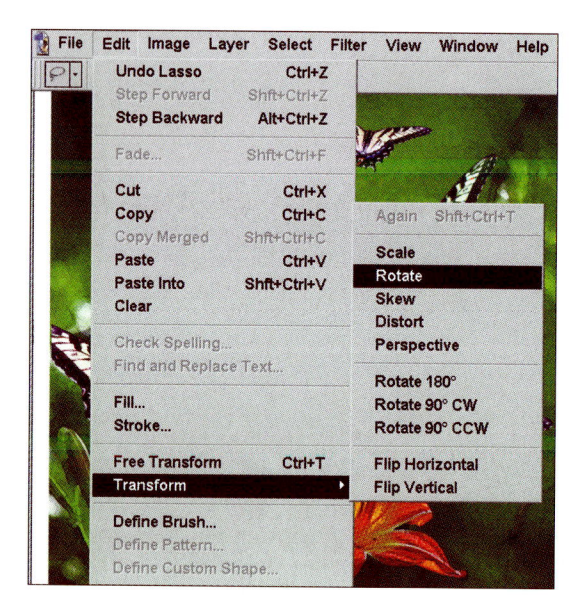

As promised, you now know all that you need to know to make a picture of yourself pulling a rabbit, or even an elephant, out of a hat. All you need is a picture of yourself holding a hat with one hand and have the other hand look like it is pulling something out of the hat. Find an image of a rabbit or an elephant and select it; then copy and paste it into the first image. Size, rotate, and transform the image as necessary. Presto! You are a magician pulling an elephant out of a hat!

Changing colors

Our image is looking good, isn't it? No? I thought we might still have a few skeptics among us. I agree. It would be unusual to have so many butterflies with exactly the same colors all clustered around two flowers. But we are qualified image editors, so let's change the colors of a few of those butterflies.

Select a few of the butterflies, one at a time, and select either Image, Adjustments, Hue/Saturation, or Image, Adjustments, Replace Color. Use the slider, like the one shown in Figure 6.7, to adjust the colors to suit your taste.

Figure 6.7
We can change the colors of the butterflies with Adjustments, Hue/Saturation.

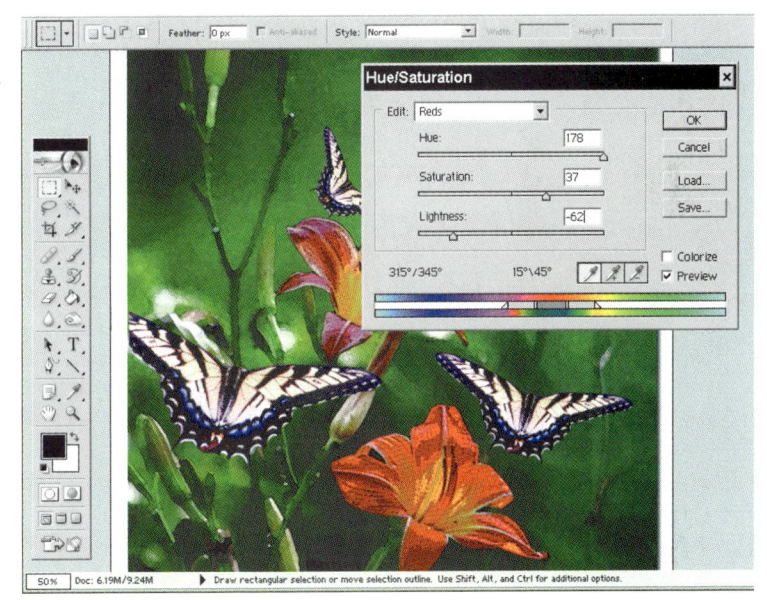

Layering objects

As you move objects around in an image, you may introduce some new problems. If you look at Figure 6.8, you can see I've moved one of the smaller butterflies so that it actually appears closer than a larger butterfly because one of its wings is on top of the larger butterfly. In addition, in this arrangement, one butterfly appears to be farther away than the flower size suggests, and yet it is covering part of the flower. We can fix both of these problems by using layers. Each time we added a butterfly, we added another layer, which can be likened to a transparent overlay sheet that can hold images. In the end, we have one background and five layers, with a newly added butterfly on each layer. You can see the layers by looking at the Layers palette in Figure 6.8. By clicking each of the two butterflies with overlapping wings,

http://www.muskalipman.com

you can determine that they are in Layers 5 and 6. Layer 5 is in front of Layer 6, but it should be behind it. Just drag and drop the layer in the Layers box, and the smaller butterfly's wings will be behind the larger butterfly's wings, just as if you had changed the order of a few transparent sheets containing images.

Figure 6.8
You can use layers to correct image "order" problems.

To fix the problem of the flower being covered by the wing that appears to be behind the flower, we have to select a part of the flower, copy it, and then paste it as a copy into the image at exactly the same place. We can now order the layers and have the flower correctly cover the wing of the butterfly. After you have the layer order correct, you can go back and move all the butterflies around until you get them where you want them.

Painting with an image

Our image showing two daylilies and six butterflies is looking good, but what do you think about adding another daylily? There is room for one in the lower-right corner of the image. We can actually paint another one simply by using the Rubber Stamp or Clone Stamp tool.

Before we use the Rubber Stamp tool, you need to create a blank layer for the new flower. To get started on the new flower, first pick a place on the image that you want to copy from—in this case, we'll pick the leftmost petal of the deep-orange daylily. Then select the new layer from the Layers dialog box and start painting. After we paint the flower and some of the surrounding background, we can once again go to our transformation tools and make this flower look different from the one we copied. This flower looks good just as it is, so we'll rotate it just a little and slide it into the bottom-right corner of the image, as shown in Figure 6.9. You'd never know that the third flower was a copy, would you? That is why this chapter is titled "Performing Digital Imaging Magic"—it's as good as magic!

Figure 6.9
We can add a third daylily with the Rubber Stamp tool.

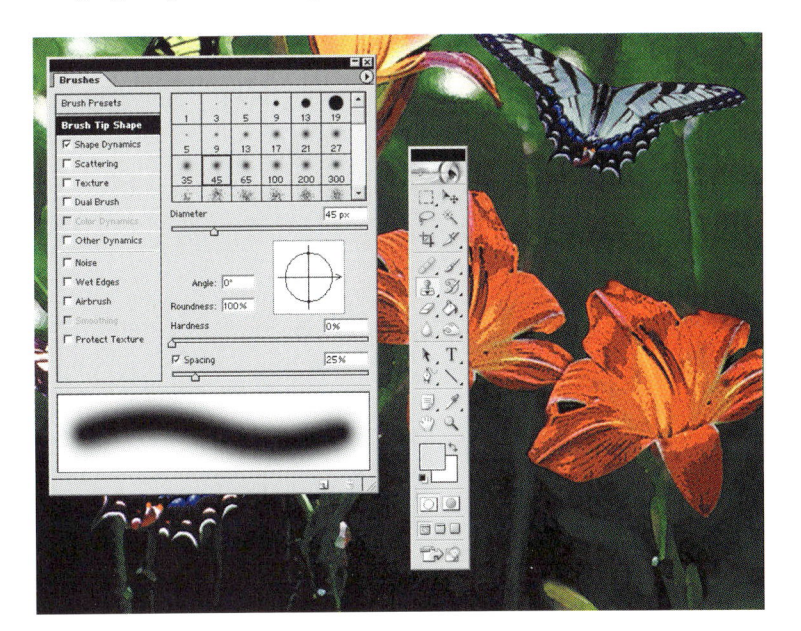

As one final step, to add a little genetic diversity, I added one additional butterfly that I cut out as an example of using Photoshop's Extract command. I also scaled and rotated it just a bit to make it fit where I thought it should be. The image is now complete, as shown in Figure 6.10.

Figure 6.10
Here's the completed image.

Removing objects from an image

In the previous technique, we did quite a bit of adding to images—not removing. Often, however, you need to remove something that is already in an image. Depending on your intentions, there are many ways to remove things. In Chapter 5, "Getting Images into Shape," the downtown Chapel Hill image had some unwanted stoplights and wires. If you recall, we used the Rubber Stamp tool to paint parts of the sky over the stoplights and wires to remove them. In other cases, you can cut and paste one image over the part of the image that you don't want, which effectively removes the part you don't want.

NOTE

One of the more well-known and often-used image magic techniques is to paste a new spouse over the top of an ex-spouse to fix an otherwise perfect family photo. You might think that I'm kidding, but I'm not—this is done quite often.

On a more serious note, by using a combination of the techniques already discussed, you can add to a family picture those family members who weren't able to attend a family get-together. It is also fun to add your favorite TV star, sports hero, or politician to an image containing yourself or someone else that you choose. Just be careful which politician you choose to pose with!

Using masks

At this point, this eighth and final technique might not seem particularly useful to you. However, Chapter 7, "Filtering for Special Effects," will make this one of your most used techniques. Masks enable you to do exactly what their name sounds like they do—mask certain parts of an image, which in turn enables you to perform your magic on the rest of the image. Because you can use a wide range of selection techniques to create the masks, you can end up with masks that enable you to perform some awesome feats. Masks also enable you to create vignettes, such as the one shown in Figure 6.11.

Figure 6.11
This vignette was created with a mask.

NOTE

A woman who had successfully published several cookbooks decided to illustrate her next cookbook herself. Using several inexpensive digital image-editing tools on digital images that she had taken with a digital camera, she created high-quality images for her cookbook. To complete the images, she applied several filters that transformed them into distinctive images for her cookbook. Besides saving the cost of an artist and photographer, she completed the book sooner and all by herself. To help sell her books, she is now planning to make some of the recipes, complete with images, available on a Web site, which is easy to do with her current software.

Creating magical images

In the previous section, we looked at eight of the more important ways to digitally edit an image. In each of these cases, we used one of the most sophisticated digital editors on the market: Adobe's Photoshop. To see the difference between the professional products that require considerable skill and the consumer-level products, we will now perform our digital magic on three images by using less-expensive image editors that offer presets for instant success.

Putting up the rainbow

To get our soccer goalie to "put up the rainbow," we will use Paint Shop Pro. By now, you probably can tell me how to create this image. First, we need to select the goalie from one image by using one of several available selection tools, as shown in Figure 6.12. After opening the background image, we can copy and paste the goalie into the open image (see Figure 6.13). After the goalie is sized correctly and properly positioned, we can then remove part of the rainbow with a Clone Brush by copying part of the sky just slightly next to the part covered with a rainbow (see Figure 6.14). After these few steps are done, our image will be complete, as shown in Figure 6.15.

Figure 6.12
Paint Shop Pro is used to select the keeper.

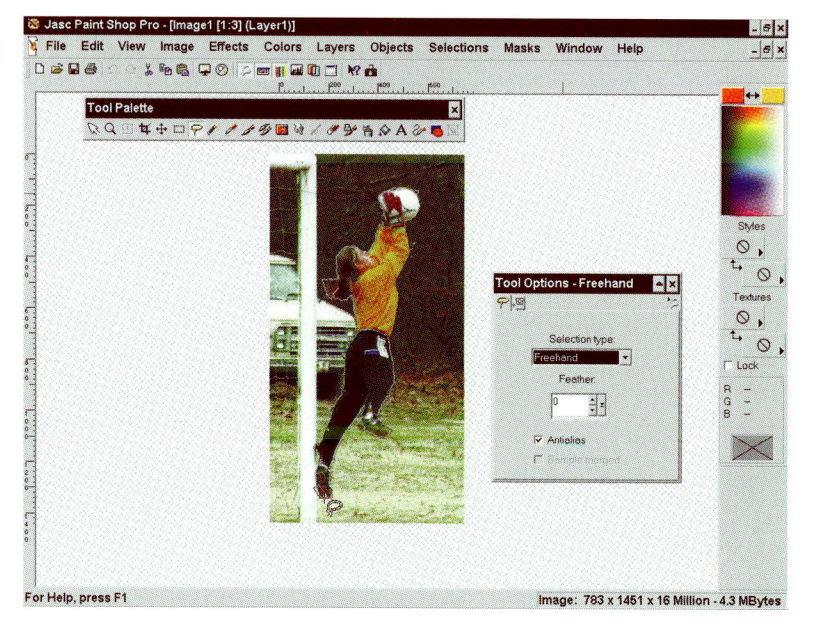

Figure 6.13
The soccer goalie is pasted into the image at its original size.

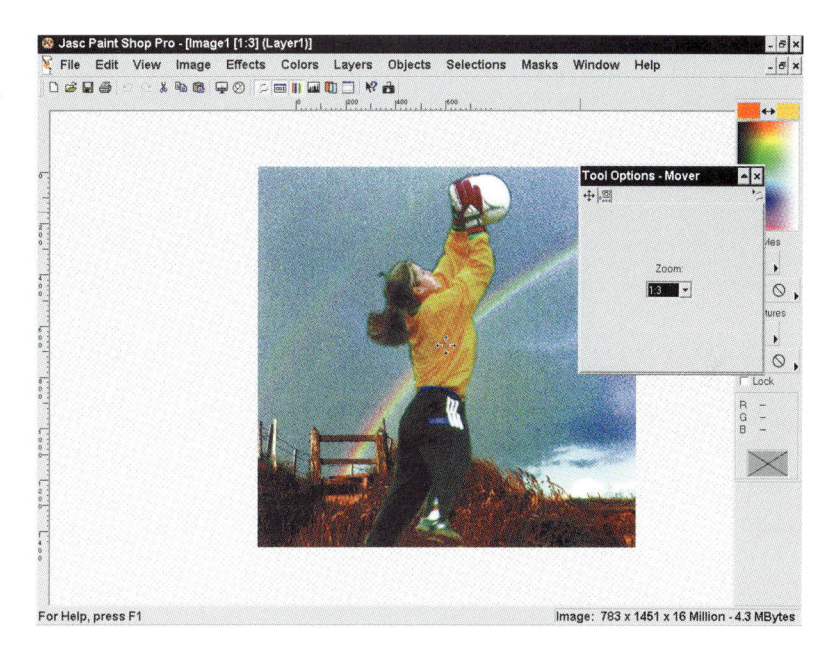

Figure 6.14
We can remove part of the rainbow with the Clone Brush tool.

Figure 6.15
Here's the completed image.

Paint Shop Pro makes creating this image easy, assuming that you have an understanding of some of the fundamental concepts of digital image editing. If you don't have this understanding, there are even easier products to use, as is demonstrated when we create the next magical image.

The mushroom garden adventure

The daylilies and butterfly image that we created earlier in this chapter required that we be able to select objects, layer them, and transform them into the appropriate size. In this example, we'll do similar things, only this time, we'll use PhotoSuite, and we'll create a fun image instead of a fine-art image. This product differs significantly from Photoshop and Paint Shop Pro. Notice particularly how PhotoSuite has been designed to make it easy to complete this image without having an understanding of digital imaging concepts.

Figure 6.16 shows how we were able to select and copy the image of a boy to be used in our image. On the left side of the application is a list of the steps and a button to click when each step is completed. There is even a Reset button for those of us who have to restart occasionally. We did the same thing to get a butterfly—every image needs a butterfly! After we select, copy, and paste the boy and the butterfly (which you can't see at this zoom setting), we need to resize (see Figure 6.17) and position them where they should be.

http://www.muskalipman.com

Figure 6.16
We can use PhotoSuite to select and copy the boy. We'll add a butterfly later.

Figure 6.17
Here we're resizing the boy.

To add a little humor to the image, we can now insert a few of the props that come with PhotoSuite. We can add a green hat, a shovel, and a soccer ball, as well as a text bubble for adding text. After throwing in one cat face for good measure, we end up with the image shown in Figure 6.18.

Figure 6.18
The completed image was fun and easy to create.

PhotoSuite is a good example of how you can accomplish some of the same things that we did in an earlier example with Photoshop. With PhotoSuite, all the steps were obvious because there was always a step-by-step process laid out in the left sidebar, which makes it easy to use. With Photoshop, you have no guidance; you simply must know what you are doing.

Adjusting light in the North Sea

In this example, we'll get a firsthand look at the value of using presets to change colors. The image shown in the PhotoImpact screen in Figure 6.19 is the North Sea with an unusually warm golden glow. Double-clicking the Twilight color adjustment button on the EasyPalette instantly changes the colors to the more dramatic twilight colors shown in Figure 6.20. Alternatively, we can double-click in the EasyPalette, as before, but this time choose from the Season menu and select Spring, producing the results shown in Figure 6.21.

Figure 6.19
Here's the original North Sea image.

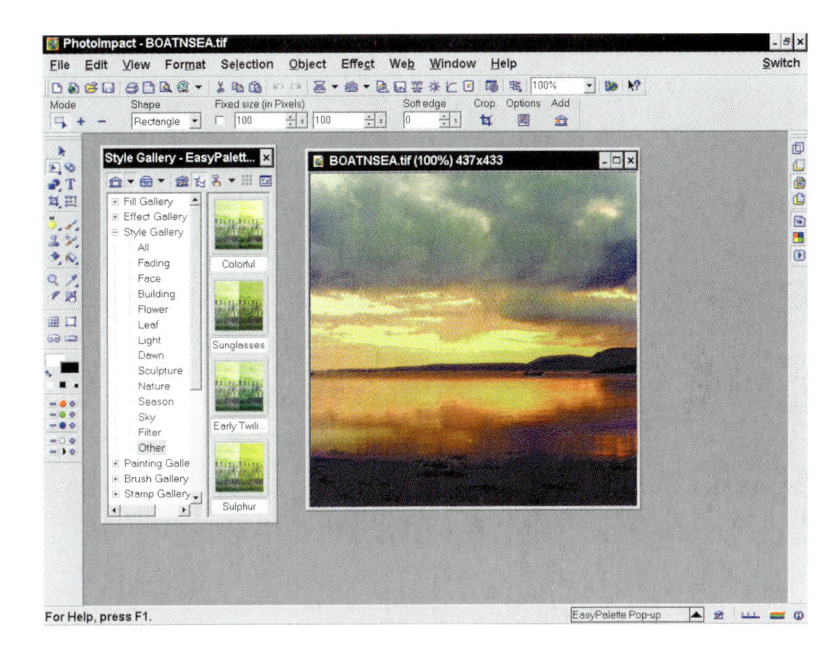

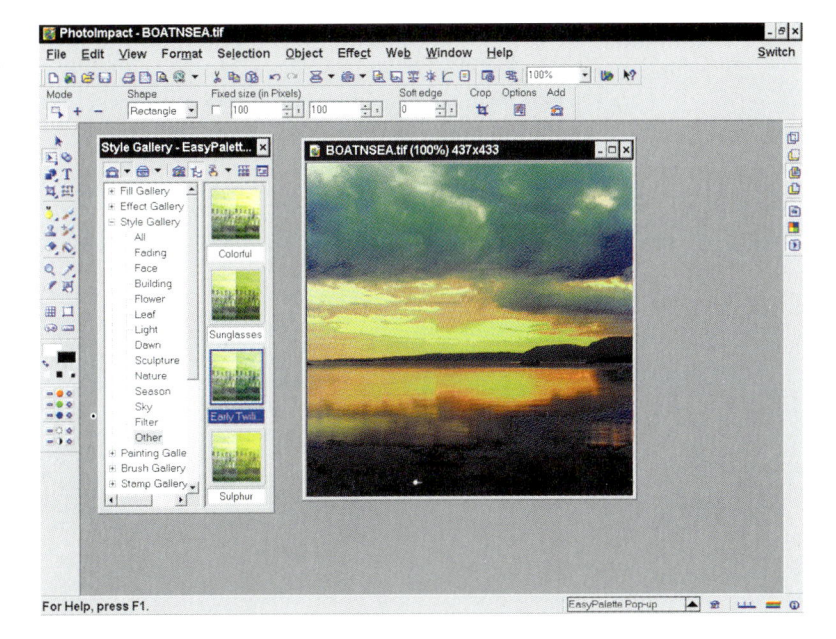

Figure 6.20
This is the North Sea in early twilight.

Figure 6.21
And here's the North Sea in Spring.

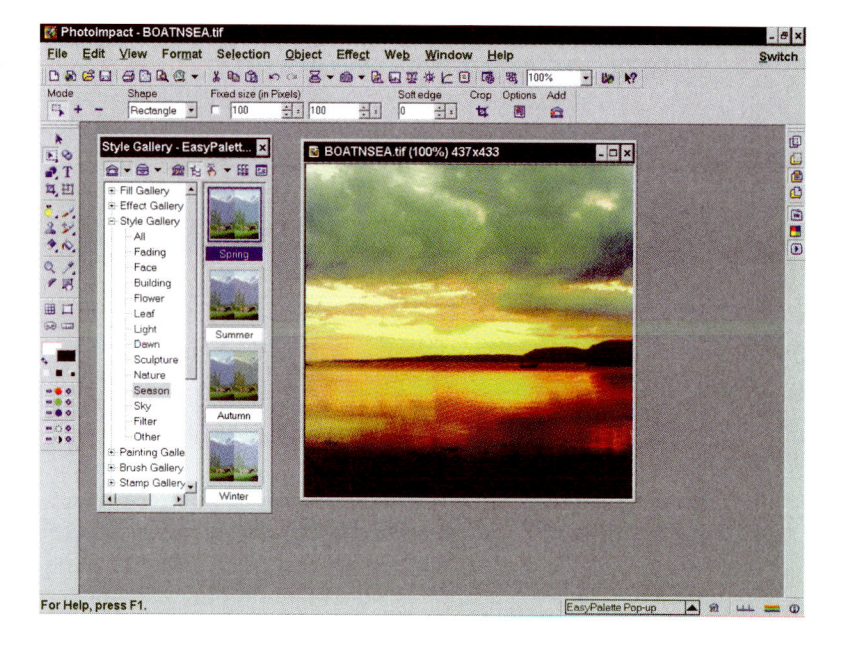

These are just two of the many presets in PhotoImpact, which enable you to make major or subtle changes in an image with a single mouse click. To see a more dramatic change, you can use presets to change a red flower to a blue flower, or you can use one of the Face presets like Sunburned, Heavy Tan, Pale, or even Green to dramatically change the look of a face. These presets might look simple, but if you had to select multiple colors and make the changes yourself in an application such as Photoshop or Photo-Paint, you would appreciate their value. On the other hand, if you understand the fundamentals of digital colors and how to use selection tools and masks, you can do much more than what is available with just those presets. It's a tradeoff between power and ease of use.

We have now reached the end of this chapter. I hope you enjoyed getting an inside look at what digital image magicians feel is proprietary knowledge. Now when you look at the images on music CD covers, glossy magazine advertisements, or book covers, you'll be able to see how the feats were performed. Digital imaging brings a completely new meaning to the notion of "trick photography."

In the next chapter, we'll use the techniques we learned in this chapter to create exciting images that begin to look less like photographs and more like works of art or graphics.

http://www.muskalipman.com

7
Filtering for Special Effects

Applying filters to digital images can be one of the most fun and rewarding parts of image editing. An image that was once boring and unspectacular can instantly become fascinating and spectacular. The nearly perfect landscape image with a truly awful sky can suddenly be made into a prized image by selecting just the sky and applying the appropriate filter to it. Applying multiple filters to an ordinary image can transform it into an absorbing, dreamlike image that can entrance the viewer.

Of course, transforming a sow's ear into a silk purse isn't pure magic. Some really bad images will end up as highly manipulated really bad images. The secret comes from using your vision to spot the weaknesses in an image and then applying some filters in imaginative ways. A certain amount of trial-and-error is involved, too, but the results are worth it.

Filters can be used to transform a single digital image into an endless variety of entirely different images. The transformed images can look like fine art or like a surreal image from a place that doesn't exist on Earth. Filters can turn a photographic image into a line drawing, transform an okay-looking image into a stunning image, help an image that is unsuitable for the Internet become a perfectly suitable one, or make a black-and-white engraving from a color photo. Filters can add a shadow to an image to make it look more realistic, or they can be used to add fur, lightning, smoke, reflective spheres, and fire where they previously did not exist. In this chapter, we will look both at what you can do with filters and at the software that enables you to apply filters to your images.

What can you do with filters?

First, what is a filter?

Image filters are software modules that modify an image in some way. They might increase the contrast between edge pixels, providing a sharpening effect. Or they can decrease the contrast at the edges, adding some blur that masks dust spots or other defects. Filters can move pixels around in your image to provide distortion effects, add random pixels to create a grainy look, overlay textures, or transform colors.

In some ways, digital image filters are similar to the glass filters that photographers have used on their camera lenses for decades. The most common traditional glass filter is the skylight filter, which is a protective and UV-absorbing filter that absorbs a significant amount of UV light and also adds a slightly warm tint for better colors. If you have a 35mm camera with a removable lens, you are quite likely to have this filter. Another common glass filter is the polarizing filter, which helps you to catch a rainbow, enhance subtle clouds in the sky, and reduce reflection and unwanted bright spots on an image. There are many other special effects filters, such as star filters, fog filters, sepia filters, color-graduated filters, color-conversion filters, warming and enhancing filters, and color-compensating filters. Each of these filters is used to make a photograph look more like reality, less like reality, or otherwise alter its appearance.

A "before" and "after" image sampler

Before we begin looking at filter software, let's look at four sets of "before" and "after" images so that we can see firsthand how to change an image with the application of one or more filters. Then we will look at 10 additional things that we can do with filters. Figure 7.1 shows an image of an old automobile parked in a garage. The picture was taken with a digital camera and then slightly enhanced to make the colors richer and the image sharper before a final filter was applied.

To make the image look a little more exciting and eerie, a single filter was applied to create the light reflections that are shown in Figure 7.2. You might think that it wasn't that easy, but it was. It was just a matter of selecting the filter and applying it with two mouse clicks. The

Filtering for Special Effects – Chapter 7   155

whole process took under five seconds to complete. The secret is a lens flare filter available in Photoshop and some other image-editing programs.

Figure 7.1
This original "old car in a garage" image was created with a digital camera.

Figure 7.2
Here's the "old car in a garage" image after applying a lighting filter.

Now let's see how we can take another ordinary image and make it interesting enough to use as a base image for a Christmas card. The original image shown in Figure 7.3 is an unexciting picture that definitely would not make a very attractive Christmas card. Once again, we are going to transform this image with two clicks of a mouse. Select the poster edges filter available with many image editors and click to apply the effect. The result is the image shown in Figure 7.4. The white foreground almost looks like snow. With a few Christmas objects placed in the image, it will make a superb card for the holidays. There is even plenty of room for a greeting at the bottom of the picture.

Figure 7.3
Here's the dull "before" image of a house.

Figure 7.4
Here's the house after applying a poster edges filter.

Part II Transforming Images

http://www.muskalipman.com

Now imagine that you need a dozen images for use on the front page of each of 12 chapters in a cookbook that you are writing. All you'll need is some time to arrange a few items on your kitchen counter and a few shots with a digital camera. Figure 7.5 shows one such image of a collection of cooking oil bottles.

After two mouse clicks to select and apply a watercolor filter, you now have the image that is shown in Figure 7.6. Ah, the magic of filters! With the success you've had with this one, aren't you curious to see how a similar image showing a few red, yellow, and green bell peppers would turn out? You might also be able to take a picture of your stove showing multiple pots and a skillet with steam rising from one or two of them. Using the same watercolor filter, you can quickly create the dozen images that you need in a similar style. As you can see, you can create a dozen high-quality images suitable for printing in just a few hours and with as few as 24 mouse clicks to apply the filters. Now imagine what you would have to go through without a digital camera and the magic of filters to get a dozen good images!

Figure 7.5
Here's a "before" image of cooking oils taken with a digital camera.

Figure 7.6
Here are the cooking oils after applying a watercolor filter.

Filters can be wonderful tools to alter the look of an image. They can also be used for other important purposes, which we will discuss later in this chapter. For our fourth and final set of images, we are going to apply several filters. Figure 7.7 shows a lake and mountain range outside Granada, Spain. The photo was scanned from a 35mm color slide. Although I used the Rubber Stamp tool to spot out most of the dust that had gotten embedded in the slide, there are a few that remain. In addition, the cloning process removed some detail, especially in the sky (which used to have more clouds in it). Applying a dry brush filter adds some texture, and judicious use of a sharpening filter accentuates that texture, as you can see in Figure 7.8. The final picture looks a lot like a painting.

Figure 7.7
Here's the original image of a mountain lake.

Figure 7.8
Here's the lake after applying several filters.

Learning more about what filters can do

We have just looked at four sets of "before" and "after" images to see how filters can change an image. In this section, we'll look at 10 additional uses for filters.

http://www.muskalipman.com

Filtering just for the fun of it

At the top of the list of things that you can do with filters is having fun using them. Those who really enjoy doing what they do do it better! If you have the luxury of digitally editing images just for the fun of it, do it. This is the best way to learn how to use filters and explore their possibilities so that you can do what you need to do when you have a specific project to complete. When you have the time, find 5 to 10 images that you like and spend a few hours trying as many filters on them as possible. Try sequentially applying multiple filters on the same image. Adjust and readjust the settings for your filters until you begin to understand how they work and what kinds of images they work best with. You'll be surprised to see how certain filters combine to produce truly amazing (and some not-so-amazing) results.

Figure 7.9 shows one variation of a "just-for-the-fun-of-it" image that was made by applying multiple filters. In fact, seven PhotoImpact filters were applied, including one that created the stars and another that made the fancy frame to fit the image. Check out those frame colors; don't you think it fits the colors of the butterfly image perfectly? You might not like this image, but it sure was fun to create, and I know much more about each filter now that I have used them. It is now your turn to create a few images just for the fun of it.

Figure 7.9
This just-for-the-fun-of-it image was created with seven PhotoImpact filters.

Making an image look better

One of the most common expectations of using filters is that they will make images look better. This is a reasonable expectation, and there are hundreds of filters on the market that can help you improve the look of your images. Easy-to-make improvements include heightening contrast between highlights and shadows, sharpening image focus, and adjusting image brightness. In particular, images that are taken with many digital cameras can be improved considerably with one of the many varieties of sharpen filters, which help bring images into sharper focus.

Blur, Sharpen, Dust & Scratches, Sharpen More, Sharpen Edges, Auto-Level, and Auto-Contrast are just a few of the many powerful image-fixing filters that Photoshop offers to improve the overall appearance of an image. The Darkroom filter category in Professor Franklin's Instant Photo Effects includes single-click filters for Auto Correct, Brightness/Contrast, and Focus. When you begin using these filters or others like them, you'll love seeing how much they can improve almost any image with just a few mouse clicks.

Changing colors in an image

Being able to change colors in an image is another common capability of filters. Filters are available that enable you to change colors in just about any imaginable way. Most of the more powerful high-end image-editing applications offer a filter that is similar to the one shown in Figure 7.10. By using the sliders, you can change the color balance of the entire image—or you can individually or in combination change colors in shadows, midtones, or highlights.

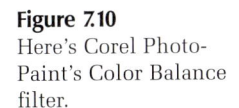

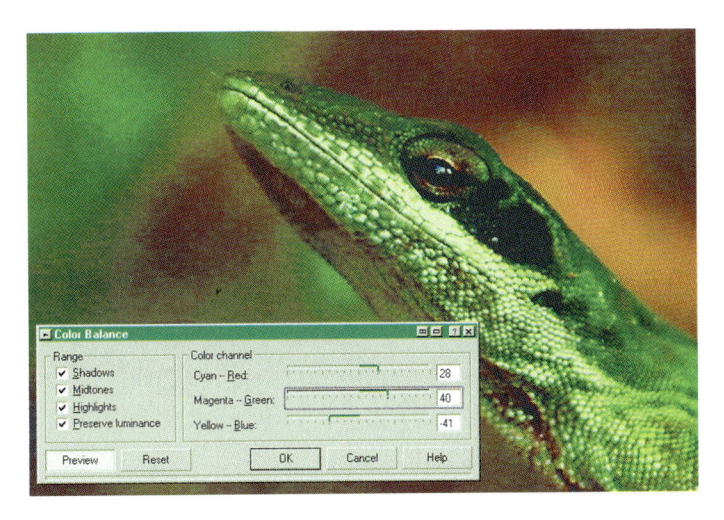

Figure 7.10
Here's Corel Photo-Paint's Color Balance filter.

Other filters enable you to change the hue or saturation of a particular color. For example, you can change a red rose into a yellow rose or increase the saturation of the color green in an image to make it look more like a summer image than a soon-to-be-winter image. Using an Eyedropper tool, you can even select small parts of an image and change those colors to any color that you want. You might recall that we used this capability in Chapter 6, "Performing Digital Imaging Magic," to change the color in a butterfly's wings.

Most of the consumer-level products do not give you the fine-detail control that you get with the professional products, but you can still change the color in your images in many ways. Consumer products typically give you color controls such as "more red," "more green," or "less blue." The more times that you click these features, the more they apply the same filter, resulting in more or less of the chosen color.

Making an image look like it was painted

In recent years, computers have become powerful enough to quickly perform numerous mathematical computations and enable software developers to offer natural-media painting tools and filters. Several programs allow fine artists to paint with digital paintbrushes, pens, pencils, chalk, or even an airbrush. To create works of art, you must have some artistic skills to use these tools successfully. The best of these real-time painting applications are procreate Painter and Right Hemisphere's Deep Paint.

For those who don't have the time or artistic talent, software developers have created filters that can take a photographic image and turn it into an art-like image with a few mouse clicks. There are two kinds of paint filters:

▶ Those that are named after one of the natural-media techniques but don't produce results that look like the intended medium

▶ Those that are named after a natural-media technique and create an image that looks like the intended medium

Sadly, more paint filters fall into the first category than into the second. However, many filters that have a natural-media name can still create an excellent image even though the filter bears little or no resemblance to its natural-media namesake. A good example of this is one of the many filters named watercolor that was applied to the image shown in Figure 7.11. Even though the watercolor edge filter was applied, the image bears little resemblance to a real watercolor painting. However, when the image is printed on watercolor paper, it makes a fine piece of artwork.

Figure 7.11
This fine-art image was created with a watercolor filter.

Besides using a single-click art-like filter to instantly create a watercolor painting, you can also apply a variety of filters to get an even better result. Just as learning how to paint a watercolor painting with watercolors and a brush takes time, learning how to create an unusually good digital watercolor painting with filters also takes time.

To make a print that truly looks like a watercolor, you need to begin with a digital image that has certain characteristics. You then need to learn which filters to apply to the image to get it ready for your chosen effect and filter. As a final step, after you have carefully chosen the best watercolor settings and have applied the watercolor filter, you might want to apply one or two more filters or adjust the color saturation before your image will be complete. With experimentation, you can create exceptionally good results, especially when you print your work on real watercolor paper that has been created specifically for an inkjet printer. Chapter 11, "Turning Digital Images into Prints," covers the topic of printers and paper in more detail.

http://www.muskalipman.com

> **NOTE**
>
> After taking a family vacation in Europe, a family decided to create a set of watercolor paintings from some of the photographs that they took. Each member of the family selected two of their favorite photographs and transformed them into watercolor-like images. One image was of them sitting around a table in front of an Italian restaurant. The bright red-and-green umbrella and the flowering plants in the planters against the sunny, brick wall of the restaurant made an excellent image. Several other favorite images were of English castles and a Dutch windmill. The father particularly enjoyed an image he created of an Irish pub where he and his wife had sampled a few Irish brews.
>
> The set of 10 watercolor images was then printed on watercolor paper on their home inkjet printer, framed, and hung on the walls of their home. Over the years, these prints are likely to become a family treasure. The best part about having the digital images is that when the children grow up and leave home, they will be able to easily print another set for themselves to be used as artwork in their own homes.

Distorting an image

In addition to the filters that are available for fixing or improving images, there are a tremendous number of filters for distorting images. For example, Photo-Paint offers several useful filters under the Distort menu. The filters are Blocks, Displace, Mesh Warp, Offset, Pixelate, Ripple, Shear, Swirl, Tile, and Wet Paint. There are also filters that enable you to change the perspective in your image and apply 3D effects. Additional image-distortion techniques include Pinch, Punch, Sphere, Zigzag, and Boss. Photoshop and Photoshop Elements have similar filters.

Many of these image-distortion filters might not seem useful to you now, but as your skills develop and you begin to do extensive work on your images, you'll find some of them to be immensely valuable—or at least fun and entertaining.

Adding objects to an image

All filters do not simply alter what is already in the image. Some filters actually add things to an image. Later in this chapter, you'll learn about filters that create fire, fur, lightning, and other things that you would not imagine being able to create with a few mouse clicks. Figure 7.12 shows a particularly well-executed filter that creates bubbles. The bubbles even reflect the environment of the English countryside at sunset. After the bubbles were added, a second filter was applied to make the entire image look more like a painting than a photograph.

Figure 7.12
These reflective bubbles were added with a Ulead PhotoImpact filter called Particle Effects.

Creating a background image

One of the significant advantages of being able to digitally edit images is that you can put your subjects into the background that you want. When you're taking a picture with a camera, have you not often thought that the subject was perfect, but the background could be better? After you begin editing your images, you will enjoy having the option of selecting your subjects and carefully placing them into a new background image of your choice.

For some projects, you might just want to create your own background image from scratch. One of my favorite filters for creating background images is procreate KPT Effects. Figure 7.13 shows a picture of a youth lacrosse player who was placed on top of an image that was created with KPT Effects. After the background image was created, a second filter was applied to smear the clean lines of the original KPT filter. The ability to create your own backgrounds enables you to save lots of time because you won't have to find an image for or shoot a picture of a background; just create your own and complete your project.

Figure 7.13
This interesting background was created in procreate KPT Effects.

Transforming a photographic image into graphic art

Some of the filters that you can use to transform a photographic image into graphic art have names like Poster Edges, Poster, Posterize, Cutout, Emboss, and Etching. These filters typically reduce the number of colors and the detail in an image. Figure 7.14 shows an image that was turned into graphic art to be transferred onto a cotton T-shirt. The soccer player was digitally cut from an image that was made from a scanned photograph. She was then pasted into a background image that was created in KPT Effects, and the entire image was framed with a frame filter. Finally, a Poster Edge filter was applied after the image was changed to a duotone image to produce the final graphic image. The rich dark-brown color of this graphic image looked terrific on a white, cotton T-shirt.

Figure 7.14
This graphic art image was created with multiple filters.

Many of the graphic-art-style filters reduce the total number of colors in an image. This makes the images good for use on Web pages because the file size becomes relatively small and downloads faster than a comparable photographic-quality image.

Framing an image

After you complete an image, you might want to consider using one of the many frame filters that are available. You'll find frame filters included with many image editors and most consumer-level photography applications plus a few that are "plug-ins" or stand-alone filter applications. Framing images has become popular, and rightly so. Frames can make your images look much better, whether they will be displayed on a Web page, in printed form, or on a computer screen.

http://www.muskalipman.com

There are many variations of frame filters. Some produce good-looking results by creating a rough edge all around the image; the edge might look like brush strokes, torn paper, or even something stranger, such as computer paper or a roll of camera film. Other filters enable you to pick up and merge the colors from your image, such as the one shown in Figure 7.15. The Ulead products even enable you to add frames that look like real wood, plastic, or metal frames, such as what you can buy in a frame shop.

Figure 7.15
This frog image was framed with an Auto F/X Photo/Graphic Edges filter.

Adding special effects to an image

Now we come to special effects filters. What makes one filter a special effects filter and another one just a filter is not clear to me. I think most filters are special, especially when I consider the mathematics behind them. For our purposes, we'll consider any filter that can do something relatively exotic a "special effects" filter.

A few examples of special effects filters include Fragment, Mosaic, Clouds, Lens Flare, Emboss, Electrify, Origami, Puzzle, Motion Trail, Squint, and Star. There are lots more, but you get the idea of what this basic set can do; their names are indicative of the results they produce.

Using applications with filter effects

The growth of the digital camera and imaging market has helped fuel the growth of applications that offer filter effects. You can even find Web sites that will apply filters to your images free of charge. Even though there are many available filters, they do vary greatly in three ways. Depending on your skill level and the projects that you want to complete, you should consider the following three items when evaluating filters:

- **Ability to control settings**. Some filters are single-click filters, whereas others offer one or more controls that enable you to fine-tune the filter to get results that more closely match your intent.

- **Effectiveness of the application's user interface**. If you work on projects such as Web sites or slide shows and need to apply filters to twenty or more images, the ease of accomplishing your task will be important. Some applications offer macro capabilities and are easy to use; others simply make you work hard.

- **Output image quality**. The most important aspect of a filter is the quality of output. Some applications or plug-ins offer many filters that simply do not produce useable output. When choosing filter tools, look for filter sets that produce results that match your requirements.

In the next section, we will quickly look at a variety of tools—either applications that offer filters or filter plug-ins. This overview is not intended to be a complete list of filter tools; rather, it provides you with an excellent idea of the kinds of tools that are available.

Adobe Photoshop and Photoshop Elements filters

Photoshop has earned its reputation as being the premier image-editing tool by featuring a full range of capabilities that help you to efficiently achieve the finest-quality output for Web, print, or online use. Photoshop Elements is developing a reputation of its own as a full-featured tool that's a bit easier to use than its older sibling. Depending on exactly which features are counted as filters, there are around 95 of them in both Photoshop and Photoshop Elements. The programs categorize all the filters into 13 general categories: Artistic,

Blur, Brush Strokes, Distort, Noise, Pixelate, Render, Sharpen, Sketch, Stylize, Texture, and Other Filters. One of my favorites is the Liquify filter (even though Adobe spells Liquefy in an odd way!), which gives you the power to "fingerpaint" your photos, as shown in Figure 7.16.

Figure 7.16
"Fingerpaint" your image with the Liquify filter, applied here using Adobe Photoshop Elements.

Broderbund's The Print Shop

Even though The Print Shop is a consumer-level product, it offers a considerable number of filters that can create fabulous images. If you are interested in a desktop publishing application and an image editor, The Print Shop range of products is a good choice. One of my favorite images ever is one that I created with a filter in the image-editing module contained in The Print Shop. The picture, which was taken in a small, abandoned Wyoming town, shows an old car and a suitcase after applying the Antique filter, as shown in Figure 7.17.

http://www.muskalipman.com

Figure 7.17
The Print Shop can create this fine-art image.

Corel Corporation's Photo-Paint

My bet is that Photo-Paint offers more filters than any other image-editing application (with the possible exception of PhotoImpact). Photo-Paint offers so many filters that I would not want to have to count them. The Effects menu alone offers 16 categories of filter effects. Most of the submenus, such as the Art Strokes menu, list 10 or more filters. In addition, you can access other filter effects under the Image menu. Just in case none of these filters creates the look that you want, a User Defined filter enables you to create your own filters, or you can go online to find others.

Photo-Paint not only offers many filters, but most of them are also highly configurable and come with a wide variety of presets. A good example of the power of these filters is the Bump-map filter, which has so many settings that it takes three tabbed views—Bump Map, Surface, and Lighting—to display them all. The Style preset option on the Lighting tab lets you choose from predefined texture maps.

The best aspect of Photo-Paint is not that it offers so many highly configurable filters and presets, but that the final rendered images produced by the filters are spectacular. The filters are as good as they get.

http://www.muskalipman.com

procreate's Painter

Painter is the ultimate painting tool for fine artists who want to be able to create digital paintings. Besides offering a wide range of excellent filter effects, Painter offers tremendous control over an automatic process of applying configurable brush strokes to an image. This technique, or filter, is called Auto-Clone. Painter also offers an Impasto painting technique that adds extreme realism to artwork by interactively rendering painted surfaces in 3D.

If you are interested in creating fine-art prints, you will also appreciate the filters that make any other filter that you apply look like it has been applied to a specific kind of canvas or art paper.

Ulead Systems' PhotoImpact

Figure 7.18 shows PhotoImpact's EasyPalette and the many filter galleries that it features. One of the unique strengths of this product is that the EasyPalette enables you to see a thumbnail image of each of the many filters offered instead of just a filter name on a menu. This enables you to get an idea of what each filter does before you take the time to apply it to your image. PhotoImpact has filter galleries for Material, Deform, Warp, Type, Button, and Frame, as well as a gallery where you can put filters that you have created yourself.

Figure 7.18
You can use PhotoImpact's EasyPalette to apply filters.

http://www.muskalipman.com

Besides offering a large number of preset filters, each filter typically has a dialog box that enables you to change settings for that specific filter. If you use filters, PhotoImpact probably has one to meet most of your needs. It's also a top-notch image editor that comes with a fantastic image-management application.

Using plug-in filters

A plug-in application generally requires a host application, such as Photoshop, Photoshop Elements, PhotoImpact, or Paint Shop Pro. When purchasing a plug-in filter, it is wise to carefully ascertain what additional software you might need to use it. In this section, we will look at the capabilities of several filter plug-ins so that you can get a good idea of what you can do to a digital image with a plug-in.

Alien Skin Software's Eye Candy

Eye Candy offers 21 filters, most of which are actually useful (as opposed to being merely cool, meaning that you might or might not ever need to use them for anything practical). Eye Candy's filter collection includes the aptly named filters Antimatter, Carve, Chrome, Cutout, Drop Shadow, Fire, Fur, Glass, Glow, HSB Noise, Inner Bevel, Jiggle, Motion Trail, Outer Bevel, Perspective Shadow, Smoke, Squint, Star, Swirl, Water Drops, and Weave. These filters are tremendous time-savers. Many of the things they do can be done with any good digital image editor, but not without lots of skill, knowledge, and experimentation. With the Eye Candy filters, you have lots of control and can get your work done well and quickly.

Each Eye Candy filter has its own user interface, with plenty of sliders to adjust the outcome to look unique and appropriate for your specific image. An Auto-Preview option enables you to make changes to the filter effects and view the effects that you select in real-time mode.

If you are serious about enhancing digital images, Eye Candy offers filters that you probably will need—especially if you create images for use on the Internet.

http://www.muskalipman.com

Alien Skin Software's Xenofex

Xenofex, like Eye Candy, is full of filters that you can use for standard purposes as well as to create unusual and wonderful results when they are creatively applied. For example, with the right adjustments, the Lightning filter can be used to make terrific cracks in marble-like surfaces.

Xenofex consists of the following 16 filters: Baked Earth, Constellation, Crumple, Distress, Electrify, Flag, Lightning, Little Fluffy Clouds, Origami, Puzzle, Rounded Rectangle, Shatter, Shower Door, Stain, Stamper, and Television. The filter names quite accurately describe what each of the filters can do.

Many of the Xenofex filters are exceptional, such as the lightning filter. If you need lightning in an image, you can select from 17 presets. In addition to the presets, 10 additional adjustments can be made so that you get just what you want. Each filter has its own user interface, such as the one shown in Figure 7.19, which shows the outstanding lightning bolts that were added to an image of a place near the Scottish coast. With all of these options, you can create almost as many different lightning effects as you might find in real life—well, almost.

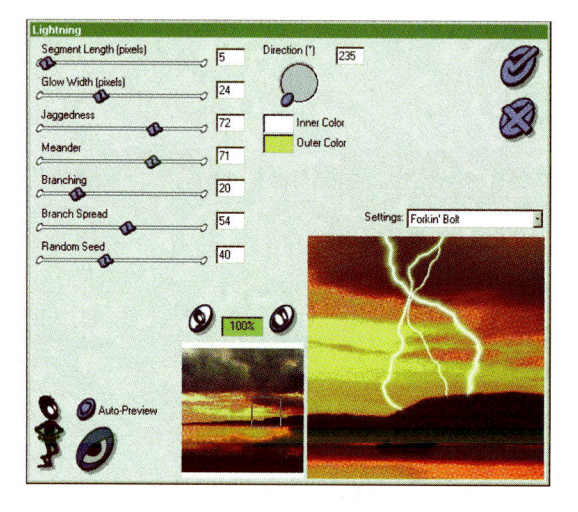

Figure 7.19
You can create lightning with Xenofex's Lightning filter.

Alien Skin Software's Splat

Alien Skin comes up with some odd names to suit its odd filters. Splat is another collection of interesting filters with names like Border Stamp, Edges, Fill Stamp, Frame, Patchwork, and Resurface. You can use these to create interesting edges, picture frames, textures, and other effects. Figure 7.20 shows three of the effects you can choose from.

Figure 7.20
Here are three different Splat effects: Edges (top), Patchwork (middle), and Resurface (bottom).

Andromeda Software Inc.'s Series 3: Screens Filters

Have you ever had the perfect color photograph or color digital image for a project and wondered what you ought to do to it before printing it as a black-and-white image? Although the cost of color printing keeps dropping, and the time that it takes to print a color page keeps decreasing, the vast majority of printing is still done in black and white. Screens Filters is a filter application that helps you get better-looking black-and-white prints.

Screens Filters comes with six categories of ready-to-use presets to help you get your work done quickly. The categories are Mezzotints, Mezzograms, Mezzoblends, Patterns, Special Effects, and Text Effects.

Screens Filters initially starts in Novice mode. When the Novice presets are not enough to meet your needs, you can select the Expert mode.

With a good image and some experimentation, you will be able to use Screens Filters to make engravings, etchings, and woodblock prints that will rival those of the masters from centuries past. However, you need to experiment with this filter to get the excellent results that it is capable of producing.

Xaos Tools' Terrazzo

When you need the effects that Terrazzo creates, there is no substitute for this filter. Figure 7.21 shows the results of applying the Terrazzo filter. To reduce some of the repetitiveness of the filter, small portions of the image were altered with the Rubber Stamp tool, and the image was cropped to put the game table off-center. Wouldn't that image make a great graphic for an invitation to a Halloween picnic? Would you like to come?

Figure 7.21
This Halloween image was created with the Xaos Tools' Terrazzo 2 filter.

You can also use Terrazzo to make background image tiles and patterns. It is an exceptionally fun filter to use. Used creatively, Terrazzo can make your work unique.

Auto F/X DreamSuite

DreamSuite has dozens of interesting effects. You can add a painterly look, create textures, adjust colors, and perform other dramatic modifications. You can even create your own jigsaw puzzles in minutes, as shown in Figure 7.22. Just take a favorite photo, apply DreamSuite's Jigsaw effect, make a color print, and then glue to a piece of foam board and cut the puzzle out. It's that easy.

http://www.muskalipman.com

Figure 7.22
Create your own complex jigsaw puzzles in minutes with DreamSuite.

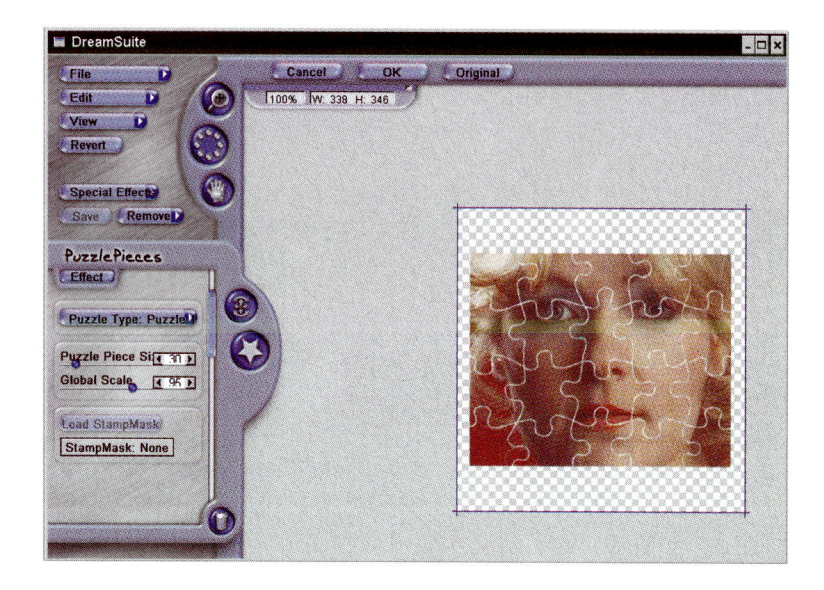

At this point, you're probably thinking that there is a filter somewhere that can do anything that you might be able to dream up. After seeing the magnificent digital imaging work done on the last two installments of The Matrix, which blew everybody away in 2003, I, too, am a believer that there isn't much that you can't do with digital images. With the combination of good filter tools, quality images, some skill in using filters, and a wee bit of creativity, you can do some outstanding work. The possibilities are endless.

Just as two oil painters can sit down next to each other with the same set of brushes and oil paints and not create the same work, so, too, can digital photographers use the same image editors and filters and yet not create the same digital images. It takes great talent, expertise, and passion to create good digital art. Just start and see where it leads you.

That's about all the time we have to cover the fun and useful topic of image filters. The end of this chapter signifies the end of Part II, "Transforming Ordinary Images into Extraordinary Ones." In the next part, we'll begin the first of two chapters that are dedicated to showing you useful and cool ways to use your images. See you there!

http://www.muskalipman.com

Part III
Useful and Cool Ways to Use Your Images

8 Displaying Digital Images Electronically 179

9 Other Useful and Fun Things
   You Can Do with Images. 199

8
Displaying Digital Images Electronically

For those of you who like to view and share images, this chapter and Chapter 10, "Sharing Images," are the two chapters to read. In this chapter, we look at all kinds of cool things that you can do with digital photo albums, slide shows, and screensavers, each of which provides easy ways of sharing your images. Photo albums are screen-based shows, often with more than one image to a page. They also can include textual information about each image. Slide shows show a series of images, one at a time in full-screen view. Screensavers are special versions of slide shows that run when a computer is not being used. Screensavers essentially are slide-show versions of computer desktop wallpaper, except that a screensaver is active only when the computer has not been used for a user-specified number of minutes.

As my digital image collection has grown to an almost unthinkable size, these three types of applications have become my preferred way of storing, sharing, and enjoying my images. Some of my favorite shows include portfolios of digitally edited photographs, slides of our three gray cats, and various screensavers showing action shots of my kids playing soccer, lacrosse, and hockey. I have created a CD that contains about 30 of my favorite albums and slide shows, which makes it easy to find or share my best images.

If you have taken many film-based photographs, you'll understand how difficult and time-consuming it is to create photo albums. Sadly, soon after family photographs are taken, they often are stored in drawers, shoeboxes, plastic containers, or other kinds of boxes and left there indefinitely. We all love to take pictures and we plan to enjoy them, but contrary to our intentions, rarely do we have time to make a photo album or slide show and share it with others—which often is the reason that we took the pictures in the first place. Digital versions of photo albums, slide shows, and screensavers have four distinct advantages over film- and print-based formats:

▶ Making multiple copies doesn't cost extra.

▶ Digital images are extremely easy to share.

▶ The same image can be used in multiple photo albums, slide shows, and screensavers without the need to find a negative, order copies, and pay for them.

▶ The creation process can be easier for digital images.

NOTE

Eight geographically remote college friends met for a week of skiing in Colorado. It was the first time they had been together since they graduated from college eight years earlier. Five of them took photographs and had their film developed at a local photo finisher who then uploaded their digital images to the Internet. One of the friends selected the 30 best images, downloaded them, and organized them into an electronic photo album. The album was then e-mailed to the seven others, as well as to six other friends who weren't able to make the trip. The album included entertaining comments as well as an invitation to meet again in five years on Utah's ski slopes. It took under two hours to create the entire show and e-mail the copies to everyone.

Just imagine the effort it would take to identify and collect all the necessary negatives needed for the reprints—what a pain! Then factor in the time and cost involved in creating a photo album for each of the 14 friends mentioned in the previous story. Thirty photographs for each of the 14 friends at $.40 per photo would cost nearly $170, plus the cost of 14 albums, envelopes, and postage! Would it be worth the time, money, and effort? Not likely. Now we have all the benefits of electronic photo albums, slide shows, screensavers, and the Internet— enjoy them!

Using a photo album to store and view images

Photograph albums are certainly useful for holding and viewing photographs from a family vacation, a wedding, or an award-winning show-dog. However, consider some of the other, not-so-obvious reasons to create a photo album:

▶ As an inventory or asset register

▶ As an art-portfolio presentation tool

http://www.muskalipman.com

- As project documentation
- As part of a personnel or interview-candidate record
- As insurance records
- As a product catalog
- As a real estate inventory portfolio
- As a news and events library

You might use a photo album to display and maintain a record of your Lenox china set, an old book collection, or even a 10-year collection of photographs of your prized roses. You can easily inventory your woodworking tools, jewelry, or music CD collection. Use a photo album to present your artwork—sculptures, paintings, photographs, and handicrafts. You can use a photo album to store and display not only photographic images but also scanned newspaper or magazine articles, or word processing or spreadsheet documents that have been converted into bitmapped images. You can document the work being done on a building project, such as a kitchen being remodeled or a new beach home being constructed. The list of uses for a photo album is endless.

When you combine the instant availability of digital images from a digital camera and a feature-rich photo album, you can easily keep records of things that you normally would have found to be too time-consuming and too expensive to do. If you are a parent, imagine having an electronic portfolio of all the artwork that your children have ever created, without the difficulties of keeping those large finger-paintings, the glued-glitter drawings, or the large papier-mâche sculptures that you love but just don't want to store forever. You can even have a photo album of all of those complex and weird LEGO projects. You can create photo albums for all kinds of home and work projects.

Using an album with database capabilities

By now, you probably have many ideas as to how you would like to use an electronic photo album. Before you begin to make one, however, spend a few minutes looking at the fantastic possibilities of one of the more feature-rich photo album applications—Ulead's PhotoImpact Album. PhotoImpact Album, which is a companion product to PhotoImpact, the image-editing application, is a powerful tool for managing and viewing files. In addition to the file-management and viewing capabilities, PhotoImpact Album enables you to organize your files visually by using thumbnails to represent the contents of a file. After you create thumbnails, you can append additional information, placed in fields, for a more detailed description of the image. You can then search and sort based on these fields to help you locate thumbnails or specific record information.

How about getting some "hands-on" experience with PhotoImpact Album? Let's create a photo-album-based asset record of tools in a woodworking shop. Such an inventory would be useful as documentation for insurance purposes in case of fire or theft, as a tool asset record, and as a system to help track warranties and repair information. The first thing to do is to get images of each of the tools. The easiest way to get images is to place each tool on a white background and take pictures with a digital camera. Obviously, a film-based camera can be used if you don't have a digital camera and are willing to scan each image with a scanner.

Using PhotoImpact Album, we can create a new database by using one of the templates, as shown in Figure 8.1. Alternatively, we can customize a database template to meet our particular needs. In this case, we'll modify the Product Catalog template specifically for our tool asset register by simply renaming a few existing fields.

Figure 8.1
Here we select an album template.

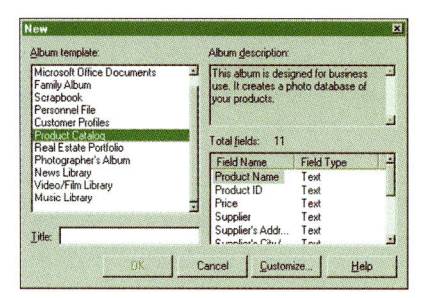

Next we insert all the images into the database by using the Collect Files from Folder function. By selecting View Mode, Thumbnails, we can see thumbnail images that were created for each image. To further divide the database into "types of tools," we can add a "list" type field and include names for the categories of tools that we want. After the field has been created, we need to select the correct tool category for each tool record. Figure 8.2 shows how the database can be separated into power tools, hand tools, large power tools, accessories for power tools, air tools, and so on. By clicking the tab labeled Air Tools, for example, the database can be reduced to show only air tool images.

Displaying Digital Images Electronically – Chapter 8   183

Figure 8.2
Here's a woodworking tool database with tool category tabs.

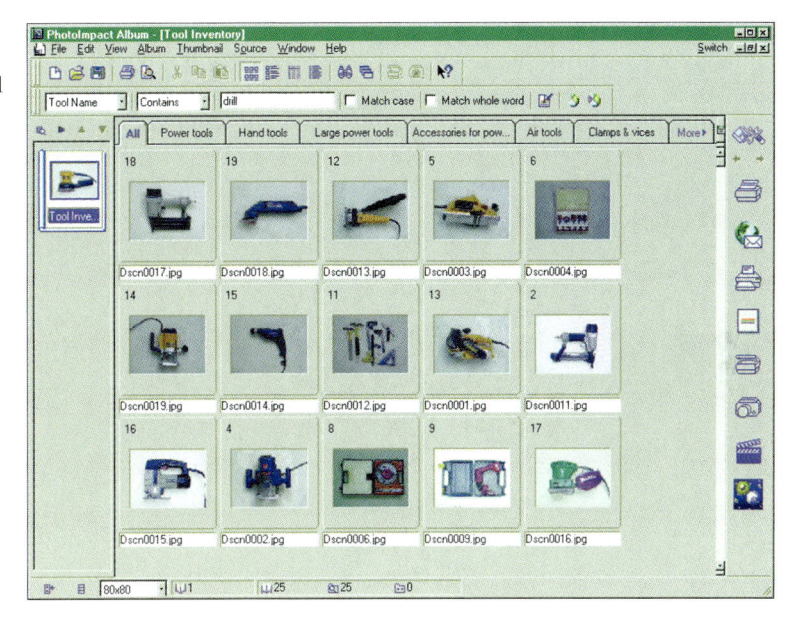

Now that we have the database built, we need to go back and add the necessary textual information to each record. By selecting View, Mode, Data Entry, we get to the screen shown in Figure 8.3. Using this screen, which includes a dialog box for entering key words such as tool types, you can enter the data for each tool that is to be recorded.

Figure 8.3
In the tool database data-entry screen, you can enter the data for each tool.

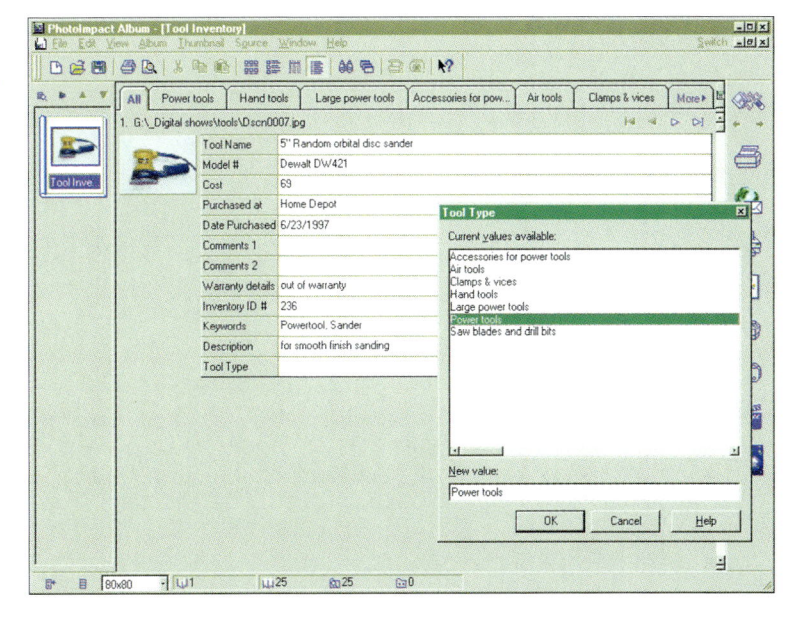

http://www.muskalipman.com

After you've entered all the information, you can export it to a comma-delimited file and import it into other kinds of applications, such as a spreadsheet, another database, or a word processor (see Figure 8.4). This step is as simple as checking the desired fields to export and then exporting them.

Figure 8.4
In this screen, you select the database fields to be exported.

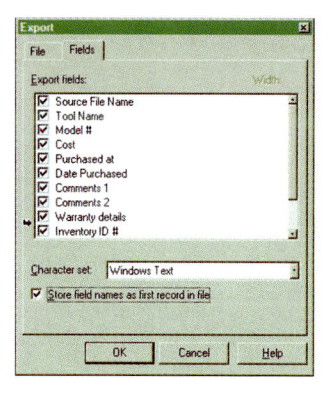

You can also search the database. For example, if you want to find all records containing the word "drill," you can use the search tools found under the toolbar just below the menu bar in in Figure 8.2. Likewise, you can perform more complex searches by using the Search dialog box shown in Figure 8.5. As the final step, if needed, you can print a color hardcopy of the entire database by using any one of several different layout styles, including images and database information. Just think of what we have accomplished. In less than two hours, we have created a database of the tools in an entire woodworking shop, complete with images, without ever touching a pencil or paper! Tell me that was not fast, easy, accurate, and fun—well, almost fun, considering the alternative ways of completing an inventory.

Figure 8.5
PhotoImpact Album's advanced search feature allows you to perform complex searches.

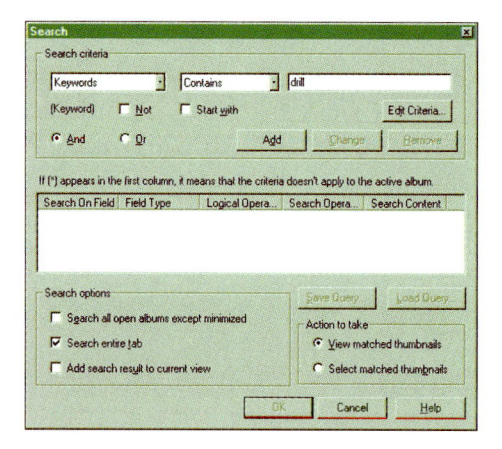

http://www.muskalipman.com

Creating a book-like picture album

We've just looked at the feature-rich PhotoImpact Album and its capability to add database information to each image. However, what if you just want a photo album—a realistic, book-like picture album with pages that turn? It also would be nice to be able to attach bookmarks to mark favorite pictures, choose images for the front and back cover, and have a table of contents and an index.

Well, that is what Adobe Photoshop Album offers you. This great new product for both Macs and PCs can create albums for you in a variety of styles and then publish them as Portable Document Format (PDF) files that you can view with Adobe Acrobat Reader. You can also print your albums, send them as an e-mail message, burn them to a CD, or order a fancy printed version online.

The first step is to choose Album from the Creations menu. A "workspace" that you can use to temporarily store images from one of your Photoshop Album catalogs appears. Drag the photos from one or more catalogs to the workspace, and rearrange them into the order you want for your album, as shown in Figure 8.6.

Figure 8.6
Drag the photos that you want to place into your album to this workspace.

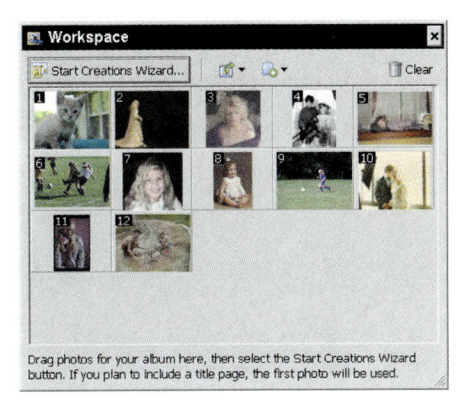

Click the Start Creations Wizard button to activate Photoshop Album's automated album-generating process. Then choose from the selection of album styles. Examples of each style are shown in a preview window, as you can see in Figure 8.7. Click Next to proceed.

Figure 8.7
Choose an album style from the available templates.

On the next screen, you can enter a title for your album, specify how many photos should be displayed on each page, and indicate whether you want captions, page numbers, or headers/footers at the top or bottom of each page. Figure 8.8 shows the available choices. Click Next to proceed to the following screen.

Figure 8.8
Choose options for your pages, including number of photos displayed on each page.

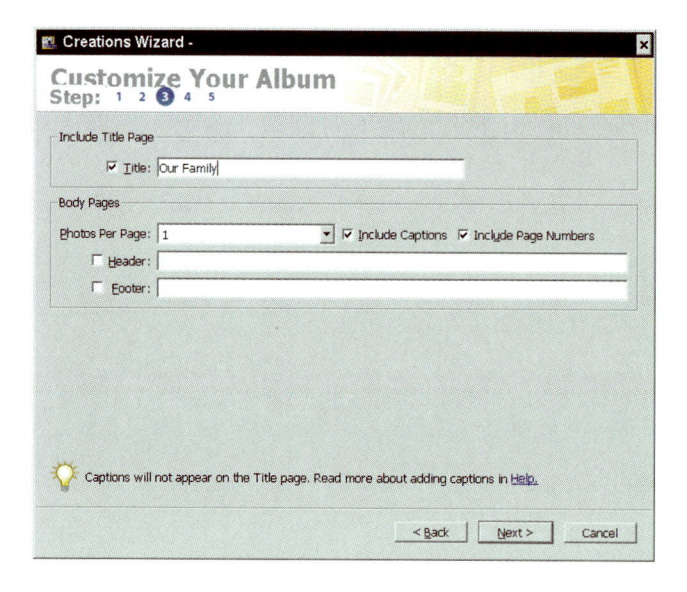

http://www.muskalipman.com

A preview window appears with Forward and Backward buttons. You can actually page through your album to see how it looks, as shown in Figure 8.9. You can preview any page in full screen mode or rearrange the order of the pages by clicking icons at the bottom of the screen. Click Next when you're satisfied.

Figure 8.9
Preview your album and make any final changes.

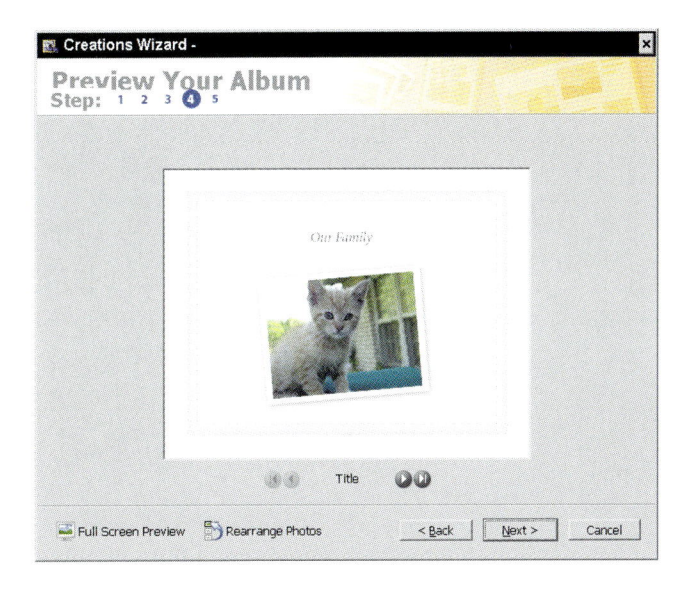

Finally, choose how you would like the album to be output. You can publish an Adobe Acrobat Reader document, print the album, send it via e-mail, burn a CD, or order a printed version from an online service. Click Done to publish your album, as shown in Figure 8.10.

Figure 8.10
Publish your album in your selected format.

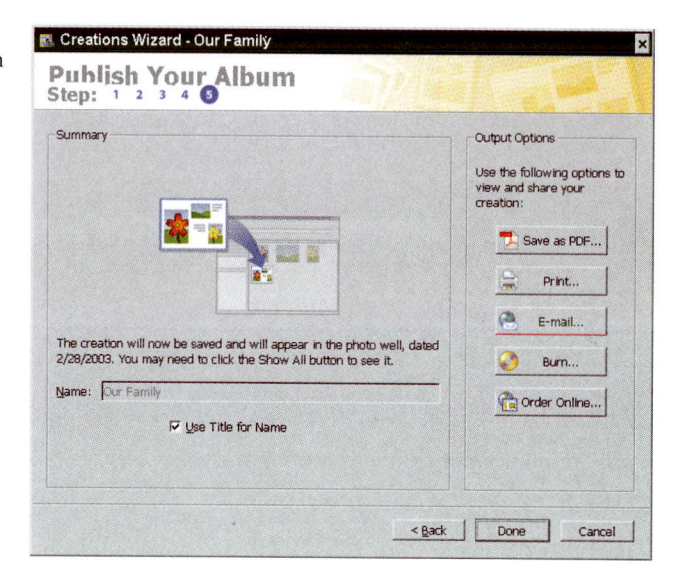

If you select PDF format, your album can be viewed by anyone who has the ubiquitous Adobe Acrobat Reader software, as shown in Figure 8.11.

Figure 8.11
View your albums in Adobe Acrobat Reader if you wish.

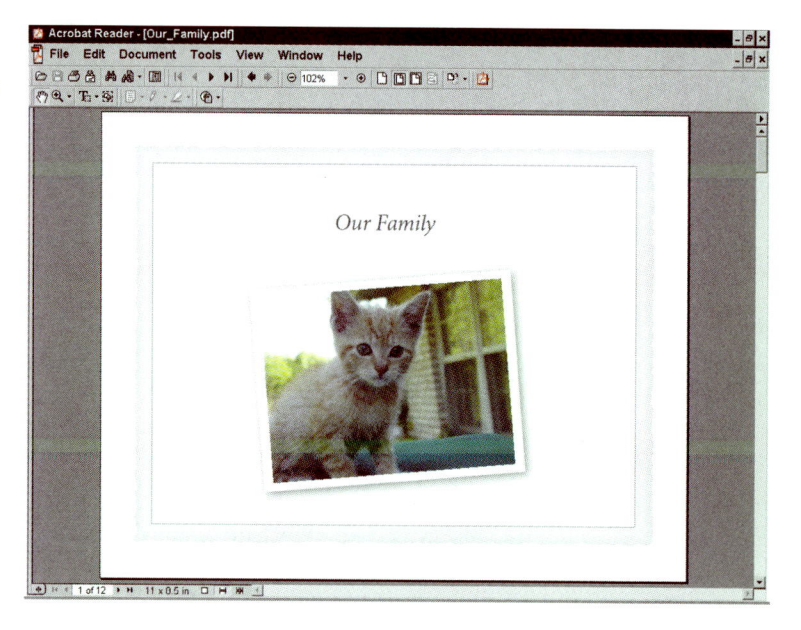

Using slide shows to view images

Traditionally, one of the best ways to view photographs is as a 35mm slide show, shown against a white screen in a dark room. Unfortunately, you have to decide to make slides at the time that you buy the film. When using slide film, it is more expensive to get prints if you want them—and without prints, it is hard to see the images without using a slide projector or a light table. A 35mm slide show also requires a dark room and a smooth, bright-white background or screen; usually, neither of these is readily available. In contrast, we'll now look at what you can do with a digital slide show application.

Creating a multimedia slide show

Both PhotoImpact Album and Photoshop Album have slide show capabilities. Both are easy to use and offer outstanding text and slide transition effects, plus audio and music capabilities. Most important of all, the finished slide shows are as good as slide shows get. They can be rich multimedia shows that are highly educational, informative, persuasive, or just plain fun.

Normally, when I get ready to put together an album or a slide show, I sit down in the middle of my living room floor and spread photographs all around me. I then begin making piles—a pile of photos that I won't use, a pile of photos that I might or might not use, and several different piles of photos that I intend to use. After I have all the piles arranged, I begin to sequence them in a large area directly in front of me. When they are in order, I then begin assembling them into bound albums.

With my creation process in mind, you'll soon understand why I especially like Photoshop Album. It is the perfect slide show for me—and possibly for you, if you are one of those "in the middle of the living room" types, like I am.

Photoshop Album's slide show module operates much like the album component we already looked at. It uses a wizard that leads you through dragging images to a workspace, selecting a template, and organizing your slide show. The main difference is the ability to specify transitions between slides, the length of time each slide will be shown, and any music you want played during the show. You can include play controls on the screen to allow the viewer to choose when to move forward or back in the slide show, or you can hide those controls and opt for a fully automated display. You can even repeat the show endlessly if you want (say, to display your wares at a trade show). Figure 8.12 shows the customization page where you can add these effects.

Figure 8.12
Add transitions, music, and other options here.

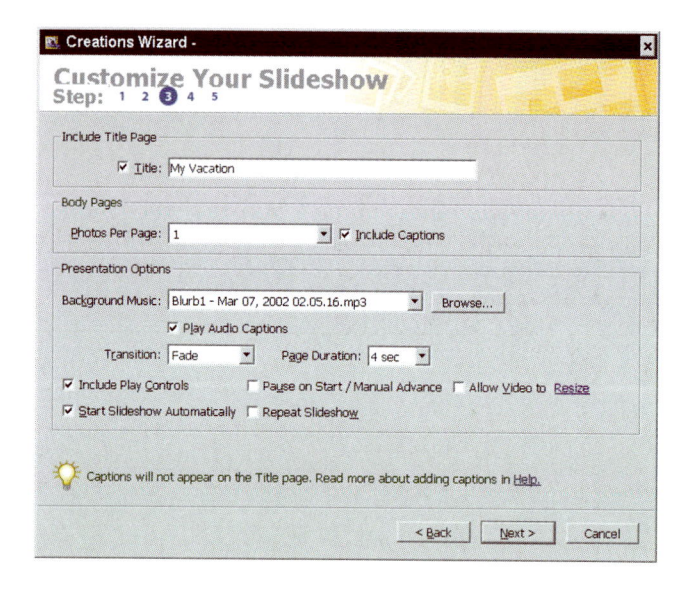

> **NOTE**
>
> An artist who works with glass and steel and specializes in creating unusual gazing globes for gardens created a slide show that presented a dozen globes that she has created. Significantly, the images showed the globes in each of the owners' gardens, instead of just the globes themselves. The last slide ends with the question: "Doesn't your garden need a gazing globe?" After mailing 100 inexpensive floppy disks containing the show to a preferred customer list, she received enough commissions for new globes to keep her busy for four months. She also uses the same show in both slide show and screensaver form on her computer in her studio.

Displaying images with a screensaver

Does your computer screen show pictures or animations after the computer has been idle for a while? If so, that is a screensaver at work. Screensavers are essentially slide shows that your computer turns on automatically after it has been idle for a specified number of minutes. By right-clicking your computer desktop and selecting the Properties menu, a Display Properties window opens. Click the Screen Saver tab to see all the options for screensavers (see Figure 8.13). (Your options might vary, depending on the version of Windows you are using.) Screensavers can be used just for fun, as a corporate billboard, or even as a sales tool.

Figure 8.13
You can select a screensaver with the Windows Display Properties dialog box.

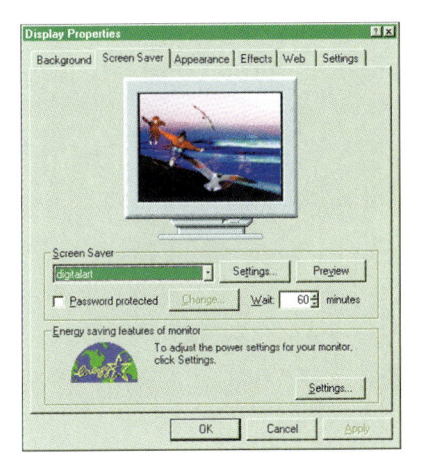

NOTE
A kitchen designer uses a screensaver to show 20 "before and after" photographs taken of kitchens she has designed and helped to remodel. When clients visit her office, they see this screensaver instead of an open software application that she might have left on her desktop. It makes a great sales tool!

Creating a screensaver

Many image editors, image-management tools, and software packages that are bundled with scanners, digital cameras, and even printers include a screensaver creation tool. If you are interested in creating screensavers but you don't have an application that enables you to create them, I recommend Screen Saver Toolbox (SST) from Midnight Blue Software.

Of course, in Windows XP and Mac OS X, you can simply place pictures in the My Pictures or Pictures folders (respectively), and then choose that folder as your screensaver. Those using Windows 98, Me, NT, or 2000, or XP users who want to share their screensavers with others, can use the tools discussed in this section.

> **TIP**
>
> SST is a good tool to use to create your own screensavers. You can get a trial version of this shareware application at http://www.midnightblue.com.

Screen Saver Toolbox enables you to easily select images, add music, and generate screensavers. It is a two-step process. Just select the images that you want and then generate the screensaver (see Figure 8.14).

Figure 8.14
You can generate a screensaver with Screen Saver Toolbox.

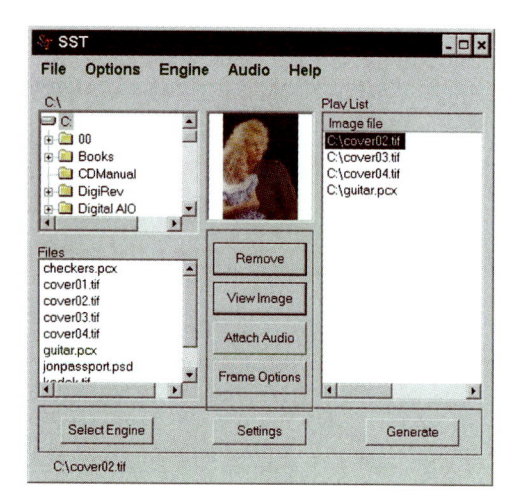

SST provides a few selectable options, which can be changed by clicking the Settings button. From there, you can change things such as image quality and size, as shown in Figure 8.15, or click the Preview Initial Settings button to change the transition mode, background color, and image position.

Figure 8.15
Screen Saver Toolbox's screensaver configuration dialog box lets you change image quality and size, transition mode, background color, and image position.

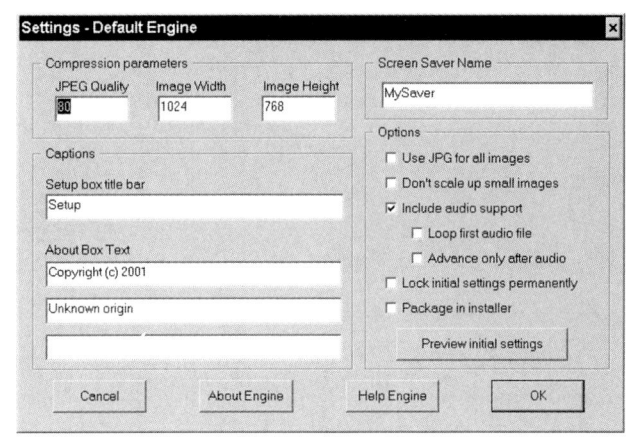

One of the most useful capabilities of SST is that it lets you generate a single file that contains an installation program and all of the show's images. You can put this single file on a disk or e-mail it, and you can install it on any PC without requiring the recipient to have additional software.

Now that you see how easy it is to create your own screensaver, what will you create? On your home PC, you could display photos from a recent overseas vacation or a family gathering or display photos of your pets or children. Alternatively, you might want to display the 20 best photos you have taken or images of a new boat or antique automobile, for example. At your office, you can use a screensaver to help promote a project or a new product design that you are currently working on. Or you might simply want to make a screensaver containing 10 funny images of your face. A little humor every now and then is surely worthwhile.

Incidentally, using the Display Properties dialog box shown in Figure 8.13 (or Desktop tab in Windows XP), you can select the Background tab and then select any image to be displayed as wallpaper for your desktop. You probably have many images that would make a great replacement for the background image that shows up when you install Microsoft Windows.

Guidelines for choosing the best application for your needs

The first part of this chapter gave you some firsthand experience with four excellent tools. However, these are just four out of literally hundreds of such tools that are available on the market to create photo albums, slide shows, and screensavers. Capabilities vary greatly among these applications. Without a doubt, you might inadvertently buy a product that won't meet your needs. For example, you might buy an application to create slide shows so that you can send a portfolio of all of your new artwork to prospective buyers, but if the application creates a slide show that requires the viewer to have the software, too, then you have the wrong application for your needs. This is just one example of the many ways you can get the wrong product.

> **TIP**
>
> You can often find the capability to create digital photo albums, slide shows, and screensavers in applications that you already own. Before you buy new software, first look carefully at any software that you have already purchased, especially applications that are bundled with printers, scanners, digital cameras, or even rewriteable CD-ROM drives. Finally, look carefully at any media-management applications that you might have, such as those that enable you to create thumbnails of each image in a directory. If you have Microsoft Office and it includes PowerPoint, then you already have an excellent slide show creation tool under the guise of a business presentation tool.

The goal of this section is to help you understand more about what you can do—or not do—based on a few key features. It will help you to decide which products are the best for you, based on how you intend to share your images.

Sharing your images with others

If your intent is to share your photo albums, slide shows, or screensavers with others, make sure that you select an application that does not require each of your recipients to purchase that application. Some slide show products create small, run-time programs that allow the show to be shown without additional software. (If you want to share this mini-program by e-mail, however, you may find that some e-mail programs will prevent your recipient from receiving it. So many executable programs sent by e-mail are viruses that they are often deleted by default!) Others require each viewer to have the application that it was created with.

Output options

Will you want to have printed copies of your albums and shows? If so, make sure that you have the options that you need. Do you want to show your work on the Internet? To post albums or slide shows on a Web site, you need an application that can create the necessary HTML code.

File and program size

File and program size might or might not be important to you. If you create small albums and slide shows, then the file size is likely to be small. If your shows contain rich multimedia effects and numerous large images, then your show will be large. Many e-mail providers have limits on the size of files that you can send. If you want to send e-mail and attach albums, slide shows, or even screensavers, the files and necessary viewers or programs must be compact. Some programs are excellent at creating tiny files, whereas others aren't.

Getting images from many sources

You can get digital images in many different ways. Digital images can come directly from a digital camera, a scanner, a digital image storage card, another PC, the Internet, an online gallery, an e-mail message, or a CD-ROM, as well as many other places. Obviously, it would really simplify the creation process if you could access all of these sources from within your application. If you don't make many albums, slide shows, or screensavers, having limited access might not be a problem.

Sorting, searching, and ordering images

The capability to sort, search, and order your images might or might not be important to you. When you're creating an album that can be used as an asset record, as discussed earlier in this chapter, you're likely to need searching capabilities. Likewise, if you are creating a slide show with more than 50 images to choose from, you will find that a variety of sorting and ordering features can be exceedingly valuable. In other cases, these features become essential. Imagine having to create a slide show from a CD-ROM full of sequentially numbered images taken with a digital camera. Without powerful sorting, searching, and ordering capabilities, you could go crazy!

Adding nonphoto "things"

In most cases, you will simply add digital images to photo albums, slide shows, and screensavers. However, every now and then you might want to create something much fancier. You might want to add sound or animated text or a few elegant slide-transition effects. You might also need to be able to add textual information to each of the images. Now that you know what is possible, you can decide what you want to do and then choose a product that will meet your needs.

Adding multimedia effects

You can create an effective photo album with just static images—and you can create an even more impressive photo album with multimedia effects. Besides image and graphics files, many photo album applications allow video and animation files, audio files, and even music from a CD-ROM. Adding these effects often is as easy as adding another image. If you want to do these things, look for an application that offers these features.

> **NOTE**
> A friend of a husband-to-be wanted to create a photo album of his friend's wedding as a wedding gift. He used one of the new digital recorders to record the wedding vows and a few conversations throughout the wedding. Using a digital camera, he took pictures of all the special moments—both of those being married and of those attending the wedding. Within a few hours, he created a multimedia photo album complete with wedding music from a CD-ROM, wedding vows, and many amusing comments. Using a writable CD-ROM drive, he was able to create a priceless 60-image multimedia gift for less than $1. The bad news: He had more than 30 requests for copies within two weeks of the wedding!

Adding text effects

Depending on how you intend to use your photo album, you might or might not want to add text. Some images would be entirely ruined with text placed over them. On other images, text makes the image much more understandable, informative, or entertaining. Another option for placing text is to create a separate slide for the text. The text can be placed on an image, on a background, or even on a graphic that is especially designed or chosen for the purpose. It is much easier to add these kinds of effects in your album or slide show application than it is to keep jumping out of one application into another.

Adding a database to your image collection

As your image database grows and you find yourself using photo albums or slide shows in more innovative ways, you likely will want a way to add textual information (or a database record) to each of your images. A good example of the use of a database with an image photo album is the asset-record application, discussed earlier in the chapter.

Applications to consider

Many high-quality, easy-to-use, feature-rich photo album, slide show, and screensaver applications are available on the market. The following list includes a few applications that you might want to consider:

- **Broderbund The Print Shop Photo Organizer**. This is a standalone product that also comes with The Print Shop Deluxe and The Print Shop Pro Publisher. The Print Shop Photo Organizer is an unusually simple, feature-rich product that enables you to create photo albums, slide shows, and screensavers.

- **Cerious Software ThumbsPlus**. This is a great product that, as Cerious claims, is ". . . the most effective, elegant, and inexpensive way to locate, view, edit, print, and organize your image, metafile, font, and multimedia files." ThumbsPlus is a shareware product that compares favorably against most of the commercial media-management applications.

- **Roxio PhotoSuite**. Not only is PhotoSuite one of the easiest applications to use, but it also offers a wide range of ways to save and share digital images. You can save a collection of images as an album to a disk or as an attachment to an e-mail, save them as a Web page, set one image as wallpaper, and create a slide show.

- **Microsoft PowerPoint**. This is a highly capable slide show tool that, as part of the Microsoft Office suite, is readily available on many PCs. Even though PowerPoint has been designed as a business presentation tool, you can use it to create excellent image slide shows. In addition, PowerPoint allows your slide shows to be uploaded to the Internet.

http://www.muskalipman.com

- **Ulead PhotoImpact Album.** This is a companion product to PhotoImpact, which is an unusually powerful image-editing tool that has some of the best features for creating Web images. PhotoImpact is unquestionably one of the best values in the graphics tool market.

- **Freeware and shareware versions.** Numerous freeware and shareware versions of photo album, slide show, and screensaver applications are available. In the Mac world, iPhoto is included with OS X, and is therefore free to users of that operating system. You can find other low-cost or no-cost programs in the Downloads section of CNET at **www.cnet.com**.

There it is—the chapter on photo albums, slide shows, and screensavers. Anyone who enjoys photography and owns a PC will enjoy viewing and sharing their digital images with these tools. Now we're off to the next chapter, where we'll look at other useful and fun things that you can do with your images.

9

Other Useful and Fun Things You Can Do with Images

Having the capability to take pictures and turn them into extraordinary digital images is good, but actually getting some practical value from your efforts by using your images is an entirely different challenge. This chapter is the second chapter that will help you learn more about what you can do with your digital images after you create them. This is a project-oriented chapter that provides you with plenty of good ideas about how you might use your images for work, home, or fun in a printed form.

In addition to giving you some ideas on how to use your images, this chapter introduces you to several software products that will help you complete your projects easily and professionally. Because the majority of PC users use Microsoft Office, we'll also look at ways to use your images with applications such as Word, Excel, PowerPoint, and Access.

Before we get started, though, let me make one suggestion: Don't underestimate your skills or your ability to successfully complete projects that you can be proud of. You might not think you are particularly talented, and you might have little graphic or artistic background, but fear not; with a little work and the right software products, almost anyone can complete projects that they are pleased with. With the combination of new and better computer hardware, software, supplies, and service companies, creating useful digital images yourself has never been easier. Moreover, you can produce digital images when you want to and the way you want to, and sometimes even for less money than with conventional film products. Therefore, have confidence and try a few of these projects. You'll see how talented you really are!

All the projects in this chapter have been created with consumer-level software products that cost well under $100, with a majority of them costing less than $40. As you will soon see, wizards and templates enable you to create all of these projects by following a series of simple steps. This means that you do not have to be a design or layout expert. It's almost like painting by numbers!

Image projects for business

No matter what kind of business you are in, you can improve your business's profile by using digital images. Dozens of software products are available that can help you create everything from business cards, letterhead, newsletters, and display signs to customized invoices, product catalogs, pamphlets, and brochures.

In this first section, we look at projects for creating business cards and letterhead, a project quote sheet prepared for a prospective customer, a product catalog, two postcards announcing a new chair design and a new studio gallery, and certificates for readers of this book.

Business cards and letterhead

Professional-looking business cards are essential for almost anyone in any kind of business—large or small. If you are not artistically talented, you might be asking yourself whether you are capable of creating a good-looking business card. With a good digital image or two, a few ideas about the design you want, and one of the better software products, you can. Let me show you how easy it can be.

First, you must decide what information you want to include on your card. Then, you need some idea about what you want the card to look like. If you are planning to use one or more images, you must also decide which ones to use. Often, the image that you want to use isn't as good as you would like it to be.

For this first example project, we'll create business cards for Windo-Bachs Flowers, Inc., a fictitious organization. We'll use two applications: Adobe Photoshop Elements and Roxio PhotoSuite. You could use just PhotoSuite if you wanted because the Roxio product includes easy-to-use photo-editing tools, but for this project, I wanted to have access to the more powerful tools available in Photoshop Elements. They're easy to use, too!

The first step is to load a flower photo to be used as a background into Photoshop Elements, as shown in Figure 9.1. It's a full color photo of a purple blossom that would look good on a full-color business card, but, unfortunately, our budget allows only a small color picture. We can spring for a toned background, though, if the picture can be converted to a less vivid sepia-colored rendition.

Figure 9.1
Transform a color photo into an old-fashioned sepia-toned version for a business card.

Fortunately, Photoshop Elements has a variety of recipes in its How To palette, including one for creating an old-fashioned or tinted photo. Click the link in the palette and follow the instructions using the wizard, and the photo is sepia-tinted in no time. As a final step, I used Photoshop Elements' Layers palette to give the image a faded, semi-transparent look. With the flower on its own layer, I adjusted the transparency of that layer to 50 percent.

202   Other Useful and Fun Things You Can Do with Images – Chapter 9

Then I loaded PhotoSuite, clicked the Compose button, and from the Business menu, selected Business Card. From a template I liked, I inserted the sepia flower folder, and then I added a single red rose from PhotoSuite's own library of images. After adding text, the finished business card, shown in Figure 9.2, was ready.

Figure 9.2
This business card was created in Roxio PhotoSuite.

PhotoSuite provides a variety of templates you can use. Figure 9.3 shows a business card being created for Specialty Mushrooms, Inc. In this case, a different template was used, but this card features only a single image. After you change the text and contact information, the card is done. The whole process takes less than 10 minutes.

http://www.muskalipman.com

Figure 9.3
A rich selection of templates gives you many layout options.

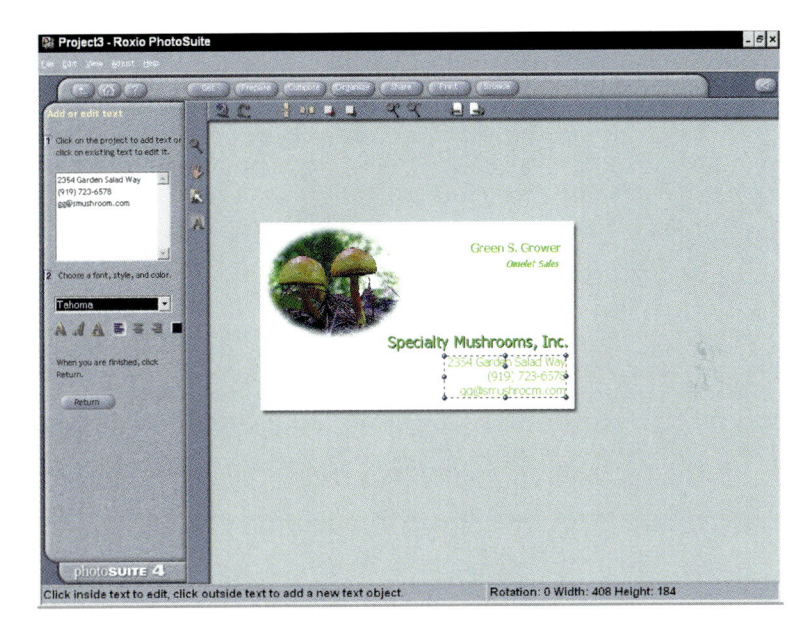

After you create a business card that you are happy with, you will need to print it. If you have a photo-quality inkjet printer, you can purchase business card paper especially created for inkjet printers. You can learn more about these business cards in Chapter 11, "Turning Digital Images into Prints." With specially formulated inkjet paper that features laser-perforated cards that tear as if they were cut, you can easily have professional-looking business cards printed, as you need them, directly from your computer on your own printer.

What if you don't have a good color printer or you want to have your design printed professionally? You have several choices. First, you can save your design to a removable disk in a standard file format and take it to a local printer. With the file on your disk, the printer can use your design to print your cards professionally. The cost of getting a printer to print your cards is more expensive than if you do them yourself. You also will find that most of the cost associated with printing is in the printer setup; therefore, printing 500 or even 1,000 cards is nearly as cheap as printing just a few hundred.

Another option for getting professionally printed business cards is to use the printing services of one of the many online Internet service companies. The number of such companies is growing and you have many choices, but I suggest iPrint.com (**www.iprint.com**), one of the early leaders in this market. iPrint.com does a fantastic job on business cards and letterhead. If you use iPrint.com, you need to supply your own image, if you want to include one. However, you don't need software other than your Internet browser. Simply visit iPrint's Web site and follow the steps. You can select from a wide variety of templates and then make changes to text, graphics, color, fonts, card size, and layout, as shown in Figure 9.4.

Figure 9.4
You can use the iPrint Web page to order customized business cards.

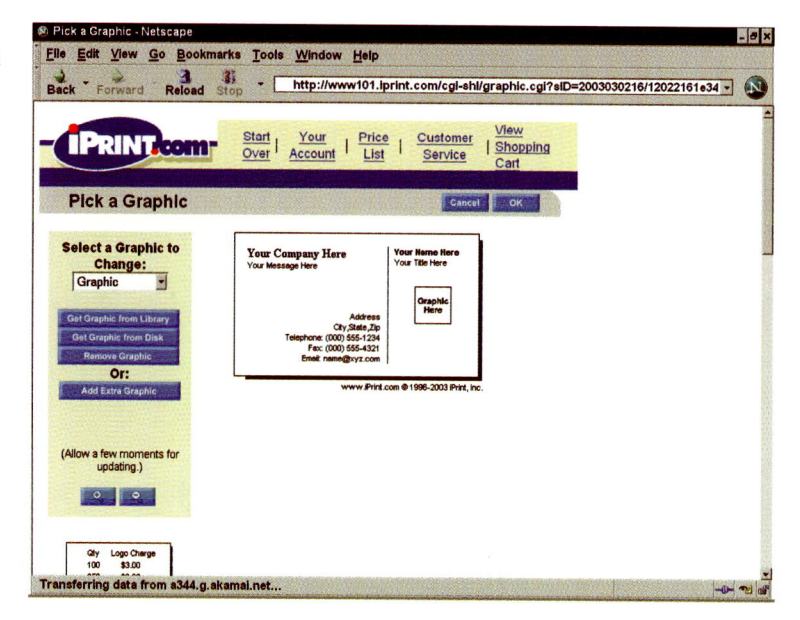

After you complete the design of your card, you can even print a "proof" on your own printer. When you are satisfied with the results, save your work and add it to the shopping cart. A few minutes later, your work is completed. Your cards will be ready to be printed and shipped directly to you within a couple of days. It doesn't get much easier than that. In addition to business cards, iPrint.com prints greeting cards, letterhead, business checks, envelopes, invitations, labels, and many other documents.

Project quote sheet

Are you good with a spreadsheet? If a spreadsheet is your tool of choice for calculating quotes for projects, then consider using it as the application to make project quote sheets for that new business you are pursuing. One way to increase new business is to improve the presentation of product and service offerings during the sales cycle, including the initial quote to prospective buyers. Figure 9.5 shows how the fictitious company, Garden Furniture Company, Inc., displays digital images of each proposed piece of furniture in its quotes. The images were taken with a digital camera and show each piece of furniture in a natural garden setting.

Figure 9.5
This project quote was created in an Excel spreadsheet.

This Project Quote sheet was easy to create. After the spreadsheet was set up, the images were cut and pasted directly from a digital image-editing application. Excel enables you to resize the images and move them around the page for precise placement. Each time a new product is created, an image is saved in a directory. This spreadsheet makes it easy to create new project quotes, which is just a matter of making sure the correct items are entered along with the order quantity. The spreadsheet then computes the total cost, including tax, shipping, and handling.

http://www.muskalipman.com

Product catalog pages

The Garden Furniture Company builds low-volume, high-priced, and—frequently—customized outdoor furniture, so having a catalog printed doesn't make sense because the products that it offers constantly change. However, the company still needs to be able to show its products on catalog pages. Using Microsoft Word, the company can easily create catalogs showing the exact pieces that it wants to show for any given purpose. Within a few minutes, employees can add and delete new or old products and quickly update the catalog, as shown in Figure 9.6.

Figure 9.6
You can use digital images and Microsoft Word to create a product catalog.

If Garden Furniture Company's product catalog needed to include more than just a handful of products, the company could use Microsoft Access to create its catalog pages. Access, the Microsoft database application, enables images to be stored as part of the database. After those images are stored, you can format them and print them as needed. The Microsoft Office applications are powerful tools that can be used to do many things. If you use Microsoft Office applications, it is worthwhile to learn more about how digital images can be used in each of the applications. You can find many additional ideas and application tips for Office products on Microsoft's Web page at **www.microsoft.com**.

Postcards

Sending a postcard is a good way to announce a sale or a new product line to prospective customers. Postcards can also be used to announce a new business offering, a new partner, a change of address, or just to let others know that your company is doing well and has recently won new business. Adobe Photoshop Elements and its watercolor filter were used to create the postcard shown in Figure 9.7, announcing a new bench design produced by The Garden Furniture Company. Hand-painted lettering was added to maintain the natural media design.

Figure 9.7
This postcard was used to announce a new garden bench design.

Figure 9.8 shows another example of a postcard, but this one was designed with a template. The postcard announces the opening of a new studio gallery. After you have a postcard design that you like, it is easy and inexpensive to have several thousand of them printed for little money. Online companies such as VistaPrint (**www.vistaprint.com**) print high-quality postcards for as little as $.04 each. You can design your own card online using the company's Web design tools.

Figure 9.8
These postcards announce the opening of a new studio and art gallery.

Certificates

A positive pat on the back is good, but a written certificate is even better. Using Ulead's Photo Express Platinum 2000, you can choose from a dozen templates for making certificates. Deciding that most readers of this book will be close to being digital image professionals when they complete it, I created the Digital Imaging Professional certificate that certifies each reader as being a digital imaging professional (see Figure 9.9).

Figure 9.9
Here's a specially created certificate for readers of this book.

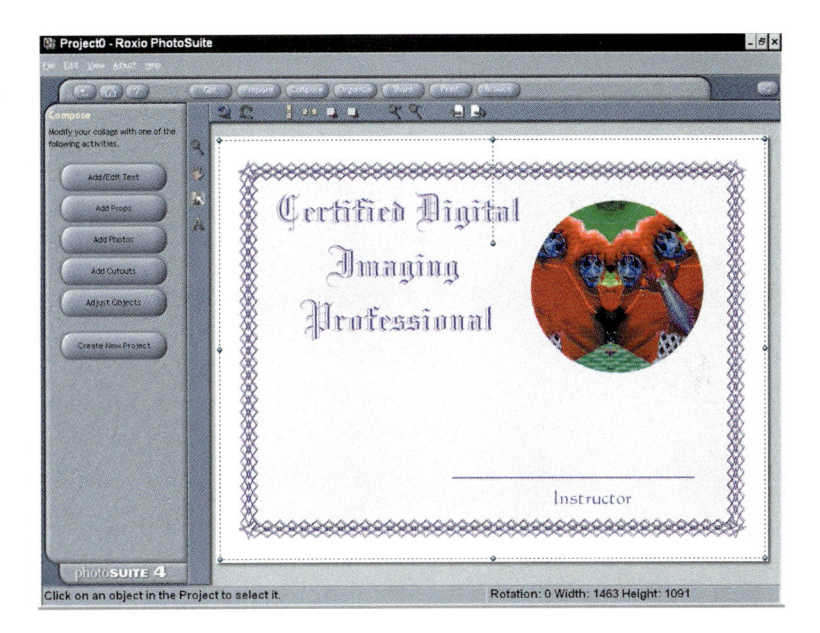

So far, we have looked at designs for only five different kinds of business projects out of many possible projects. You can also create signs, information cards and tags, pamphlets or brochures, banners, newsletters, and a million other kinds of projects.

To obtain other ideas for business projects, just think about your current business issues. Are you just about to roll out a new product or complete a large project? Do you need to improve the teamwork in a group of new employees? Maybe you need an entirely new business image or are in need of a regular employee newsletter. The use of appropriate digital images in your business documents can help you be more successful in accomplishing your business objectives. If you are still not sure how you can use images for your business, purchase one of the consumer image-editing products that offer many large "content" collections (images, clip art, project templates, and so forth). The Print Shop and PhotoSuite are excellent products for doing useful projects for both business and personal use, and they all have huge content collections.

http://www.muskalipman.com

Image projects for home

The previous section gave you a few ideas of how you might use digital images for projects for your business or work. Now we'll look at a few sample home projects. More specifically, we are going to look at ways to improve the ordinary look of personal letters and how you can create a collage, greeting cards, a wine bottle label, a calendar, photo album pages, a family tree picture, and a flyer. The Print Shop screen shown in Figure 9.10 shows a variety of other home and community projects that you might like to do.

Figure 9.10
The Print Shop screen shows a variety of items you can create for home and community.

Personal letters

If you are like me, you enjoy receiving a letter every now and then. It is nice to get an envelope in the mail with a return address indicating it is from someone you are excited to hear from and not just your local utility company. The more e-mail I get, the more I seem to value getting a letter. If someone has included photographs or digital images—that's even better. With the hope of starting a resurgence in sending real letters in the mail, let's look at how we can easily create letters that people will love to receive.

Chances are good that you have Microsoft Word (or Works), so let's use it to create a letter. To add a little tradition to our letter, how about selecting a font, such as Courier, that resembles the output of an old typewriter? Now how about adding an image? For the sake of this example, assume that both the sender and recipient enjoy cooking. If you have a digital camera, you could arrange a variety of things on your kitchen counter—maybe a few different kinds of fruit, vegetables, pasta, or even a row of cooking oil bottles. Just take a few pictures; don't fret too much about the quality of the pictures because quality won't matter much. Download the pictures from the camera to the computer and pick one that you like. That is exactly what I did for this example; I chose cooking oil bottles.

Using a masking technique from Chapter 6, "Performing Digital Imaging Magic," you can select the part of the image that you want to use and allow it to blend into the white background. Just before saving it, you will need to lighten it by about 50 percent. From a new document in Word, select Insert, Picture, From File, and then select the picture that you saved. After the picture loads, right-click it and select Format Picture from the pop-up menu. In the Format Picture dialog box that appears, select the Layout tab, select Behind Text, and then select Center as the choice for horizontal alignment. Click the OK button, and you are ready to type your letter, as shown in Figure 9.11. You should choose the Washout or Watermark color setting on the Picture tab of the Format Picture dialog box to tone down the image so the text is readable. In more recent versions of Word, you can choose Format, Background, Printed Watermark to insert a watermark.

Figure 9.11
You can use Microsoft Word to create an image watermark.

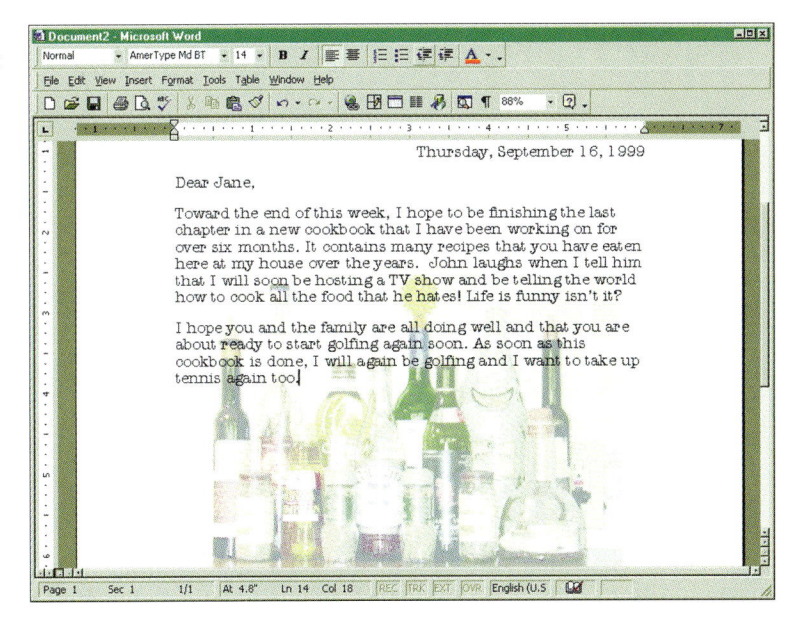

This process enables you to use any image as a watermark for writing paper. When you begin typing, you type right over the top of the image as if it were watermarked onto the paper. When you print it on a color deskjet printer, you will be pleased with the results. After you do this a time or two, you'll find that you can shoot a picture, adjust and place the watermark image, and begin to type in less than 10 minutes. This means that you can create great-looking letters to suit your taste any time that you need them.

You can make a watermark with any image you would like to use. It can be the face of a family member, an image of your new home, an old pet, or even a picture of one of your favorite roses from the garden. After you complete one watermark successfully with full color, check whether your digital image editor will create duotones. If so, try using a duotone (a two-color image) as a watermark; duotones make great watermark images. If you can't create duotones, just desaturate your image (remove all the color) and then tint it with one or two colors; you'll get the same results. To learn more about these techniques, see Chapter 7, "Filtering for Special Effects."

Microsoft Word has several other features that enable you to vastly improve the look of personal letters through the display of digital images. In the same dialog box that you used to set the watermark image, you are given a choice of aligning text square against an image, wrapping text around an image, or picking one of a few other text-formatting options. Learn about these features and create images with your digital image editor so that you can make text wrap around your image. Using the wraparound feature, you can, for example, have text run right up to the sloping edge of a Christmas tree on both sides. You can keep typing until the Christmas tree is surrounded by text.

While we are on the letter-writing topic, let's see what we can do with holiday letters. For the past several years, it seems that more and more people are getting into the tradition of writing and sending family holiday letters around Christmastime. These letters usually tell what each family member has done during the year and end with best wishes for the new year. Unless these letters (or sometimes poems) are well written and interesting, they often just sit in the Christmas card pile, unread. Using appropriate digital images and a few less words, you can say more and in a more interesting way. Consider sending a Christmas letter this year with a few digital images to differentiate your letters from the others in the pile.

I have always liked the idea of a Christmas letter but have never been able to get them out by Christmas. Therefore, each year, I plan to send a Christmas letter, and when it's not done until well into January, I send it as a New Year's letter—appropriately ending the old year and wishing the best to all for the new year. This past January, I combined a variety of pictures into one letterhead image for our New Year's letter, as shown in Figure 9.12.

Figure 9.12
This digital image used on a New Year's letter combines duotones and color images.

Although this image was not difficult to create, it did take time because it was made from 10 images carefully selected and cut from 10 different photographs. After copying and pasting the four larger faces into a file, the file was converted to a duotone. Then each of the other six images was scaled and placed on top of the duotone in full color. The combined image was then placed at the top of a sepia-colored 8 1/2 × 11-inch paper on which the New Year's letter was written.

Creating a photomontage

Sometimes you'll want to combine more than one image into a single image to get the results that you desire. Combining photographs is an old technique that has been used for years. Until now, however, you had to cut and paste without all the benefits of the new digital cut-and-paste techniques. With any digital image editor, you can quickly create an image such as the one shown in Figure 9.13—without fuss.

214   Other Useful and Fun Things You Can Do with Images – Chapter 9

Figure 9.13
This photomontage was created with PhotoSuite.

With a little more effort and a lot more time, you can even create an image such as the one shown in Figure 9.14. After carefully selecting six images from six separate photographs and inserting them into a single image, the picture looks like five goalies are in the game. After all the images were placed, a watercolor filter was applied to give it an artsy look. It sure looks like it's hard to score a goal against the team with the goalie wearing the yellow jersey, even if you use more than one ball!

Figure 9.14
Here we combined soccer goalies from a variety of images into a single image.

http://www.muskalipman.com

Another technique that has become popular in recent years is creating an image composed of hundreds or even thousands of other images. When I first saw one of these images in a shopping mall, I began to wonder who would take the time to create such an image. Many of these merchants would offer dozens of these posters! Now you can create such an image in the time that it takes you to fix and eat a sandwich—which you might want to do because the creation process takes more than a few minutes, depending on the speed of your computer. Figure 9.15 was created by using PhotoSuite and the PhotoTapestry effect. PhotoTapestry re-creates any photograph by using small, thumbnail photos from a large thumbnail database that comes with the product.

Figure 9.15
You can create a PhotoTapestry with PhotoSuite.

In case you were wondering, the PhotoTapestry print shown in Figure 9.15 was made with 1,500 separate images. It took 20 minutes to create. That's not too bad, considering how long it would have taken to do manually. The final print was 11 × 16 inches and was printed on photographic quality paper. It turned out quite well—well enough, in fact, to generate lots of questions asking how long it took me to pick and place all of those separate images!

Greeting cards

Greeting cards might be one of the most popular projects to create for those who have a color printer. Most greeting card creation software, unfortunately, offers far more cards with no space or little space for images than cards with space for images. This means that you have to

http://www.muskalipman.com

get creative and make your own cards by extensively modifying one of the predesigned templates included with the software. When a friend fell off her horse and broke a few ribs, we decided to add a little humor to the painful event. I found an old photograph of her horse that I had taken a year or so earlier, and I used a few filters on it to make it look more like an image for a humorous greeting card. The result of this work is the card shown in Figure 9.16.

Figure 9.16
This get-well card features the recipient's horse.

If you have a favorite image or two, you might want to make your own note cards, like the one shown in Figure 9.17. That particular cat image was printed on an embossed greeting card stock, which made it look wonderful. For someone who likes cats, this card would be hard to throw away because the eyes are bright and magical; in fact, the eyes appear to be looking straight at you. It's almost a work of art.

Figure 9.17
This embossed note card features a cat image taken with a digital camera.

Wine bottle labels

Not too long ago, I attended a wedding at which an impressive touch was added to the occasion—they served wine and a sparkling beverage in wine bottles that had custom labels made especially for the wedding. With a little creativity, you too can add such a special touch to a wedding, a birthday party, or other special event. Using PhotoSuite, you can pick from a good selection of wine bottle templates or create your own from scratch. Add an image and some appropriate text, and you have created a unique label for a bottle that someone is likely to want to keep forever. Figure 9.18 shows a wedding label that was created especially for Jack and Jill. If you have an anniversary coming up, consider making a special label for the occasion. My wife is considering making one for me when this book is finished!

Figure 9.18
You can create a wine bottle label with PhotoSuite.

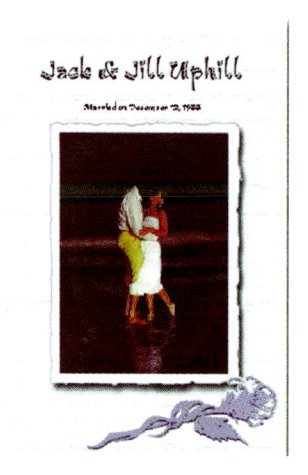

Image projects for kids

If you have children, you will probably have more ideas about how to use your images on projects for the kids than you have time to complete them. To make sure this chapter is complete, however, I will list a few useful and fun projects you might like to do.

Birthday party invitations

First, how about creating a birthday party invitation? You'll be a hero to little Johnny as well as his guests if you use a little imagination and create a personalized birthday party invitation. Maybe your child is into cars, gymnastics, or baseball. Use these or other topics to create cards specifically for your child, or just use a standard template and create one similar to Figure 9.19.

Flyers

Sometimes families need to create one or more flyers. Flyers are good for selling used sports equipment, finding a babysitter, selling a car, or even finding a lost turtle (see Figure 9.19). Kids can use flyers to get jobs mowing lawns or raking leaves. Flyers are easy to create with any word processor or desktop publishing package, or programs like Photoshop Elements, PhotoImpact, or PhotoSuite.

http://www.muskalipman.com

Other Useful and Fun Things You Can Do with Images – Chapter 9   219

Figure 9.19
Here's a birthday invitation and lost turtle flyer.

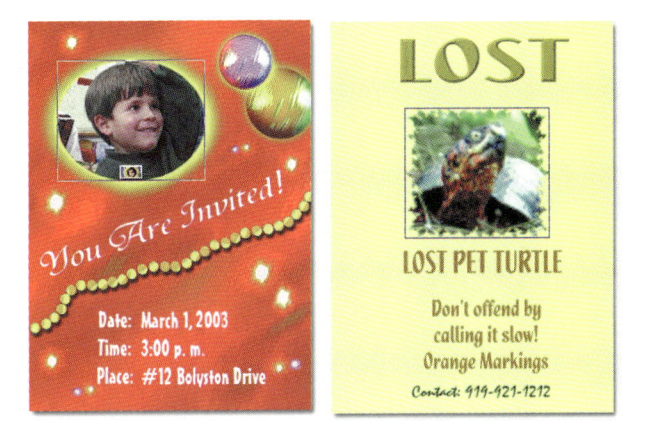

Creating fun pictures

One of the advantages of living in a neighborhood is that children often get to be close friends as they grow up together. Think about creating an image of your children's friends that they can put on a T-shirt or use on their notebook covers. The image in Figure 9.20 was created for a greeting card that invited the neighborhood gang to a birthday party and a movie. It was a big hit—both the evening and the card!

Figure 9.20
Here's a picture of the "neighborhood gang."

http://www.muskalipman.com

Sometimes it's fun just to create things with no real purpose in mind. The images in Figures 9.21 and 9.22 were both created just for the fun of it.

Figure 9.21
This newspaper was created with Microsoft Picture It!

Figure 9.22
This magazine cover was created in PhotoSuite.

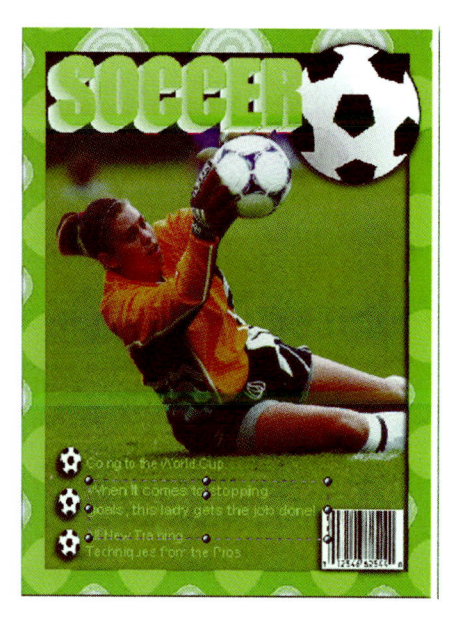

Images for coaches

Youth sport coaches donate a tremendous amount of time and effort to coach teams. Unless you have coached a team, it might appear to be much easier and more fun that it oftentimes is. Thank your child's coaches for the efforts they put into teaching your child how to play a sport by presenting them with a signed and framed image of the team. Figure 9.23 is an image that was created for a coach whose son played on the team. The coach's son was a tremendous lacrosse player and led the team in goals. If you look carefully, you can see that there are four pictures of the player wearing 21 on his jersey—that is the coach's son, and in three of those four images, he had just scored. The collage on the bottom was created by digitally cutting, pasting, sizing, and adjusting parts of four other photographs. The final image was set in a matte border and framed. Each player wrote his jersey number and signed his name on the border. This gift will be valued for a long time.

Figure 9.23
This season-end photograph was created for a parent coach.

Sports cards and posters

After you are able to create quality digital images and projects from your pictures, you might be able to use this talent to help raise funds for your child's sports teams. At the end of the lacrosse season one year, I chose the best photograph of each player and digitally edited and printed it on a high-quality fine-art paper or photographic paper, depending on the style of the work. These images were then made available to the parents for $20, with the understanding that the entire amount would be donated back to the team to purchase new jerseys for an upcoming season. Nearly all of the images were sold, and the team was able to buy new jerseys in the following year. Five of these images are shown in Figure 9.24.

Figure 9.24
These digitally edited images of lacrosse players were created to raise money for the team.

If you have limited time for creating these projects but you need them done, consider teaching your children how to use the applications. Help them come up with a few ideas for projects that they would like to do. Suggest things such as a book or notebook cover, bookmarkers, or pages for school reports. After the kids experience a little success, they will continue building on it and can become your own in-house design staff. It is amazing to see how quickly children can become experts on computer technologies. Who knows—maybe your kids can even help you do things for your own business or work, which will give you a little more time to get them to all of those soccer practices, while still keeping up with the other household chores!

http://www.muskalipman.com

Image creations just for art's sake

When you were a child, did you spend most of your free time drawing or painting? Have you always wanted to be able to create artwork that was good enough that you could frame it and put it on the walls in your own home or office? If a part of you is just dying to be creative, my advice is to begin creating art—just for art's sake.

Skip a few evenings of watching TV or aimlessly surfing the Internet and instead spend your time working with a digital image editor. Go back through your old photographs and pull out a few dozen that look interesting. Scan them and then experiment to see what you can do with them. Buy a digital camera and begin shooting pictures specifically to create digital images. Chapter 2, "Learning to Take Better Pictures," offers a "starter set" of digital-imaging techniques that will help you shoot images that you can use to create work that you will be pleased with.

Artwork to be framed

About 10 years ago, I stopped on a long, desolate stretch of highway to take a few pictures of several old rusty cars. When I looked for a few photographs to use for this book, I found those pictures and immediately realized how good they might look after a few filters were applied. Twenty minutes later, one of those photographs had turned into a 6 × 10-inch print on fine-art paper. The highlights in the window, on the headlights, and in the open suitcase make this a spectacular print (see Figure 9.25).

Figure 9.25
This art-quality print depicts an open suitcase and old cars.

http://www.muskalipman.com

After adding a signature, a date, and a border, this picture looked like a real painting. Figure 9.26 shows a second image that was transformed into an art-like print. There is no reason why you can't create images like these. Try it.

Figure 9.26
This photograph was turned into artwork with filters.

Images to accompany short stories

Do you enjoy writing, as well as taking photographs and creating digital images? If you do, here is an idea that might appeal to you. Take 10 or so of your favorite digital images, transform them into similar types of images with a few filters, and add an appropriate frame to them. Use each one as the basis for a short story. You can choose to use images with a common subject and write stories for children, or for anyone for that matter. You might even want to write these stories just about the real events that surround the images that you have chosen. The transformed images can often be a strong impetus to help you write a great story with more clarity and detail than you might have written without the images (see Figure 9.27). Who knows—your stories might be so good that you can get them published!

Figure 9.27
Here's one of several duotone images that were created for a series of short stories.

The point here is that if you enjoy being creative, then create. Buy a few software applications and a good color printer and enjoy yourself. You'll never know how good you can be until you try.

Stitching images together to create a panorama

Anyone who has taken pictures with a camera has, at one time or another, felt the frustration of not being able to get the full view of what you want in the picture. Until recently, solutions to this problem were limited. You could use an expensive wide-angle or fish-eye camera lens, which has a tendency to warp the world to make it all fit in an image. Alternatively, you could shoot multiple photos and tape them together, which I've done before. Now we have digital image-stitching software—software that enables you to digitally stitch a series of digital images together in a seamless and continuous manner for perfect panoramic images, prints, or even movies.

http://www.muskalipman.com

With digital image-stitching software and a printer that enables you to print on paper wider than 11 inches, you can create those panoramas that you have always dreamed about. As one of those work-at-home types, I am a member of the Small Office/Home Office (SO/HO) Club. For my Web page, I wanted to include a view of my office, which has windows on three sides. Without digital-stitching software, this office is terribly difficult to photograph and even more difficult to show online. I took eight pictures in the fall with all the rich fall colors showing through the windows. After I scanned the images and put them into a folder, I was able to flawlessly stitch them together in about 10 minutes. The result is the image shown in Figure 9.28. Ah, how right you are—the image is too wide to show on a single book page.

You can scroll the image inside your browser's window to see the entire image. Pretty cool, wouldn't you say? If you think that's cool, read on to learn how you can create a full 360-degree panoramic movie with zooming, panning, and tilting capabilities.

Figure 9.28
This panorama view of a home office was made by digitally stitching multiple images together.

NOTE

Hoping to create a different kind of art that would sell well in galleries, an artist decided to create exceptionally wide and narrow panoramic views of famous landscapes and cityscapes. Using multiple photographs, digital image-editing software, and some digital image-stitching software, the artist was able to create some unique and outstanding prints. A commercial printer of tourist posters saw several of his images and commissioned him to complete panoramic views of 25 cities to be sold in stores attracting tourists.

PhotoSuite includes simple stitching software, which is sufficient to stitch a few images together. It even enables you to choose from several stitching methods, including wide (for horizontal panoramas) or tall (for vertical scenes). You can use images that are already stored on your computer as image files, or you can acquire them directly from your scanner or digital camera.

http://www.muskalipman.com

Other Useful and Fun Things You Can Do with Images – Chapter 9

Adobe Photoshop Elements also has a powerful stitching capability called Photomerge. Photomerge can find the overlapping areas of photos and merge them for you automatically. All you have to do is locate the image files you want to merge, as shown in Figure 9.29. Photomerge then imports the pictures and stitches them together. If need be, you can manually move any of the photos around to get a closer match, as you can see in Figure 9.30.

Figure 9.29
To use the Photoshop Elements Photomerge capabilities, simply locate the files you want to stitch together.

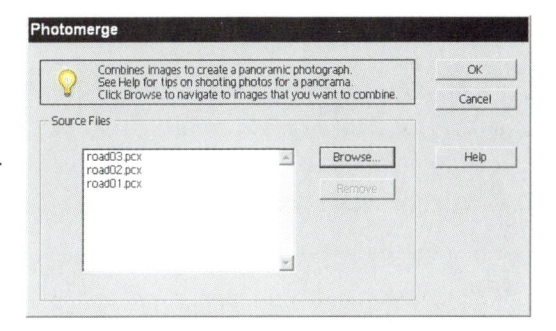

Figure 9.30
Photomerge finds the overlapping areas and combines the photos automatically.

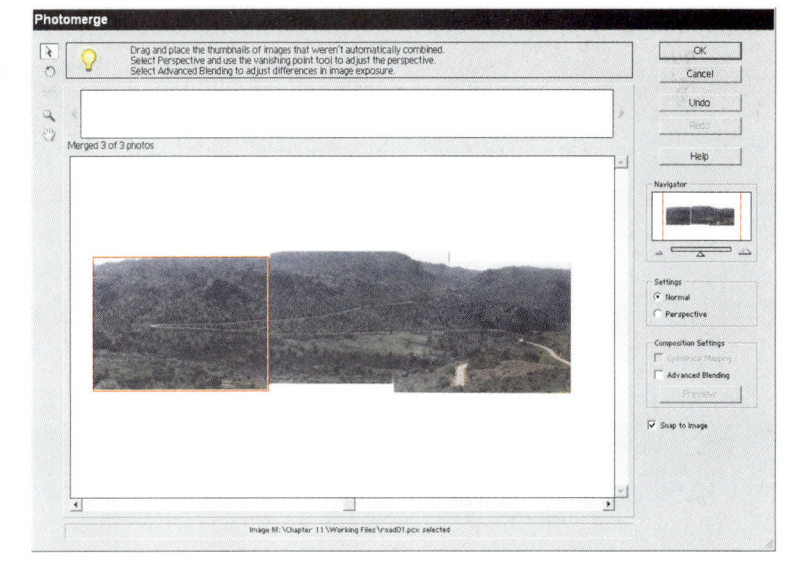

TIP
Before you spend money on a digital image-stitching application just to create wide panoramic views, check all of your current software to see whether it might have the capabilities to stitch together images. Some digital cameras come bundled with a lite version of image-stitching software.

Other cool things to do with images

Most of the projects covered in this chapter so far have resulted in images that were to be printed on one kind of paper or another. Your images can be put onto many other objects, such as T-shirts, mouse pads, coffee mugs, sweatshirts, puzzles, hats, ties, aprons, buttons, tote bags, and a wide range of additional items. Check with your local photoprocessor to see what items they offer. If you don't find something that you like, visit one of the Internet sites.

In the preceding pages, we looked at projects for home, work, kids, and you. Don't forget that you can also use digital images in projects for your church, special-cause groups, and other organizations. Tradition is the basis for many of these types of organizations. Often, these traditions can be strengthened and grown by creating some documentaries of people and events. Help make your church bulletins or newsletters more interesting by adding some appropriate digital images. Scan photographs to document fundraising events or work done by charity groups. People enjoy seeing themselves in pictures, if the pictures are good.

The projects in this chapter are just a few of the millions that you can do. The point of this chapter is a simple one: You can do many more things with your digital images than simply using them digitally (on a Web page or as an e-mail attachment) or printing them like photographs. Be creative and invent your own projects, or use templates and modify them to suit your own needs.

At this point, if you are going to be caught in the vicious circle of digital imaging, you are in it now. This vicious circle begins when you reach the point at which you can create images that you really like, and you begin using those images to make things such as those mentioned in this chapter. The more you use your images to complete projects, the more projects you will want to do—and the more images you'll need to complete these projects. I am most certainly caught in this circle and hope that you will join me. Life is supposed to be fun, and digital-imaging projects can certainly be fun—especially when you start seeing the joy that others experience when they receive your work. I hope that you will experience the joy of seeing someone else truly appreciate your work. That makes it worth the time, effort, and money.

In the previous chapter, we looked at ways to create digital things—digital photo albums, slide shows, and screensavers. This chapter introduced you to many projects that resulted in nondigital things, such as printed calendars, greeting cards, business cards, sports cards, and bookmarks, to name just a few. In the next chapter, we'll return to the digital world and learn how to share images electronically.

Part IV
Sharing & Enjoying Your Images

10 Sharing Images 231

11 Turning Digital Images into Prints 263

10
Sharing Images

As you learn to create quality digital images and your digital image portfolio grows in size, you probably will want to share your work. In this chapter, you will learn how to use e-mail, e-postcards, and e-greeting cards, and the Web to share digital images. Additionally, you will see some exciting new possibilities for sharing images in real time by using chat applications or one of the new instant messengers (IMs). The use of IMs is growing incredibly fast, and one of the reasons is related to the interactive capabilities that IMs offer. Such interactive capabilities are wonderful for sharing digital images.

Several of the more significant benefits of working with digital images are gained only when you take advantage of the capability to share them electronically. Using the Internet makes sharing images incredibly easy, with virtually no cost involved. You can send a digital image to 100 friends almost as easily as you can send it to one friend, and for little cost—which surely isn't the case for traditional, film-based photographs!

Not too long ago, I completely gutted my kitchen down to the wall studs and floor beams. I enjoy woodworking and building projects, so I opted to do it myself. Many business colleagues, family, and friends knew I had undertaken the project and were always interested in how it was going. I posted images to a Web site and frequently sent e-mails telling them where on the Internet I had posted images of newly completed electrical, plumbing, or sheetrock work. Occasionally, I had questions and was able to e-mail images to friends who were contractors and could help. With the benefit of the images, they could offer good advice. Likewise, twice I got advice from builders on home-building or kitchen-design forums. It was a great building experience that I was able to share with others who cared—and that made it even more enjoyable. Now two of our friends have decided to redo their kitchens, and they say that they have enough experience to tackle the project based on watching ours being done.

Expertise in using these new communication technologies can be rewarding. At the very least, it enables you to communicate more effectively, share images without cost, renew old friendships, communicate more frequently with geographically remote contacts, and more fully enjoy your images through the interactive sharing capabilities of IMs. This is a valuable chapter that I know you will find useful.

Sharing Images

To share images, everyone involved must have the right stuff. What is the right stuff? First, some examples of what it means not to have the right stuff might be helpful. Have you ever

- ▶ Received e-mail that you could not read?
- ▶ Had someone send e-mail to you at the right address, but it never arrived?
- ▶ Received e-mail with an attachment and, upon opening it, got an incredibly long file full of strange characters?
- ▶ Received an electronic document, such as one created in a word processor, but didn't have the software or the correct version and couldn't open it?
- ▶ Had someone send e-mail to your office while you were home, but because you have a different e-mail service at home, you could not receive it?

If any of these examples is familiar to you, then you know what can happen when you don't have "the right stuff."

So what exactly is the right stuff? The right stuff is whatever is required to make communications work as intended. That means that you need the right hardware (sometimes, although increasingly rarely, a PC instead of a Macintosh computer), the right communications link (a network or networks that can connect), the right viewer (an application that lets you view what was sent), and the capability to receive the file (not too large, because some e-mail providers limit file size). Finally, you have to be able to access your e-mail, meaning that you must be able to physically get to a machine that has the right software and communication capabilities to get the e-mail. If any one of these variables is not correct, you will experience frustration instead of successful communication.

Accessibility is everything

Taking a simplistic view, there are two types of e-mail applications:

- Desktop-based e-mail applications, such as Microsoft Outlook, currently offer more features than browser-based e-mail applications and integrate well with other desktop applications.
- Internet browser-based e-mail applications, such as Hotmail, and some office e-mail systems enable you to send and receive e-mail anywhere in the world that has Internet access.

Note that neither application type is necessarily superior—they are just different. The point here is to recognize what you can and can't do with your e-mail and your intended recipient's e-mail configurations. Some e-mail providers let you use both. For example, if you use America Online (AOL) at home, you can use the AOL application to send and receive e-mail. However, you can still access your AOL mail from any computer that has Web access by going to the AOL Web page at **www.aol.com**. There, the AOL Anywhere feature can log you in using your regular AOL screen name and password, and then it can take you directly to a Web page where you can send and receive mail messages.

If you have a desktop-based e-mail service, you can add flexibility to your e-mail capabilities by also signing up for a free, Internet-based e-mail service. The downside with free e-mail services is that they typically allow a maximum of 2MB of storage, so if you receive many images, you'll have to clean out old e-mail frequently.

TIP
If you want to sign up for a free e-mail service, visit **www.cnet.com** and search for "e-mail." CNET provides a recommended list of free e-mail services.

In conclusion, if you want global accessibility, then sign up for an Internet-based e-mail service; you'll be able to access your e-mail from anywhere that you can get access to the Internet and on any kind of computer.

> **NOTE**
> A professional photographer who travels frequently uses an Internet-based e-mail application so that he can easily send and receive e-mail, often with digital images. This enables him to read or send e-mail or view images from any hotel, library, or office in the world that has a connection to the Internet.

It takes the right kind of viewer to view

If something goes wrong with an e-mail message, odds are that it has an attached image file. Many e-mail servers either mutilate image files or reject them because they exceed a predefined maximum file size. If the image file is successfully sent and received, then the next step is for the recipient to view it.

To view an attached image, an appropriate viewer is needed—either the application that was used to create the image or a viewer application that can read a variety of image file types. If you send the image in one of the more standard formats, such as BMP, TIFF, or JPEG, your recipient is likely to be able to view it with a standard viewer that comes with the operating system. These standard viewers are limited in their capabilities, though. If you send large images, using one of these viewers makes viewing them difficult. If an image is turned sideways (which is common when you shoot a picture in portrait mode), the recipients might have to turn their heads sideways to view it.

File size matters more than you think

When sending e-mail, it is considered rude to send large image files—unless the recipient has requested that you do so or has agreed in advance that you send them. You'll understand this the first time that you are in a hurry to get your e-mail and it takes 10 minutes or more to download a single e-mail loaded with images.

To avoid annoying others with excessively large e-mail attachments, consider one or more of the following:

- ▶ Reduce the size of an image (such as from 1280 × 1024 pixels to 640 × 480).
- ▶ Reduce the file size by using one of the compressed image file types, such as JPEG. See Chapter 5, "Getting Images into Shape," for a complete discussion of this topic.

▶ Combine and compress your images by using a compression utility, such as WinZip. WinZip is a compression and archiving tool that you can download at **www.winzip.com** as a free evaluation version. Be aware that when files are compressed and zipped on one end, they need to be unzipped on the other end. Therefore, both the sender and the recipient need WinZip or an equivalent application.

▶ Don't e-mail the image or images. Instead, post them to a Web site and then send an e-mail with a pointer to the URL. This approach is covered later in this chapter.

Incidentally, many e-mail services have limits placed on the file size that can be sent or received. If you exceed this limit, your e-mail is returned to you. Because many of the free e-mail services limit e-mail storage space to less than 2MB, having e-mail with image attachments returned due to insufficient storage space is a common experience.

Using e-mail to send images

E-mail is often referred to as a "killer application" because it is useful and enough fun to prompt many people to buy a computer just to have e-mail capabilities. The easiest way to share images is with e-mail. Using e-mail, you can share images in any one of the following ways:

▶ Send an image as an attachment to e-mail.

▶ Send an e-mail with a URL pointer, pointing to the Web site where the image is posted.

▶ Embed an image into the e-mail, provided that the sender and the recipient have HTML-based e-mail applications.

Most e-mail applications support the first two methods, but HTML-based e-mail is usually only possible on the newer e-mail applications, such as Microsoft Outlook. The following section looks at some of the advantages and disadvantages to each of these approaches.

NOTE

An interior designer who is making an out-of-town shopping trip for several clients thinks that she has found the perfect desk for one of her client's home office. The question is whether the client will also think it's perfect. Using a digital camera, she shoots several pictures, making sure to show the beautiful wood grain and detailed carvings. She knows that she has captured the images that she wants because she can view them in the LCD. Using her notebook computer, she sends an e-mail to her client with the images attached. Within a few minutes, she gets an e-mail back from her client saying, "It looks terrific. Buy it!"

http://www.muskalipman.com

Sending images as an e-mail attachment

The easiest way to send images is via an e-mail attachment. This is as painless as selecting Insert, File from your e-mail application and then selecting the image file by using a file browser. The e-mail application then attaches the file when you send the e-mail message and indicates in the message that it has an attached file, as shown in Figure 10.1.

Alternatively, many applications such as image portfolio, greeting card, and digital camera software make it equally easy to send images. With an image, images, or a document of some type selected, you simply select Send To, Mail Recipient. Your e-mail application is then automatically launched and the appropriate file (or files) is included as an attachment. After you complete your e-mail message, you can send the file—it's really that easy! This is one technique that you must learn how to do if you intend to share your images.

Figure 10.1
It's easy to send an image as an attachment to an e-mail message.

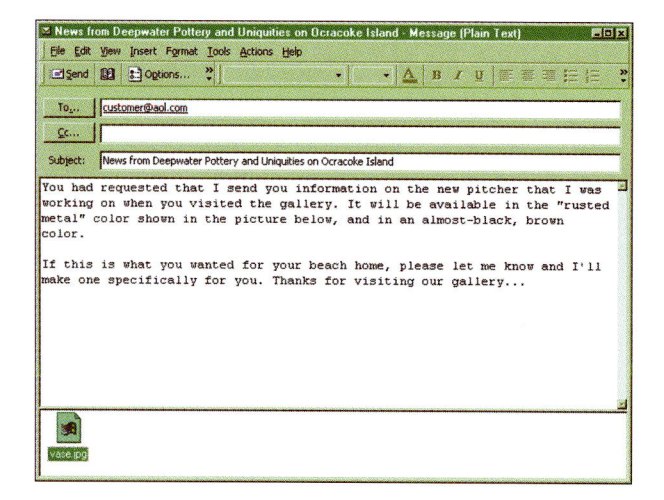

The advantage to sending an image as an attachment to an e-mail message is that it is easy to do. The disadvantages are that the recipient has to have the right kind of viewer application, and sending the image requires the recipient to download the image to get the e-mail. These disadvantages might make more sense after you read about the next two ways to send images.

When the recipients receive the e-mail, they see the image represented as a file icon embedded in the message. To view the image, they simply need to double-click the icon, and the image will be displayed in their default image viewer. The key here is that the recipients must have an appropriate image viewer for the file type that you send.

http://www.muskalipman.com

Sending e-mail with a URL pointer

The best way to avoid sending a large image (or lots of images) to someone who might not want to take the time to download and view it is to post the image to a Web site and then send an e-mail with a URL pointer, telling the recipient where the image can be viewed (see Figure 10.2). The "hotlink" pointer makes it easy for the recipient to jump from her e-mail to the images on your site by using an Internet browser. This approach also eliminates the problems that occur when the recipient does not have sufficient storage capacity or the appropriate software to view the images.

Figure 10.2
You can use a URL pointer to share a digital image.

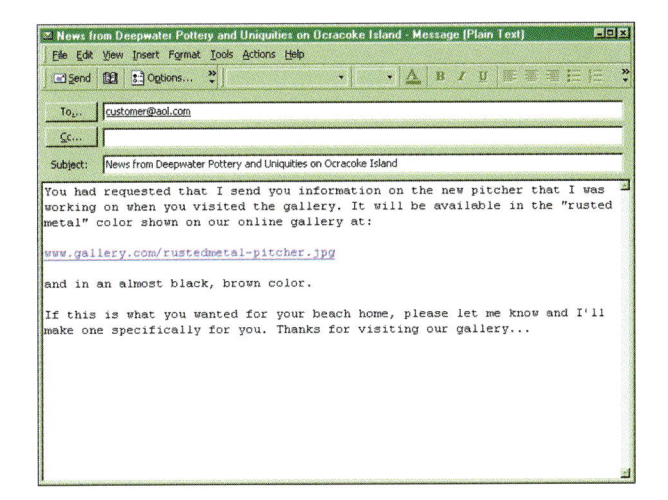

An advantage of this approach is that the e-mail will not contain the images, so it will be small and quick to download. It also enables your recipients to decide when (and if) they want to view the images. Another advantage is that if the recipient has access to the Internet, it is highly likely that she will be able to view your images with her browser. She will not need a viewer application; she can view the page by using any kind of computer, including a Macintosh, IBM PC, or one using Linux or UNIX.

One final advantage to this approach is that as long as you leave the images on your Web site, the images can be viewed from anywhere that has a browser and an Internet connection. This is in sharp contrast to having the images attached to an e-mail that is located on a PC that might not be accessible.

Using HTML-based e-mail to send images

If you have ever received e-mail that looks just like a Web page, you have received HTML-based e-mail. HTML-based e-mail is becoming an increasingly popular way to send e-mail. It allows e-mail to include anything that can be included on a Web page, such as formatted text, graphics, background colors, hotlinks, and textures.

For instance, using Microsoft Word, you can create a Web page directly in Word. You create this page just like any other Word document. Then, instead of saving it as a DOC file, you save it as a Web page file with the .htm extension. After you save the file as a Web page, you can right-click on it (either from Windows Explorer or Word's File, Open dialog box) and select Send To, Mail Recipient from the context menu that pops up, and then send it as a Web page. When you choose to do this, Word transforms into a hybrid Word and Outlook package, as shown in Figure 10.3.

Figure 10.3
You can use Microsoft Word to create an HTML-based e-mail.

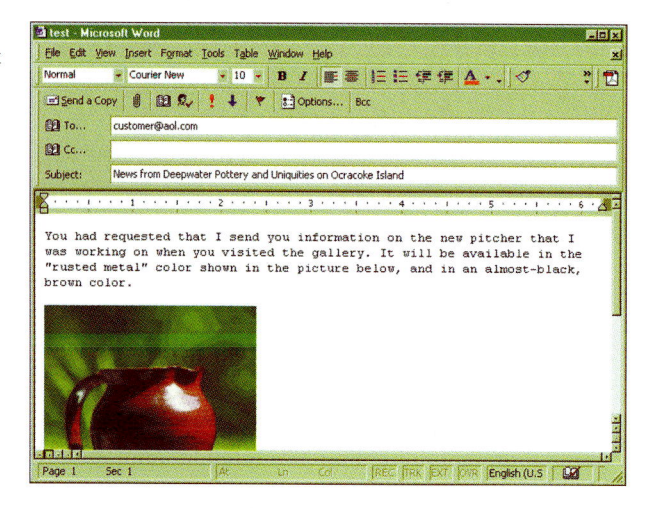

If the recipient does not have an HTML-capable e-mail application, she can view the file in a browser, as shown in Figure 10.4.

Figure 10.4
You can view an HTML-based e-mail in a browser.

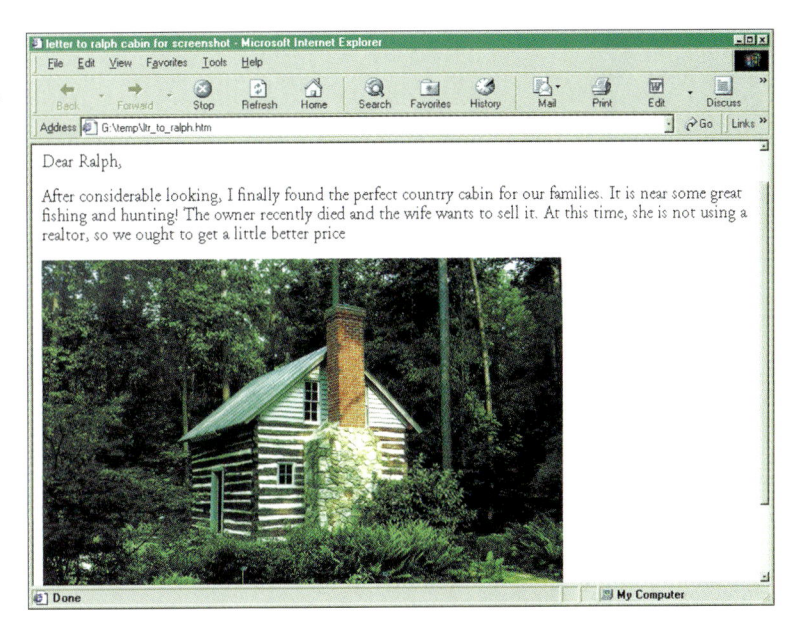

Like the other two approaches, HTML-based e-mail also has advantages and disadvantages. The advantage is that you can lay out a page containing your images by using an application that you might be used to using (such as Microsoft Word) and then use it to convert the document into a Web page. Your recipients can then see the entire layout exactly as you created it.

The disadvantage is that the recipient must have a browser or an e-mail application that can display HTML Web pages. The recipient must also download all the images on the page. The fact that the images are displayed on a Web page, however, is a good indication that they are small, compressed files. You are likely to see more e-mail being sent in this format in the future.

Now that you know about three possible ways to let your e-mail recipients view your images, you should be able to share your images more effectively. Next we'll look at some exciting variations of desktop e-mail.

http://www.muskalipman.com

Sharing images with electronic postcards and greeting cards

I have always liked postcards—one side shows an image or graphic, and the other side has a little room for a short, to-the-point message. Postcards are fun to send and fun to receive. Now you can send the digital equivalent of a postcard using your own images, which in my opinion is even better. If you want to send a card for a special occasion, you can turn your postcard into an Internet greeting card.

There are hundreds of Web sites that let you create postcards and greeting cards that you can send over the Internet. These come and go with alarming frequency, so I suggest you find one using the search engine at Google (**www.google.com**), using a keyword search such as "Internet+postcard." Most of these services include their own pictures, but some let you upload pictures from your computer to include in electronic postcards and greeting cards. I found a great service at **www.all-yours.net**. You can then choose photos to send as postcards or greeting cards, as shown in Figure 10.5.

Figure 10.5
You can create your own photo greeting card.

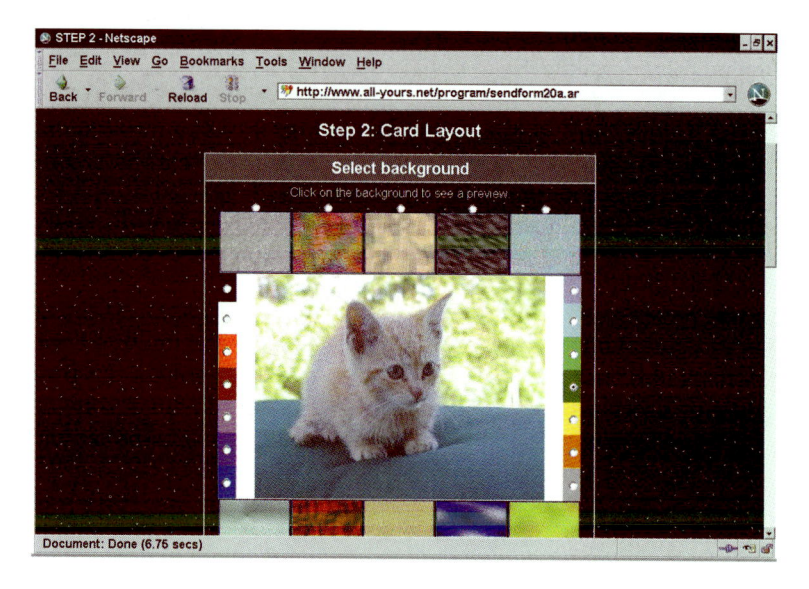

The recipient of your e-postcard gets a regular e-mail message and instructions for reading the card, which can include music and other enhancements. Large card companies, such as American Greetings, have products on the market that enable you to create e-greeting cards.

If you think a standard greeting card can say it best, then wait until you see what you can do with a greeting-card creation tool. Not only do you get to use all the artistic and creative talent that companies like American Greetings have, but you also get to take their cards one step further and personalize them for the occasion. When a friend fell off her horse while jumping a fence and broke her arm and a few ribs, it seemed appropriate to add a little humor to the event. Digging back through some photographs, I was able to find a picture of her horse. In about 10 minutes, I was able to scan the photograph, pick a card, insert the photograph, modify the text, and send it electronically. Figure 10.6 shows the American Greetings CreataCard Gold screen where you modify the card step by step. (I used the CreataCard Gold version, but American Greetings has a Platinum version now. I expect they'll have Titanium or Uranium versions during the life of this book.) After you complete the card, you click the E-Mail button, fill in the e-mail address, and add any message that you choose. Then you can send the card from your regular e-mail application.

Figure 10.6
This is the front of an e-greeting card created with American Greetings' CreataCard Gold.

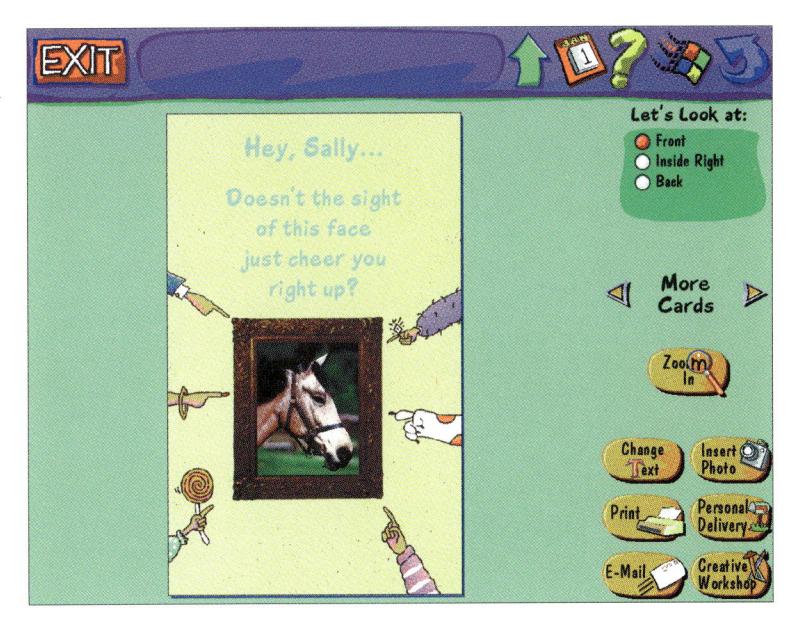

The recipient of the e-greeting card receives a normal e-mail with some instructions and an attachment. Double-clicking the attachment causes a background screen to be shown with the greeting card placed in the middle, as shown in Figure 10.7.

Figure 10.7
This e-greeting card has a background screen, created with American Greetings' CreataCard Gold.

Clicking the arrow opens the card (see Figure 10.8). One more click, and you can see the back of the card. With American Greetings' CreataCard, your recipient can also print the card on a color printer by clicking the printer icon. For those of you who procrastinate and wait until the last minute to send a card, this is a great way to procrastinate and still look good!

Figure 10.8
Here's the inside of an e-greeting card created with American Greetings' CreataCard Gold.

http://www.muskalipman.com

Sharing images with instant messenger and chat applications

Chat and IM applications are quickly becoming two of the most popular ways of communicating electronically. By the end of the last millennium, AOL claimed that there were more than 750 million messages sent per day via ICQ and the AOL IM; in comparison, there are only 500 million letters mailed each day via the U.S. Postal Service. Microsoft has its own MSN instant message service that attracts users. Even Yahoo! gets into the act with an instant messaging service. You'll find IM clients like Trillian that let you log onto several IM services simultaneously.

Initially created as a means of enabling people to chat online for entertainment purposes, IMs and chat applications are now rapidly being implemented as business tools, and many more people are using them as a serious personal communication tool. During this next year, when visiting an online store, it will be increasingly common to have a sales assistant offer to help you via an IM or chat box.

IMs enable you to send and receive messages to any computer that is connected to the Internet, enabling you to chat from work, home, school, a friend's house, or anywhere you can get on a computer with an Internet connection. IMs also enable messages to be stored on a server, so they are always accessible. An IM might be likened to a real-time e-mail application with a simulated telephone ring announcing that you are calling; there is no waiting for e-mail to be received. As you type, those whom you are chatting with can see the letters being typed. When you pause or misspell a word and go back to correct it, they see it all!

One of the more interesting aspects of IMs is that they enable you to create buddy lists—lists of people with whom you occasionally like to chat. Unless your buddies set themselves up to be invisible or hidden specifically to you, their names are listed whenever they are online. You can even assign special audio sounds for them, which will play when they either sign on or sign off. Most IMs enable you to categorize

http://www.muskalipman.com

your buddies into family, friends, business contacts, or any other category that you would like to create. You can see an IM window in Figure 10.9.

Figure 10.9
You can use AOL's Instant Messenger to chat online and exchange photos.

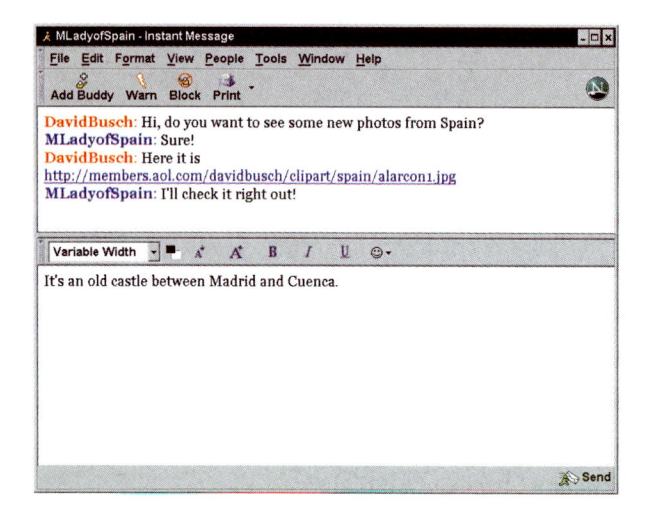

Instant messaging, by some accounts, is growing faster than any other communications medium in history. AOL says that its three instant-messaging services have nearly 80 million users, and they crossed the 50 million mark in less than two-and-a-half years—compared to five years for the Internet and 13 years for television.

You might ask why IMs are covered in a book on digital cameras and digital imaging. The reason is that using IMs is a wonderful way to share images and interact in real time. You send or post to a Web page only the images that the recipient asks for—and then you can talk about that image. For example, after taking a trip to Spain to shoot pictures of castles, you could have a chat with one or more friends and share your digital images of the castles with them.

> **NOTE**
> A college student uses an IM to chat with her parents on a regular basis. During the evenings, when she is studying, she turns on the IM. She can see when her parents are online and can instantly page them for a quick chat. Using the Send Picture feature, she can send images of friends, her soccer games, or even a ding in the new car that her parents bought her. The interactive chat capabilities of IMs make sending images even more enjoyable.

NOTE

A father watched his one-year-old son take his first step. This was a significant achievement, so he shot a picture of the second step with a digital camera. Knowing that his wife would be equally excited, he paged her at work on her IM and, using the IM's file-transfer feature, sent her the image. She got the image within a few seconds and sent back the message, "Wow, I'm coming home early today!"

Sharing electronic documents that contain images

You might want to insert your images into many different kinds of electronic documents, such as those created by word processors, desktop publishing applications, spreadsheets, or graphics and illustration tools. After you complete your work, you might need to share these documents with others. Generally, you can share these documents in two ways:

- ▶ If the intended recipient has the same application, you can send e-mail with the file as an attachment. The recipient can then click the attachment, which will launch the native application. This works well with software such as Microsoft Visio, Adobe Illustrator, or other products that have proprietary files that generally can't be shown in standard viewers.

- ▶ If the intended recipient does not have the native application, you need to either find a viewer for that type of file or identify a file type that is common between that application and any software that your intended recipient has. Again, using Visio as an example, you can export the chart as a TIFF or JPEG file, which should make it easy to view. After you export the file, you can send it as an attachment.

Working with Microsoft Office documents

Because the Microsoft Office products have become omnipresent, it is worthwhile to know how you can use them to share documents with images. The most commonly used product in the suite is Microsoft Word. Word is a wonderful tool to use to combine text with images. However, files from various versions are not always compatible. To overcome this problem, you must save the file as a Word 97 file.

http://www.muskalipman.com

WordPad, which is included in recent versions of Microsoft Windows, can view these files in their most basic form. Alternatively, your recipient can download Microsoft Word 97/2000 Viewer, which can be retrieved free of charge at **www.microsoft.com**. Microsoft moves the location of the download from time to time, so your best bet is to type "Word Viewer" into the Search box at the Microsoft Web site.

With Word Viewer, Microsoft Word users can share documents with those who do not have Word, and users who don't have Word can open, view, and print Word documents. This product also enables users who want to post rich-formatted Word documents on the Internet to expand their online audience to people who might not have Word. Users are able to zoom, outline, or view the page layout, headers/footers, footnotes, and annotations.

Microsoft's PowerPoint presentation tool enables you to share images in PowerPoint presentations by posting them to a Web site or by creating run-time versions of the slide shows. You can view these slide shows without additional software.

Using photo labs and online services to share digital images

One of the easiest and least expensive ways to share your photographs with others is to use one of the digital services provided by an increasing number of photo labs and online businesses. Using the digital services offered by a photo lab has advantages. When you shoot pictures with a film camera and have your film scanned at a photo lab, you can have the photo lab create digital images and upload them to the Internet at the same time that they develop and print your prints.

Even if you use a digital camera, online services will still be useful to you. You won't have to worry about a trip to a local photo lab, and you'll save a few dollars because you won't have to pay for the developing, printing, and scanning. However, you will have to pay for a roll of online "spaces" (online digital storage for digital images) so that you have room to upload your image files.

Obviously, the first step to being able to share digital images on the Internet is to get your image files uploaded. The three basic ways to do this are as follows:

▶ Drop your film off at a local photo lab and have the developer scan and upload your digital image files to the Internet.

▶ Use a mail-in envelope and send your film to a mail-order photo lab that can process your film, scan it, and upload digital images to the Internet.

▶ Create an account with an online service and upload your images to one of the online labs from your PC.

Some of the most popular services are Ofoto, Kodak Picture Center, and PhotoWorks, a service of Seattle FilmWorks. You can find these services at **www.ofoto.com**, **www.kodak.com**, and **www.photoworks.com**, respectively. An up-and-coming service is Shutterfly, which has the advantage of being accessible directly from within Photoshop Elements (using the File, Online Services menu choice). You can access Shutterfly at **www.shutterfly.com**.

Using any of these services to share your photographs with others is easy, quick, and inexpensive—especially when you compare it to the costs of sharing ordinary printed photographs. All of these services work in a similar way. This section explains how you get your images into the service and what you can do with the images after they are there.

The first step to getting your pictures online is to have them converted into digital image files. You can drop off your film at a local photo lab or mail-order service that is affiliated with the online photo service. The lab will process and scan the film and upload the digital files to the service's Web space; then it will notify you at the e-mail address you provide. Alternatively, you can have the photo lab scan your film and put the digital images directly onto a CD-ROM or floppy disk.

If you already have images, you can upload them to the photo service from your computer. Either way, your images will be ready to be shared. Figure 10.10 shows the screen that is used to upload photos to PhotoWorks. The procedure with Shutterfly, Ofoto, and the Kodak Picture Center is similar. When you are ready to upload photos, you're taken to a screen with three or more text boxes in which you can enter the address of the photo you want to upload (such as c:\photos\myphoto.jpg), or click the Browse button and navigate to the folder on your hard disk that contains the picture. Some services let you specify only three or so pictures at once for uploading; Shutterfly lets you collect 10 images at once.

Figure 10.10
You can upload an image to PhotoWorks.

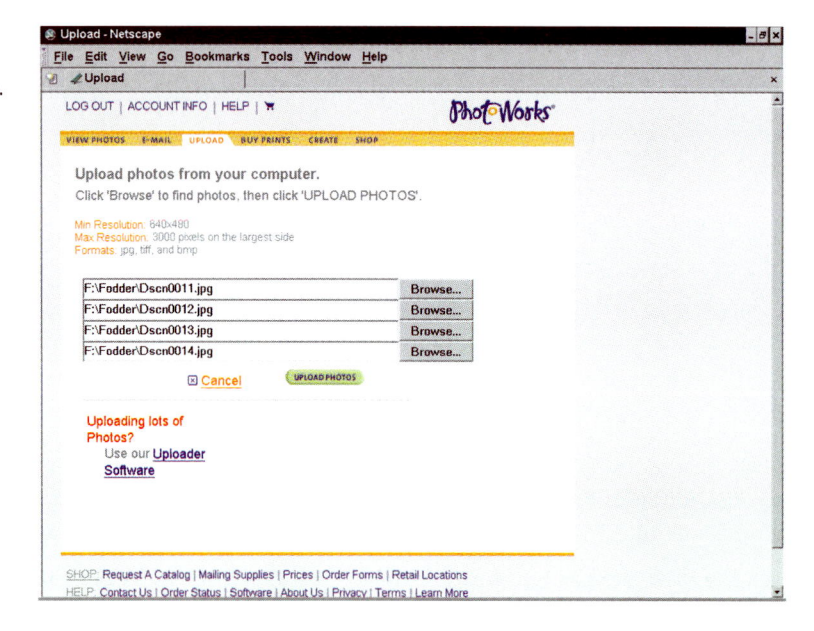

In Chapter 3, "Turning Photographs into Digital Images," you learned how to use a photo lab to put your pictures onto a CD-ROM or floppy disk. You also learned how you can scan photographs. If you used either of these approaches or took pictures with a digital camera, you need to upload your digital image files. Again, it is quite easy to do.

After you upload your images to your service, the images are available to be shared with others. You can assemble the images into albums and then select the roll that you want to share. The photo service can send an e-mail to your friends, like the one in Figure 10.11, showing them how to access your online album and inviting them to view your roll of pictures.

Figure 10.11
You can use Ofoto to send an e-mail to invite others to view your online pictures.

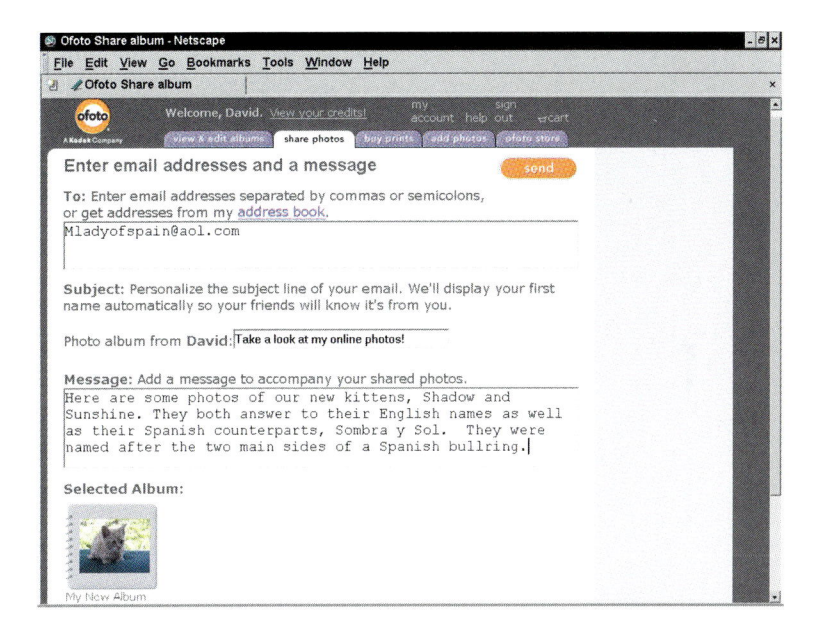

When your recipients receive the e-mail inviting them to view your roll of pictures, they need to log in to the service to view them. If the recipients are not already registered with the service, they have to create a free account. After they are logged in, they can select your roll to view. After the roll is selected, the album is displayed in their browser. They can even order their own prints, if they want.

> **NOTE**
> A part-time breeder of show dogs who travels a lot for his regular job uses **www.FilmWorks.com** to store more than 50 images of dogs that he has bred. Frequently, when he travels, he meets people who are interested in purchasing his dogs. When he is near a PC with a connection to the Internet, he can show the prospective customer the images. On several occasions, he has sold a dog to an out-of-state customer based solely on the images, which the buyers could look at and share with their families when they got home.

Getting your own Web space

If you want to share your images on the Internet but you don't want to use an online service offered by a photo lab, you need to get your own Web space. Digital images can consume considerable storage space and command lots of bandwidth when they are downloaded, so it is important to find an appropriate site to meet your needs. The good news on getting Web space is that there are many options—many of which are free.

Before you look for Web space, you need to decide whether the address or URL for your site needs to be short and simple to remember and whether it needs to look professional (as opposed to looking like it is located on a free, personal-use type of site). If you own a business that sells gazing globes to customers on a worldwide basis, for example, you don't want to have an address such as www.somefreeservice.com/member2395340xb/ttsdke32450.htm. Odds are that you'll be much happier with www.gazing-globe.com.

On the other hand, if you are just sharing personal pictures with friends and family members, the actual address might not matter because it will usually be sent in e-mail as a hot link. In this case, you have many more choices than if you want to have a "good-looking" URL.

Where should you begin your search for Web space? First, you should check to see what your current online service or Internet service provider (ISP) offers as part of the service you already have or as an upgrade. Most ISPs offer between 5MB and 20MB or more of Web space with their basic service package. America Online provides 2MB of space for each screen name. ISPs often offer home page templates, wizards, or even a proprietary or "lite" version of a commercial Web page creation tool to help you get your Web page up and going.

If your ISP offers space and you decide to use it, you need to be aware of any restrictions that might apply to the usage of this space, such as bandwidth limits. If you are just sharing images with a few friends, you aren't likely to consume much bandwidth. However, if you post images that are going to be looked at by thousands of visitors, you might find yourself being charged additional money for the excess bandwidth that is above your limit.

If you don't have Web space available with any of your existing services or don't want to use it, you need to look elsewhere.

Getting free or low-cost Web space

If you want free or low-cost Web space, you simply have to sign up for it. I know that sounds unbelievable, but many Internet companies have come up with innovative business models that enable them to provide free or almost-free services—such as photo-sharing communities and Web space.

These sites come and go, but the following sites are a few of the more popular Web hosting sites that have been around for quite a while and which provide good service and a wide variety of tools and site services. Most of them offer between 5MB and 10MB of space:

- Lycos Angelfire (**www.angelfire.com/**)
- Yahoo! GeoCities (**www.geocities.com**)
- Homestead (**www.homestead.com**)
- iVillage.com (**www.ivillage.com**)
- Familypoint (**www.myfamily.com**)
- Tripod (**www.tripod.com**)

If you are serious enough about your Web space that you are willing to register and pay for a domain name and the monthly fees, then you probably ought to consider many other issues that I won't take the time to cover in this book. You can search for Web hosting companies at **www.cnet.com**.

Using software that automatically creates image-based Web pages

So far in this chapter, we have looked at how you can share images online by using services that photo labs offer. We also have seen how fun and easy it is to share your images in a photo-sharing community. Then we covered the topic of how to get your own Web space. In this section, we look at software that makes it extremely easy to create image-based Web pages that you can post to your own Web site. More specifically, we will look at ways to do the following:

- Create an online image portfolio
- Create an online slide show
- Create an online rotating picture cube

Creating an online portfolio

Creating an online portfolio is a feature that is available in many image-management software applications. To give you a good idea of the kinds of things that you can do with such software, we will look at creating image portfolios with several different software packages.

Using ThumbsPlus

Cerious Software, Inc.'s ThumbsPlus, one of the more feature-rich image-management tools (discussed in Chapter 4, "Managing and Storing Images"), offers a wide range of options for creating an online image portfolio. Creating a portfolio with ThumbsPlus is as easy as answering a few questions posed to you by the Web Page Style Wizard shown in Figure 10.12. This wizard enables you to choose from, modify, and save templates, which determine how your Web portfolio will look. Selecting the number of columns and rows per page, table border size, thumbnail size, file format, and thumbnail JPEG quality are just a few of the many other options available to you.

Figure 10.12
You can use ThumbsPlus' Web Page Style Wizard to create a Web page image portfolio.

The portfolio can contain one or more pages. You also have an option to have thumbnails only or thumbnails and full-size images, as shown in Figure 10.13. If you use both, click the thumbnail image or hot link below each image to cause a full-size image to display. To return to the thumbnail page, just click your browser's Back button.

Figure 10.13
This Web-based portfolio was created with ThumbsPlus.

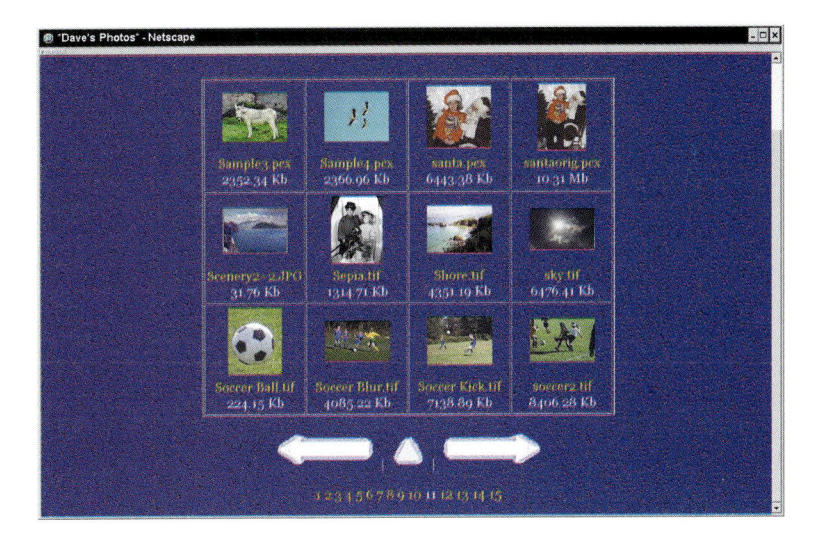

If you have ever tried to write HTML code for an image portfolio, such as the ones that are created by ThumbsPlus in a few seconds, you'll love this feature; it really saves a tremendous amount of tedious coding, which is highly prone to errors.

After ThumbsPlus has created the necessary HTML code and thumbnail images, it stores them in file directories that you specify. From there, you must copy these file directories to the Web site on which you want them to be displayed. A good software utility to use to do this is WS_FTP, which is covered toward the end of this chapter.

NOTE

A woodworker creates multiple digital images of each project that he has built over the years. He manages these images with ThumbsPlus. Every December, he adds the work from the prior year to the work from all earlier years. File directories are named after the kinds of furniture that are contained in them. Images of desks, for example, are saved in a file directory named "desks," and images of chairs are in the "chairs" directory. When he has a prospective customer who wants to see his work, he loans them one of the CD-ROMs containing his work. To make the images easy to view without requiring additional software, he uses ThumbsPlus to create an HTML-based portfolio that can be viewed quickly with a standard browser.

He also uploads the portfolio to a Web site so that he can show others his work from anywhere he has access to the Internet. On many occasions, when he visits clients' homes or businesses, he gets an order for a new piece of furniture simply by showing them the work that he has done by going to his Web page on their computer. This saves him from having to create a photo album and carry it around all the time. In addition, it allows him to talk to a prospective customer on the telephone while the customer looks at his work on a Web page.

Using Adobe Photoshop Album and Photoshop Elements

Photoshop Album and Photoshop Elements each have Web Photo Gallery tools that produce good-looking Web pages for showcasing your pictures. If you happen to own the flagship image editor, Photoshop, you'll find the same capability there, too. Each lets you choose the photos you want to display on your Web page and specify formats, banners, text, and other goodies. Photoshop Album's Web Photo Gallery dialog box is shown in Figure 10.14. It uses tabbed pages so that you can define the banner text and size of thumbnails, specify larger photos, and choose custom colors. You'll end up with a Web page that shows one large picture, with a selection of thumbnails arrayed along the bottom or one side. Visitors can click a thumbnail to view that picture, as shown in Figure 10.15.

Figure 10.14
Adobe Photoshop Album simplifies creating an online photo gallery.

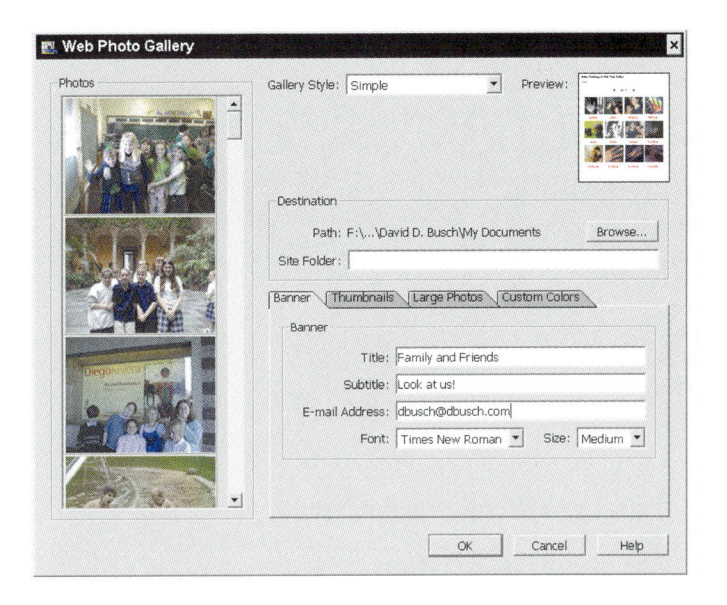

Figure 10.15
Photoshop and Photoshop Elements produce Web galleries like this.

Using PhotoSuite

Roxio's PhotoSuite has been called "The PC and Internet Photography Power Pack." As expected, PhotoSuite is one of the more Internet-enabled PC photography software applications on the market. One of the unique aspects of this program is its embedded browser that enables Web viewing from within the program. This feature enables users to save photos from the Web directly into the application simply by dragging them off the Web page into the photo library that is part of PhotoSuite. Then you can directly edit the images or use them in a photo project.

To create your own Web pages, just collect and organize the images that you want to use in the album feature, located by clicking the Organize tab. Then, in one step, the software automatically converts your album into a Web page (or pages) ready to be posted to your Web site. Figure 10.16 shows the kind of page you can create. By the way, when you click the image file name or the image, your browser will display the full-size image. To return to the thumbnails view, click your browser's Back button. Again, after the pages have been created, you must upload the images and Web pages to your Web site. Other than that, there is no more work to be done.

Figure 10.16
This image portfolio was created with Roxio PhotoSuite.

Authoring your own Web pages

"Wait a minute," you might be thinking. "Why is a section on authoring your own Web pages included in a book on digital cameras and imaging?" The answer is a simple one. If you want to be able to do something that is more sophisticated than what we have seen so far in this chapter, you need to know about the tools that can help you accomplish your objectives.

Sure, I could have skipped this section entirely, but I have included it for one reason: Some of the tools that we will look at briefly are so useful that you can do some amazing things without having to become a programmer. Without including this section, you would not have learned an important, invaluable point: You can do more than you think you can with some of the new software products. As I previously challenged those of you who don't have a digital camera to try one, I now challenge those of you who really do want to create quality Web pages to try using a Web page authoring tool or two. My bet is that you'll be surprised at what you can do with one, if you haven't tried one lately.

A few words about HTML

Web page creation is all about writing HTML code. HTML stands for hypertext markup language, which is a fancy term for a text formatting language. In the early days, just about all HTML could do was format text on a page and enable hyperlinks. Now, however, its capabilities have expanded greatly.

If you've never looked at HTML code, take a quick peek at some. The easiest way to do this is to launch your browser and visit any Web page that you like. If you use Internet Explorer, you can view the HTML code (source code) by selecting the menu item View, Source. You will see the HTML code that created the page that you are viewing. If you use Netscape Navigator, you can see the source code by selecting View, Page Source. The bad news is that the code on many pages can be pretty darn ugly stuff if you aren't familiar with HTML (or JavaScript, which also might be present). The good news is that you don't have to know much HTML to do some amazing things—provided that you are using the right tools.

Depending on what you are trying to accomplish on a Web page, you might not ever have to learn or even look at HTML code. During the past few years, a number of software vendors have worked hard to develop tools that enable users to create Web pages through what is known as WYSIWYG (What You See Is What You Get) editors. The idea behind these Web page creation tools is that you build your pages exactly as you want them to look in a graphical environment, and the software creates all the necessary HTML code without your having to look at it.

Using Microsoft Office to create Web pages

Some of the best examples of software programs that enable you to create Web pages without coding are the applications that are included in Microsoft Office. Any version from Office 2000 onward will work fine. For example, you can use Microsoft Word to create a standard document and then add a few digital images, titles, various headings, graphics, and even tables. After you compete your work and are happy with the way it looks, save it as a normal DOC file. Then you can save it again, only this time, you select the Save As menu and, in the dialog box that appears, select Web Page in the Save As Type box. You now have a Web page that looks like the Word document that you created.

Another approach is to use Word's Web page templates and start by creating a Web page instead of a Word document. To get to these templates, select File, New and then click the Web Pages tab. Notice that there is even a Web Page Wizard, which will help you select a theme, create multiple pages, and more.

After you see what you can do with Word, you might assume that you can do the same kinds of things in the other Office applications. Your assumption is correct—you can. Creating a Web page that looks like a spreadsheet is as easy as creating a spreadsheet in Excel. You can also use PowerPoint to create a slide show that uses your digital images and then have PowerPoint create a Web-page-based slide show. Even Microsoft Publisher enables you to create Web publications. Access can be used to manage images that then can be shown on a Web page.

The important point is that creating Web pages is quickly becoming a common and popular thing to do. Anyone who has Microsoft Office has the capabilities. Shouldn't you try making a Web page, either for fun or with a purpose in mind?

Using WYSIWYG editors

Macromedia Dreamweaver and Microsoft FrontPage are just two of the many highly capable WYSIWYG editors that are available to create Web pages. FrontPage is especially easy to use. Dreamweaver, on the other hand, which was designed for professional Web site designers, is widely recognized as one of the most powerful of all the reasonably priced editors and, consequently, is more difficult to learn how to use.

Just to give you an idea of how these WYSIWYG editors work, let's briefly look at how we would use FrontPage to create a page for showing digital images. We could, if we really wanted to, start with a blank page and create each element that is needed. Another option is to use one of the templates included with the software and then make a few modifications to meet our needs.

Figure 10.17 shows a Web page being created with one of the basic templates. Looking at the bottom of the window, you can see three tabs—one for Normal view, one for HTML view, and one for Preview. These tabs enable the designer to quickly switch between views. You might want to start in Normal view, which is the view that you use to insert text and other objects and to change their properties. When you want to see what the page looks like, click the Preview tab. If you need to add, delete, or modify HTML code, click the HTML view, as shown in Figure 10.18.

Figure 10.17
It's best to create your Web page in FrontPage in Normal view.

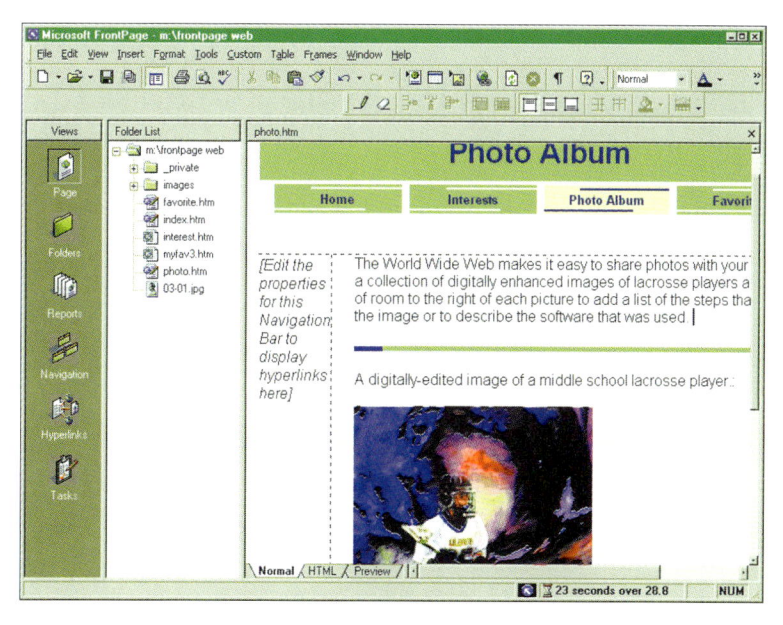

Figure 10.18
You can use FrontPage's HTML view to add, delete, or modify HTML code.

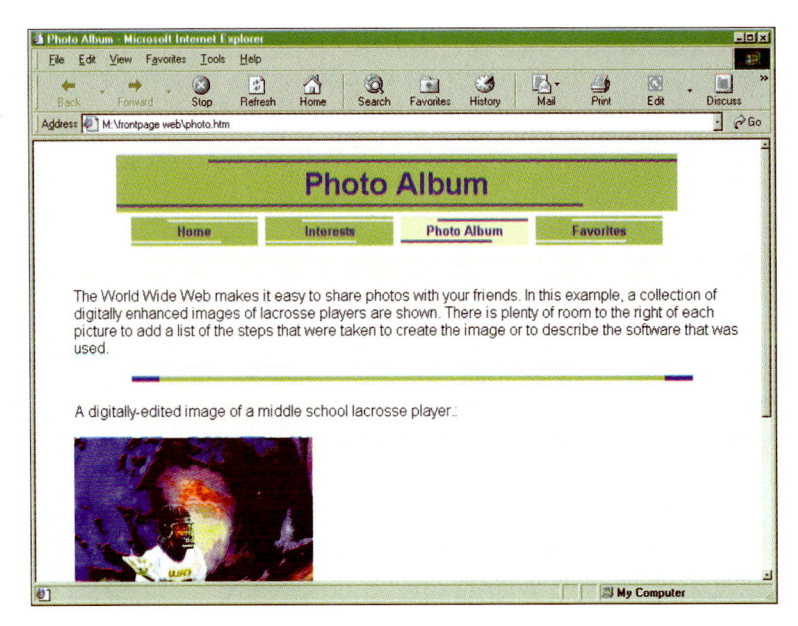

Uploading files to your Web site

Before we end this chapter, one last type of program worth discussing is FTP clients. These are the programs that are used to upload and download files between a Web site and a computer. Many of the applications that are covered in this chapter, such as those that created Web-based portfolios, create image files and Web pages on your PC's hard drive. To post those images and Web pages to a Web site, you have to transfer their files to a Web site. An FTP client is used to upload the files to your Web space. Be sure to upload the folders that are created to hold them, too.

Figure 10.19 shows one such program, WS_FTP, being used to upload a collection of JPEG images. WS_FTP is a simple application that works similarly to Windows Explorer. On the left side, you select the drive, directory, and files that you want to upload from your PC. On the right side, you select the directory on the Web site where you want the files to be transferred. WS_FTP is an efficient program that makes the task of transferring files as error-free and quick as possible.

Figure 10.19
You can use WS_FTP32 to upload images and Web pages to a Web site.

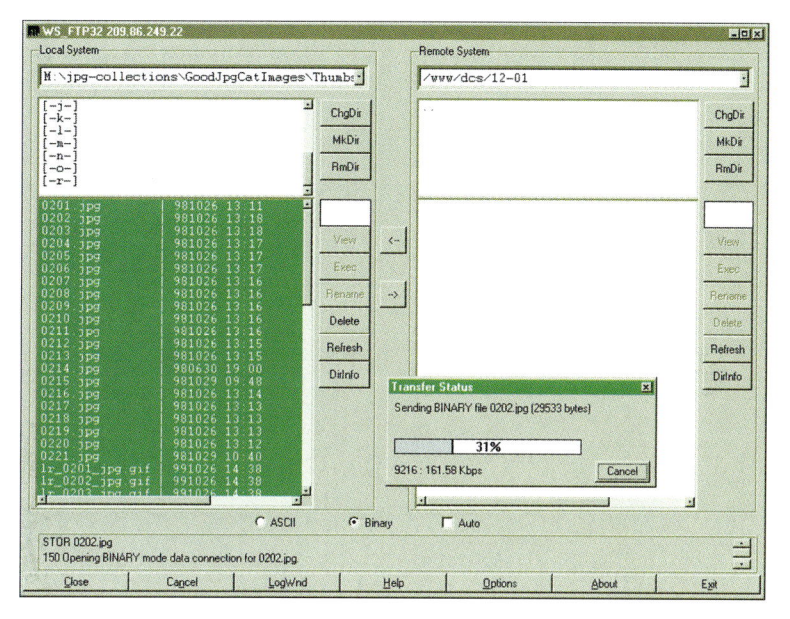

WS_FTP is available for download from CNET. Two versions of WS_FTP are available. One is free for noncommercial home users, students, and faculty, and the other is a commercial version with a few extra features for about $40. You'll find many other FTP clients at CNET. My personal favorite for the novice user is FTP Explorer. It's completely free, and almost mindlessly simple to use. When you connect to a Web site, a window opens that looks exactly like a Windows Explorer window. Open up the folder that contains the files you want to upload using Windows Explorer, and just drag them to the FTP Explorer window. It's that simple. FTP Explorer is shown in Figure 10.20. With some more recent versions of Internet Explorer, you can access FTP folders and upload files to them, too.

http://www.muskalipman.com

Figure 10.20
FTP Explorer looks like and operates like the Windows Explorer.

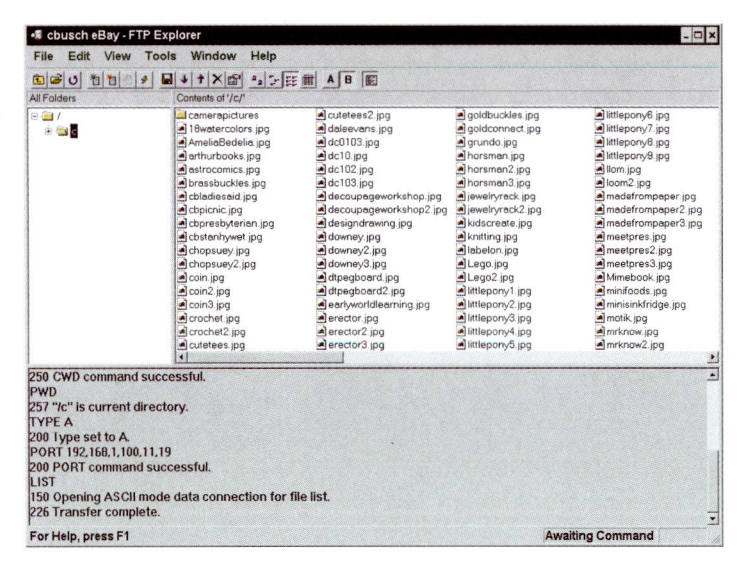

Besides the applications mentioned in this chapter, dozens of other Web page creation tools are available on the market. Many of the online services have even created their own proprietary page creation tools for creating pages on their free Web space. If you are considering buying a Web authoring tool, you might find it worthwhile to visit CNET at **www.cnet.com**. The tips, product reviews, tutorials, and other features at CNET are likely to be useful to you. You can even download trial versions of the products. It's worth a visit.

That concludes this chapter on using the Internet to share images. I hope it has given you several project ideas that you are keen to get started on. In Chapter 11, we'll continue on the topic of ways to share and enjoy your images—only we are going to leave the digital world and return to the printed world. We'll explore ways you can turn your digital images into printed images.

11

Turning Digital Images into Prints

Do you have digital images that you want to print? Maybe you've received them as e-mail attachments, downloaded them from the Internet, taken them with a digital camera, or scanned them with a desktop scanner—it doesn't matter how you got the digital images. The task now is to get them printed so that you can display them on your wall or mantle, carry them in your wallet, or share them with others in hard copy form. What options are there? What kind of printer should you use? If you don't have a printer, how can you have prints made? Can you make your own prints if you don't have a PC? What kinds of specialty papers are available? If you want the absolutely best print possible, where should you go? How can you make prints available to a friend who lives in another city? If you have these or similar questions, you are reading the right chapter!

In this chapter, you will learn how to turn your digital images into prints by doing the following:

- ▶ Uploading them to an Internet-based printing service
- ▶ Using the digital image services of a local photo lab
- ▶ Using a desktop printer
- ▶ Using the services of a custom photo lab

Looking into the future

In the past few years, the number of ways that you can get photo-quality prints made from digital image files has increased dramatically. Many companies are focused on introducing new

http://www.muskalipman.com

printing services that will revolutionize the way we use, share, and print pictures. This vision is being built on three elements that will make sharing pictures almost as easy and common as sending e-mail.

The first element consists of digital minilabs and photo kiosks. The new integrated digital minilabs will accept virtually every input source from silver halide film to digital camera media, CD-ROMs, PC cards, floppy disks, Zip disks, and more. These minilabs can also print regular photographs as well as upload digital images to the Internet. Photo kiosks are the self-serve consumer versions of a digital image lab that enable users to scan photographs or read images from CD-ROMs, floppy disks, or digital camera media. You can use these kiosks to digitally edit images, upload them to the Internet, and produce photo-quality prints. The kiosks of the near future will also enable you to download images from the Internet so that you can print them or write them to digital storage media.

The second important element is the personal computer, which is available in an increasing number of homes and offices. A large percentage of PCs can be connected to the Internet, and they are frequently connected to an inkjet printer that is capable of making photo-quality prints. If you own a digital camera, you probably have a PC, and if you have a PC, you most likely have a printer that can make great prints from your digital photos.

The final element—as you might have guessed—is the Internet. The Internet links the PCs, the digital minilabs or kiosks, and a digital picture network such as Shutterfly, Kodak Picture Center, OFoto, and PhotoWorks (all discussed in Chapter 10, "Sharing Images"). With that background, you can probably see the same vision that is driving many companies to provide us with a way to easily share our pictures with others no matter where they are. If you live in Sioux Falls, South Dakota, and you want to share a photo with a friend in Salem, Oregon, or your grandparents in Ft. Lauderdale, Florida, you can. After you have a digital image, you can upload it to the Internet and send the recipient an e-mail telling how to access it. The recipient can then download it to his PC and print it on his printer if he has one. If he doesn't have a printer, he can download the image on a photo kiosk and have it printed while he waits. Alternatively, you can send a digital image to a specific photo lab in the recipient's neighborhood where he can pick up the prints after they have been made. Your brother in Rome, Italy, could even get the print merely by picking it up at a nearby photo lab (see Figure 11.1).

Figure 11.1
Here's the process of uploading a digital image file to be printed with Kodak's Quick Print service.

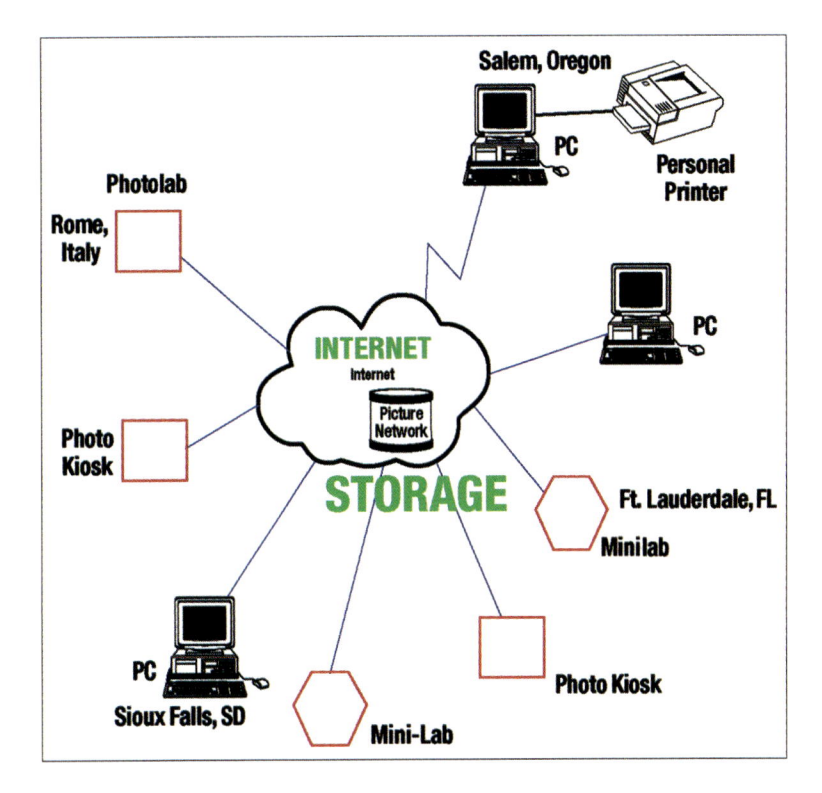

That is a quick peek at the future. Two problems are keeping this vision from becoming reality. First, most of the large chains of one-hour labs (mass merchants, camera stores, and drug stores) do not yet have their minilabs or kiosks connected to the Internet. Second, many photo labs do not have the new integrated digital minilabs or kiosks installed, or existing ones have not been upgraded to enable them to accept digital image file media such as CD-ROMs or digital camera media. Both of these problems are rapidly being addressed.

Ordering prints through the Internet

We've already looked at online picture services in Chapter 3, "Turning Photographs into Digital Images," and Chapter 10. You can deploy the same services that you can use to share photos online to create hard copies of those images. In fact, one of the easiest ways to turn your digital images into prints is to order them through the Internet. You can order these prints in many ways and through a number of companies. As you might expect, Kodak has worked hard to position itself as a leader in the digital photography marketplace. Kodak services are available through Kodak directly or through many participating Kodak photo retailers and its Picture Center online service. These services are available from as many as 40,000 outlets worldwide. This total digital solution is available through every level of the photofinishing industry, from minilabs to wholesale labs and even mail-order labs.

To use an online picture service, your image must be in one of the common image file formats, such as JPEG, BMP, TIFF, or GIF. Some services put restrictions on the size of the image (in megabytes), as well. After you've selected a file, you can either add additional files or you can continue with the order process. When your image has been uploaded, you will be presented with a screen that shows the image that was uploaded, often in album form, indicating that the upload was completed successfully. The remaining steps include choosing the number of copies and the size of prints that you want. Click on the Add to Order (or Add to Cart) button, and you are ready for the final step of entering your name, shipping address, and credit card information. These steps take place on the Web page, like the Shutterfly page shown in Figure 11.2. Within a few days of placing your order, you will receive your print in the mail.

Figure 11.2
You can order prints from a digital image file from Shutterfly.

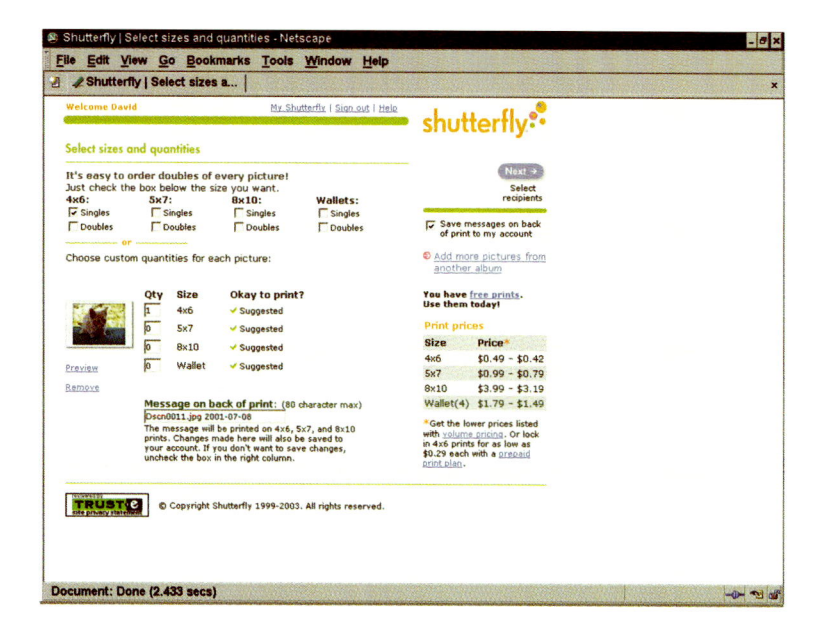

Besides printing the regular wallet-sized, 4 × 6-, 5 × 7-, and 8 × 10-inch glossy print, some services also allow you to order an 8 × 10-inch photo jigsaw puzzle, photo mugs, photo mouse pad, photo T-shirt, or sweatshirt. All the services discussed in Chapter 10 offer printing from your digital files at competitive prices.

NOTE

More than 120 friends and family members got together for a wedding. One of the family members took photographs with a film-based camera. After shooting four rolls of film, he took them to a nearby, one-hour photo-processing lab (located inside a drug store) to be developed. When he dropped off the film, he indicated on the processing request envelopes that he wanted four sets of reprints. Additionally, he checked a box to have the images uploaded to the Internet and checked another box to have the images put on a CD-ROM. In one hour, he could pick up the four sets of reprints. Within two days, he could pick up the CD-ROM, and he received an e-mail notifying him that he could view and download images for all four rolls of film from the Internet. The e-mail included his user name and an access code for each roll of film. He then viewed the images, added titles to a few, and deleted others.

Next, he sent one e-mail message to everyone he knew who had e-mail (about 60 people) and had asked to see the pictures. All the recipients of that e-mail were then able to view the images simply by clicking the link that was embedded in the e-mail message. If the recipients wanted prints of any image, they could order them from their PC, either to be mailed directly to them or to be picked up at a local photo-processing lab. Alternatively, if they did not have a PC, they could visit a local photo-processing lab and have them print the images within a few minutes.

Getting prints made at a local photo lab

Many in-store photo labs already have equipment that can read digital files on removable media such as a CD-ROM, floppy disk, or digital camera storage media. If the labs don't have such equipment, they must send your digital media to an out-of-store lab to be printed—frequently a lab that is a Kodak-participating photofinisher. If your local in-store lab is not properly equipped, you might find it easier to order your prints by uploading them to the Internet from your PC.

http://www.muskalipman.com

Alternatively, check around to find an outlet that has an appropriate kiosk like Kodak Picture Maker, as shown in Figure 1.8 of Chapter 1, "Introducing Digital Cameras." Many photo-processing outlets either have a Kodak Picture Maker or a competitive kiosk like Fujifilm's digital picture center that enables you to get prints from your removable storage media. The Kodak Picture Maker contains a Kodak printer that uses a sophisticated dye-sublimation print technology that provides high-quality prints up to 8 × 10 inches. It is a 300dpi continuous-tone print, which provides superb color and fine detail. The Kodak Picture Maker also enables you to enlarge or reduce your photos, fix red eye, zoom and crop images, adjust color balance, and add creative borders before the print is made. Kodak plans to have more than 100,000 of these kiosks worldwide, so they will be readily available wherever you might be.

Ritz Camera/ Wolf Camera is a chain of national camera stores in the U.S. They have thousands of stores or labs spanning most of the United States, which makes it likely that one of them has a store near you. Both are rapidly implementing their own plans to provide a wide range of digital imaging products and services. You can learn more about their current offerings or find a store in your neighborhood by visiting their Web sites at **www.ritzcamera.com** and **www.wolfcamera.com**.

In addition to the Internet-based services, there are thousands of mass merchants (drug stores, supermarkets, and discount stores) that provide, or will soon provide, services to process your film, scan it, and upload it to the Internet. Just about every national chain store you can think of—Kmart, Wal-Mart, Target, Walgreens, CVS, Osco Drug, Eckerd Drug, Harris Teeter, and Safeway—offers digital services.

To get your first glimpse of where the vision and reality meet, check around and find a place that has one of the newer digital print stations. Have them print a few of your images. If you have good images, the prints will be spectacular. I took the close-up picture of a butterfly that I found in my garden (see Figure 11.3) with a Nikon CoolPix 950 digital camera. The camera settings resulted in a 1600 × 1200, 800KB file. I had it printed at a Ritz Camera store as an 8 × 10-inch print. The print was outstanding. It looked as though it were taken with a film camera and processed and printed as an ordinary photographic print. Go try it!

Figure 11.3
This print of a butterfly was taken with a digital camera.

Using custom photo lab services or specialty printers

When you want the best possible print made, find a custom photo lab or a specialty printer that has the equipment and services to meet your needs. Such companies cater to a professional customer base. They are accustomed to the high expectations of professionals and have skills and equipment that enable them to do a better job than consumer-focused, one-hour photo labs. These custom labs have built their business on quality rather than volume, and they tend to charge a premium for a better quality print.

For a particularly good photographic print, get one of your images printed with a Fuji Pictography 4000 printer. That printer is a 400dpi continuous-tone device, and it offers brilliant photographic color quality. The prints are true photo-quality output, just like a conventional photograph. Images are printed on glossy photographic paper that is capable of being displayed in the same way as conventional photographs. The printer utilizes an innovative process in which photosensitive donor paper is exposed by laser diodes—a process which yields a print far superior to the more common dye sublimation print used in most consumer photo labs. If you want to

http://www.muskalipman.com

get a Fuji Pictography print from a local photo lab, you can order it at one of the online services that offer them.

Many specialty printers have high-end digital printers that can print with archival-quality ink on museum-quality paper. Prints like these can cost several hundred dollars for a 30 × 40-inch print. Several high-end printers you might want to consider using are Corporate Color (**www.corpcolor.com**), Autumn Color Digital Imaging (**www.autumncolor.com**), or Imagers (**www.imagers.com**).

> **TIP**
> To save time and an unnecessary trip, call before you visit a custom photo lab and ask a few questions. What will a print cost? What storage media can the lab read? What kinds of paper can it print on? What kind of digital image file format can it read and which ones does it prefer? What dpi setting should you use? Can the lab accept files over the Internet? How long will it take to complete the work?

Using a desktop printer to make prints

If you haven't seen a print made by a photo-quality printer, you will truly be amazed. Many printer manufacturers offer a range of photo-quality printers from around $100 to well over $1,500, many of which are capable of printing prints on photo-quality paper that closely resembles an actual silver-halide print (a true photographic print that is exposed by light). If you don't have a photo-quality printer, you might want to consider purchasing one. In this section, you will learn how to choose a printer that meets your needs and, I hope, your budget as well.

Types of printers

As you might expect, there are many different types of color printer technologies; some are good for photographic images, and some are not. There are color lasers, thermal inkjet, dye sublimation, and inkjet printers to name just a few. Because so many inkjet printers are available that can do an outstanding job of printing photo-quality prints and because most printers using other printer technologies cost in the neighborhood of $1,000 (and up), we'll limit our discussions here to just inkjet printers.

Printer features that might be important to you

I will limit the content in this section to features that I have found to be particularly important when printing digital images—either as regular 4 × 6-inch photo-quality prints or as large-format, fine-art images. You might not ordinarily consider some of these features. As you become more successful at editing your digital images and you begin to print more of them in larger sizes and on different print media, however, you'll be glad you considered them.

With our discussion narrowed to inkjet printers less than $1,000, we will now look at several characteristics or features you should consider when hunting for the perfect photo-quality printer. Key differentiating features that might be important to you, depending on how you want to use your printer and how much money you are willing to spend, are as follows:

▶ **Print quality**. Print quality is likely to be the most important thing you will consider when choosing a photo-quality printer. If it isn't, it should be. Although print resolution has a lot to do with print quality, many other factors are involved in producing a good print. Print quality is often a subjective notion, so I suggest that you look at prints from every printer that you are considering and decide for yourself whether or not it is the quality that you want. A good inkjet printer will print even, continuous gradations, and it will not show banding (straight lines that are parallel with the printer head path). The colors will be correct—not faded—and they will be close to what your computer screen shows, providing you have calibrated your printer and screen.

▶ **Print resolution**. Print resolution is specified in dots-per-inch (dpi), and the general rule (with a few exceptions, especially many of the HP printers) is that an image will be sharper and have smoother gradations, higher highlights, and darker shadows as the dpi increases. Printers with higher resolutions generally print a better image than printers with a lower dpi. Inkjet printers with 1200 to 1440dpi or more are capable of printing a good photo-quality print.

▶ **Maximum print size**. When purchasing a printer, we all envision printing large photographic images. The reality, however, is that photographic images that are larger than 8 × 10 inches require huge image files. These large files also can consume incredible amounts of RAM to process and considerable hard disk space as well. However, some inkjet printers can handle prints longer than 11 inches, enabling you to create panoramas, like the one shown in Figure 11.4.

Figure 11.4
This 4 × 24-inch panoramic picture was printed on watercolor paper.

- **Adjustable printer head height**. If you are serious about printing and plan to use some of the thicker fine-art papers, such as watercolor paper or artist canvas, look for a printer that enables the printer head to be raised. Some of the more expensive Epson printers offer this feature. Without the ability to adjust the printer head height, you will be limited to the lighter-weight media.

- **Paper-feed path**. This might not seem like an important feature until you see what happens when a thick piece of paper is fed into a printer that makes it turn around a narrow-diameter roller. Printers that enable thick paper to be fed straight into the printer enable you to use thicker paper with better results. If you want to use heavy watercolor paper or other thick media, don't consider a printer that won't enable the paper to be fed straight in.

- **I/O interface**. In the old days, the interface that was used for devices like scanners and printers was important because it was possible to connect only so many devices at one time. Today, most computers use USB or FireWire (IEEE-1394) interfaces to connect almost anything. Although I have an old HP laser printer plugged into my parallel port, my inkjet printers (as well as my scanner, digital camera, digital media reader, and other devices) plug into a USB hub. Most printers today are available with a USB connection, and I suggest you don't accept anything else.

- **Print speed**. Print speed might be an issue to you if you plan to print many pictures. Generally, photo-quality printers are not particularly high-speed printers because they are optimized for quality, not speed. One compelling reason for getting a high-speed printer is that printing large image files to an inkjet printer can slow down your PC so much that you will want to wait until the printing is complete to continue working.

http://www.muskalipman.com

▶ **Ink cartridges and print heads**. Inkjet printers are not cheap to use. The print cartridges are expensive—anywhere from $25 to nearly $40, depending on the brand and model. Full-page color prints consume lots of ink. When you are looking at inkjet printers, be aware that you can get printers that offer three colors in one cartridge, plus a black cartridge. Alternatively, you can get printers that have a separate cartridge for each color. If you print lots of landscapes with blue skies, and you have a single cartridge for red, green, and blue ink, you might end up throwing out a fairly unused cartridge simply because it no longer contains blue ink. Some printers offer six-color ink systems, which include cyan, magenta, yellow, light cyan, light magenta, and black to create an extremely wide color gamut. In this case, you simply replace one color cartridge when it runs out. Be aware that at least one printer vendor sells a multiple cartridge printer, but it only sells the cartridges in a package of four—meaning that you can never buy just one color.

Here's a question that no printer vendor seems to be keen to answer: How much does it cost to print one page with 100 percent ink coverage on an 8 × 10-inch space? It should be an easy question to answer, but I've never seen it answered. My experience suggests that a full page costs from $.75 to $1.25 or more to print one page. That is expensive on a per-page basis, but when you consider that an 8 × 10-inch photograph usually costs from $5 to $9, it seems like a bargain.

TIP

With inkjet printers costing as little as $100, it is easy to spend many times more than the initial cost of the printer on ink cartridges. Although printer vendors often claim that you save money by having a printer with separate cartridges for each color, plus black, it might not be true for you. If you are an infrequent user of your inkjet printer, you will find that your cartridges can dry out, for they do expire. If you have four ink cartridges that cost $30 each and they all dry out, you will have to spend $120 to replace them all. Fortunately, most individual cartridges cost only $10 to $15.

When you're purchasing new inkjet cartridges, especially for older models of inkjet printers, carefully check the packaging for the expiration date to make sure that you are purchasing a new cartridge rather than one that has expired or is about to expire.

Printers for the PC-less environment

Yes, there are printers that enable you to store, edit, and print photo-quality prints without having a PC. As the digital camera market continues to grow, you'll see many more of these printers. There are printers that have memory card slots (like several in the HP PhotoSmart line) and can receive pictures "beamed" directly from the camera (or PDA, laptop, or cell phone) to the printer over an infrared connection. These printers have LCD screens that you can use to choose the photos you want to print. We're even seeing printers with full-color viewing screens, like the 3.2-inch LCD on some Sony printers that actually show you the full image before printing. Expect to find more features like this in the future.

Printers are even becoming a digital camera accessory. In March 2003, Kodak introduced an EasyShare printer that serves as a dock for some Kodak digital cameras. Just plug the camera into the printer, and you're ready to make prints! This particular model makes only 4 × 6-inch prints, however, and it uses the dye-sublimation process rather than inkjet printing.

If you have a digital camera and you don't have access to a PC, but you want to be able to print your own photo-quality prints and store digital files, one of these printers would be perfect for you.

Choosing print media

The media you choose for printing makes a significant difference in the overall quality of your print—especially for inkjet printers. Because you invest your time and energy shooting a picture and working on it with digital-editing tools, you want to get the best possible print of that image. To do that, you must choose the right paper.

Types of paper

For simplicity, this section divides printer media products into five categories: low-cost inkjet paper, high-quality nonglossy papers, photographic papers, fine-art papers, and specialty papers.

▶ **Low-cost inkjet paper**. Nearly all paper vendors provide one or more grades of inexpensive paper manufactured especially for inkjet printers. These papers cost as little as $3 for a 250-sheet package. Although these papers have their uses, they don't have the weight or sufficient surface quality to use for printing photographic images. Use them for test strips and for design work and then print on a higher-quality material for your final prints.

▶ **High-quality nonglossy papers**. Often, you will want the best possible print quality without having to print on glossy photo-like paper. Numerous products are suitable for this purpose, including 36-pound heavy-duty papers that are suitable for brochures, calendars, report covers, and certificates.

▶ **Photographic papers**. Quite a few good photo-grade papers are available for inkjet printers. I use—and have been happy with the results from—Kodak, Epson, Lexmark, and HP papers.

▶ **Fine-art papers**. Unless you have experimented with digital image editors and have seen what you can create by using sophisticated filters, you might not yet appreciate the value of using fine-art papers. My bet is that you'll be hooked the first time that you change one of your favorite photographic images into a watercolor and print it on a high-quality watercolor paper. It will be a work of art that you'll want to frame! You'll soon be deciding what to do next, at which point you should look at some of the oil-brush filters, create an oil painting, and print it on real canvas that is created especially for inkjet printers. Be careful, though—don't get caught forging *The Mona Lisa*!

If you are an artist or photographer who is just getting into digital imaging, you might already have a keen interest in different paper types. If so, you might want to experiment with many of the same papers that you have been using. Although I don't advise against trying these papers because you might get the desired result, you will find that coated papers that are produced especially for inkjet printers will give you a better print more often than not. Most art papers are not coated, which enables the ink spray to soak in and spread. This turns your fine lines into fuzzy lines and, in some cases, enables bordering colors to merge and create a third color, which isn't what you want to happen. Another problem with uncoated papers is that they soak up more ink than they should, which will transform your sharp, brilliant-colored work into a muted image.

Finding fine-art paper that is created especially for inkjet printers is getting easier as the demand for it has grown. I suggest that you visit one of the large office supply stores or your favorite art supply shop. The art supply shops have lost so much business due to all the digital art tools that they usually are eager to carry products for artists who use computers for their artwork. Figure 11.5 shows a print on watercolor paper, and Figure 11.6 shows an oil-painted effect on a heavy canvas paper.

Figure 11.5
Here's a watercolor-like print on watercolor paper.

Figure 11.6
Here's an oil paint-like print on heavy textured canvas.

http://www.muskalipman.com

Specialty papers

Besides premium inkjet paper, glossy photographic paper, and fine-art papers, several other products are available on which to print. You can use these specialty products to print everything from greeting cards to business cards, stickers, labels, and transparencies. You can even use transfer sheets to print directly on cotton fabric. Some of the more fun and useful products are listed next:

▶ **Greeting cards**. Companies such as International Paper and Avery are making more greeting card papers than probably any other kind of paper on this list. International Paper produces embossed greeting cards on smooth white card stock with white vellum envelopes. These are classy cards for "fine-art" works and for formal invitations with images or the embossed card shown in Figure 11.7. You can buy card variety packs with 24 assorted cards that are high-quality, heavyweight stock with two-sided coating for brilliant color; some are half-fold, some are quarter-fold, and the balance are full-sheet. The package also includes matching envelopes. This is a great starter kit if you want to create your own greeting cards. Another especially nice half-fold card offered by Avery is called the print-to-the-edge greeting card. These cards are specially designed so that images can be printed right to the edge of the card. To do this, each card has a micro-perforated edge that can be neatly torn off after the card has been printed.

Figure 11.7
Here's an embossed greeting card featuring a cat image.

278   Turning Digital Images into Prints – Chapter 11

▶ **Calendars**. If you have a dozen or more images and the time to make a 12-month calendar, you should get one of the available calendar printing kits. These typically include sheets of 8½ × 11-inch heavyweight photo paper with gloss and matte sides, two sheets of Print & Stick Project paper, two heavyweight paper covers, two clear-plastic covers, and an easy-to-use spiral binder. Using The Print Shop or another product offering calendar-creating formats, you can create an outstanding 12 months' worth of images.

▶ **Postcards**. One of my favorite specialty papers is the Avery glossy photo-quality postcard. These cards are glossy heavyweight stock with a full-bleed format that enables you to print right to the edge. After tearing off the micro-perforated edges, the postcards are 4 × 6 inches (see Figure 11.8).

Figure 11.8
These Avery postcards have micro-perforated edges.

▶ **Iron-on transfers**. Believe it or not, you can transfer your digital images onto any white or light-colored cotton or cotton-blend fabric with iron-on transfer sheets. These transfers can be used on T-shirts, tote bags, placemats, aprons, sweatshirts, jerseys, and more. Using an ordinary household iron, you simply iron the

http://www.muskalipman.com

transfer sheet onto the fabric and then peel off the backing sheet. Designs stay bright and clear through repeated washings if the laundry directions are followed. I created the "Soccer Mom & Soccer Kid" T-shirt image shown in Figure 11.9 for a friend to wear when she attends her daughter's soccer games. Notice that the image is mirrored so that when it is ironed on to the fabric, it will show correctly.

Figure 11.9
Here's a Soccer Mom image for use on an iron-on transfer sheet.

TIP

Hanes' T-ShirtMaker Iron-on Transfer Paper comes in packs of 20 8½ × 11-inch sheets. You can download Hanes T-ShirtMaker Lite software for free from **www.hanes2u.com**. The bargain here is the Hanes Oops Proof Guarantee. If you goof up decorating a first-quality, heavyweight Hanes garment, Hanes will take it back and give you a new one—up to six "oops" per household per year! (Don't forget to keep your store receipt!)

▶ **Posters and banners**. If you want to print a large poster or banner and are willing to use the quantity of ink that is necessary to print these large formats, you can buy paper that is fan-folded and use it with printers that enable continuous page printing. If you want to print banners, make sure your printer has this feature before buying the paper; most printers don't have it.

http://www.muskalipman.com

- **Stickers**. Stickers come in all sizes and shapes and in both matte and glossy versions. If you are into brewing your own beer or creating your own wine, you can make elegant bottle labels with sticker materials.

- **Business cards**. You can create wonderful business cards by using photographic images. Various paper manufacturers offer both glossy and matte versions of business cards. Most of the better business cards are available with the micro-perforated edges that enable you to print to the edge and tear off the edges, leaving an almost perfect cut.

- **CD labels**. Have you just recorded your first music CD and are now ready for the big time? If so, use CD labels to create custom labels that include photographic images on the disc and on the jewel-case insert. You can also get removable labels for DVDs, Zip disks, audiocassette labels, videocassette inserts, and more.

- **Jigsaw puzzles**. This is a great one for grandparents. After printing an image of the grandkids, you can break up the puzzle and send it to them to put back together. Make several of them for their next visit to keep them busy.

- **Decals**. One of the more unusual things to print on is a see-through, repositionable film for creating stickers and decals for windows, mirrors, and other nonporous surfaces.

A few last words

That's about it, folks—for this chapter and the book! I truly hope you enjoyed reading it as much as I enjoyed writing the chapters and creating the images and projects that have been included. Even more, I hope that this book inspires and motivates you to do creative, fun, and useful things with your digital images, and that you will enjoy sharing the images you create with friends, family, and business colleagues.

Combining the Internet, PCs, and digital images gives you so many more options than have ever been available to share and more fully enjoy the benefits of digital imaging. Keep your eyes open for new products and services and help become a pioneer in the new world of PC photography.

My challenge to you is to buy a digital camera, if you haven't already done so. They are better than you might think. Digital cameras make it easy to create and use digital images, and they are just plain fun.

Index

A

accessing digital images, 16
Acrobat Reader. See Adobe Acrobat Reader
action photos, 12, 13, 29
    shooting tips, 52
Adams, Ansel, 55
adding objects to image
    with digital imaging, 138–139
    with filters, 163
Adobe. See also Photoshop; Photoshop Elements
    Illustrator, 245
Adobe Acrobat Reader
    with Photoshop Album, 101
    Photoshop Album and, 187–188
advantages of digital cameras, 14
afternoon light, 32
Alien Skin Software. See also Eye Candy; Splat; Xenofex
    Image Doctor, 136
all-yours.net, 240
America Online (AOL), 233
    instant messages on, 243
    Web space offered by, 250
American Greetings, 240–242
    CreataCard system, 241–242
Andromeda Software Inc. Series 3: Screens Filters, 174
animation files, adding, 196
Antimatter filter, 171
Antique filter, 168–169
aprons, images on, 228
architectural photos, 10
art galleries, visiting, 54
Artistic filter, 167
artwork
    creating, 223–224
    filters creating, 160–162
    graphic art, transforming image into, 164–1654
    painting with images, 142–143
attachments. See e-mail
Auto-Clone filter, 170
auto-contrast edges filter, 159
Auto F/X. See AutoEye; DreamSuite; Photo/Graphic Edges
auto-level edges filter, 159
AutoEye
    fixing images with, 123–124
    as plug-in, 136
autofocus cameras, 19
automatic document feeders for scanners, 70
automating image correction, 122–128
Avery
    greeting card paper, 277
    postcard paper, 278

B

backgrounds, 34–35
    bright subjects, black backgrounds, 36
    filters, background images with, 163–164
    shooting for use as, 43–44
backlit subjects, 35
backup systems, 86–89. See also Microsoft Backup
    batch file for backup instructions, 88–89
    extra copies, creating, 89–90
    in Photoshop Album, 101
    semi-automated systems, 87–89
bad images. See imperfect images
Baked Earth filter, 172
banners, paper for, 279
batch file for backup instructions, 88–89
batch processing, 124–128
    with PhotoImpact, 126–128
    with Photoshop, 125–126
batch scans, 70
batteries, 11
Billings, Josh, 5
birthday party invitations, 218, 219
bit depth for slide show images, 122
black backgrounds, 36
Blocks filter, 162
Blur filter, 159, 168
BMP format for online picture service, 266
Border Stamp filter, 173
borders and frames
    with Alien Skin Software, 136
    with filters, 165
    for subjects, 36–37

Boss filter, 162
brands, selecting, 22–23
bright subjects, black backgrounds, 36
brightness
    Photoshop Album tools, 101
    scanned image, fixing, 116
Broderbund Print Shop
    filters, 168
    Photo Organizer, 197
Bump-map filter, 169
business cards
    images for, 200–205
    paper for, 280
business projects
    business cards, 200–204
    certificates, 208–209
    letterhead, 200–204
    postcards, 207–208
    product catalog pages, 206–207
    project quote sheets, 205
buttons, images on, 228

C

calendar printing kits, 278
camera angles, varying, 34
cards. See also greeting cards; postcards
    business cards, 200–204
    greeting cards, 215–217
    sports cards, 222
Carve filter, 171
catalog pages, 206–207
CD-R drives
    saving images with, 105
    storing pictures on, 9
CD-RW drives, 11, 104
    saving images with, 105
    storage on, 82
CDs
    best images, copies of, 106
    duplicating images on, 105–106
    labeling disks, 106
    labels, paper for, 280
    as lasting technology, 104
    multiple copies, making, 105–106
    storage on, 104
    ThumbsPlus, management with, 99
    tips for storing images on, 105–106
    writing image files to, 104
Cerious Software Inc.'s ThumbsPlus. See
    ThumbsPlus
certificates, creating, 208–209
character, shooting for, 49

charity group projects, 228
charts, exporting, 245
chat rooms
    comparing cameras on, 23
    sharing images with, 243–245
Chrome filter, 171
church projects, 228
Clik, 104
Clone Brush tool, 146–147
Clone tool, 114–115
Clouds filter, 166
CNET.com
    e-mail services, free, 233
    freeware from, 198
    FTP clients on, 261–262
    models, comparing, 22
    scanners, review of, 70, 71
    Web authoring tools, information on, 262
coaches, images for, 221
coffee mugs, 228
    online print services printing images on, 267
color. See also color depth; duotone
    balance, 5
    with Extensis Intellihance Pro, 134
    filters for changing, 154, 159–160
    images, changing colors in, 140–141
    number of color bits, 61–62
    Photoshop Album tools, 101
    shooting for, 45–46
Color Balance slider, 117
color-compensating filters, 154
color depth, 61–62
    imperfect image, fixing, 114
    in scanners, 62, 68
color-graduated filters, 154
color laser printers, 270
combination scanners, 67, 68
CompactFlash memory cards, 9, 21
complex objects, 41
compression. See file compression
Constellation filter, 172
contrast
    Photoshop Album tools, 101
    scanned image, fixing, 116
controls, comfort with, 19
Corel. See Photo-Paint
costs
    of cameras, 10–11
    of inkjet cartridges, 273
    online purchases, 24
    of scanners, 65
    selecting cameras and, 18
    for storing images, 81

Courier font, 210
cropping
    for partial images, 37–38
    for slide show images, 122
Crumple filter, 172
custom photo labs, 78
    prints, ordering, 269–270
    scans from, 78
Cutout filter, 164, 171
CVS, 268

D

damaged images. See imperfect images
Darkroom filter, 159
DAT tape, 104
databases
    Microsoft Access for project catalog pages, 206–207
    and photo albums, 181–184, 197
decals, 280
Deep Paint, 135
    filters for painted images, 160–162
defects in pictures. See imperfect images
depth of field, 38–39
digital image files, 57–65
digital image-stitching software, 225–227
digital imaging. See also magical images
    adding objects to image, 138–139
    colors of images, changing, 140–141
    layering objects, 141–142
    masks, 145
    painting with images, 142–143
    parts of image, selecting, 138
    removing objects from image, 144
    sampler of techniques, 137–145
    transforming parts of images, 139–140
digital minilabs, 264
digital picture labs, 24
digital zooming, 5, 20
Displace filter, 162
display resolution, 58
Distort filter, 168
distorting images with filters, 162, 168
Distress filter, 172
documents containing images, sharing, 245–246
downloading
    HTML images, 239
    Web authoring tools, trial versions of, 262
dpi (dots per inch), 61
    printer resolution, 271
Dr. Franklin's Instant Photo Effects, 159
dramatic effects, shooting for, 53

DreamSuite
    digital imaging with, 135
    filters, 175–176
Drop Shadow filter, 171
Dry Brush filter, 156–157
duotone, 120
    in personal letters, 212
    short stories, images for, 224–225
dust & scratches filter, 159
DVDs, 11
    as lasting technology, 104
    storage on, 104
dye sublimation printers, 270
dynamic range in scanners, 68

E

e-mail, 4. See also sharing images
    attachments
        sending images as, 236
        viewing attached images, 234
    file size and, 234–235
    free services, 233
    HTML-based e-mail, sending images with, 238–239
    slide shows, sharing, 194–195
    with URL pointer to image, 237
    viewing attached images, 234
EasyShare printer, Kodak, 274
eBay.com, 13
    costs of cameras, 24
Eckerd Drug, 268
edges. See also Photo/Graphics Ediges
    filter, 173
Edges filter, 173
Electrify filter, 166, 172
Emboss filter, 164, 166
enhancing filters, 154
Epson photographic papers, 275
equipment, learning about, 53
Etching filter, 164
exposures, 5
    for backgrounds, 43
    controls, 20
Extensis
    Intellihance Pro, 134
    Mask Pro, 134–135
    PhotoFrame, 133
    Portfolio, 99–100
extra copies, creating, 89–90
Eye Candy
    filters, 171
    as special effects plug-in, 136
Eye Dropper tool, 119

http://www.muskalipman.com

F

f-stops, 20
Familypoint, 251
fantasy, shooting for, 45
fast-succession photos, 12
features
    printer features, 271
    of scanners, 70
    selecting camera and, 19–22
    surprise features of camera, 21–22
file compression. See also Zip drives
    image compression, 63–65
    quality of, 6
    requirements for, 109
    storing images and, 81–82
file formats, 6. See also specific formats
    selecting camera and, 21
    for slide show images, 121–122
file size
    e-mail and, 234–235
    for photo albums, 195
    for slide shows, 195
Fill Stamp filter, 173
film cameras
    digital cameras compared, 8–10
    uses for, 10
film scanners, 67
filters, 153
    adding objects to image, 163
    before and after images, 154–157
    background images, creating, 163–164
    Broderbund's The Print Shop filters, 168
    colors, changing, 159–160
    defined, 154
    digital camera images, 115
    distorting images with, 162
    DreamSuite, 175–176
    evaluating filters, 167
    Eye Candy filters, 171
    frame filters, 165
    fun with, 158
    graphic art, transforming image into, 164–165
    improving images with, 159
    multiple filters, using, 158
    painted images, creating, 160–162
    Painter filters, 170
    Photo-Paint filters, 169
    PhotoImpact filters, 170–171
    Photoshop Elements, 167–168
    Photoshop filters, 167–168
    plug-ins, 171–176
    quality of output, 167
    Screens Filters, 174
    settings, control of, 167
    Splat, 173
    Terrazzo filters, 174–175
    user interface and, 167
    with Xenofex, Alien Skin Software, 136
    Xenofex filters, 172
fine-art papers, 275–276
fingerpainting with filters, 168
Fire filter, 171
FireWire, 21
    printer connections, 272
    scanners, 69
fixed focus cameras, 19
fixing images, shooting, 50–51
Flag filter, 172
flash capabilities, 21
flatbed scanners, 67
floppy disks, storage on, 21
flyers, 218–219
focal length
    depth of field and, 39
    of lenses, 20
focus, partial, 38–39
fog filters, 154
folder/directory system, creating, 84
folders, image management with, 90–91
foregrounds of pictures, 34
forums, comparing cameras on, 23
Fragment filter, 166
framable artwork, 223–224
Frame filter, 173
frames. See borders and frames
freeware, 198
freeze-action photos, 12
FrontPage, Microsoft, 259–260
FTP clients, 260–262
FTP Explorer, 261–262
Fuji
    kiosks for sending pictures, 25–26
    Pictography 4000 printers, 269–270
    Pictography kiosk, 76
Fur filter, 171

G

gallery, creating, 102
geometry in photos, 39–40
GIF format
    compression in, 63
    for online picture service, 266

Index

Glass filters, 154, 171
Glow filter, 171
Google, postcards on, 240
graphic art, transforming image into, 164–1654
gray market imports, 24
greeting cards, 215–217
    electronic cards, 240–242
    specialty papers for, 277

H

Hanes' T-ShirtMaker Iron-on Transfer Paper, 279
hard disks, backing up on, 87
Harris Teeter, 268
hats, images on, 228
high-contrast images, 53
holding cameras, 19
Homestead, 251
horizontal orientation of image, 109
hot-swappable hard disks, 87–88
hotlink pointers, 237
Hotmail, 233
HP (Hewlitt-Packard)
    photographic papers, 275
    PhotoSmart, 274
    printers, 271
HSB Noise filter, 171
HTML
    capabilities of, 257–258
    e-mail, sending images with, 238–239
    exporting images to, 102
    ThumbsPlus code, 253
    with WYSIWYG editors, 259
hue of color, filters changing, 160
huge images, 54

I

I/O interface of printers, 272
image compression, 63–65
Image Doctor, Alien Skin Software, 136
image editors, 6, 93–97. See also imperfect images
    advanced consumer/business use editors, 132
    choosing, 130–137
    consumer-level editors, 132–133
    professional-level image editors, 131–132
    for slide show images, 121–122
image management
    with Adobe Photoshop Album, 100–101
    advanced applications, 97–101
    consumer-level image editors, 93–97
    with Extensis Portfolio, 99–100
    gallery, creating, 102

HTML, exporting to, 102
    with Paint Shop Pro, 93
    with PhotoImpact Album, 101
    with Photoshop Elements, 95–96
    with PhotoSuite, 94–95
    with SuperJPG, 92
    with ThumbsPlus, 98–99
    utilities, 92–93
    with Windows Explorer, 90–91
image sensors, quality of, 5
image size, 62–63
images on, 228
Impasto painting technique filter, 170
imperfect images, 109, 110–121
    AutoEye, fixing with, 123–124
    automating image correction, 122–128
    batch processing, 124–128
    deleting, 14
    digital camera, fixing images from, 113–116
    filters for, 159
    Photoshop, fixing with, 125–126
    scanned image, fixing, 116–118
    slide shows, fixing for, 121–122
improving photography skills, 53–56
inkjet printers, 270
    cartridges, cost of, 273
    papers for, 274–275
Inner Bevel filter, 171
installing
    Backup on Windows XP, 86
    screensavers, 193
instant messengers (IMs), 231, 232
    buddy lists, 243–244
    Send Picture feature, 244
    sharing images with, 243–245
instant print cameras, 8
Intellihance Pro, Extensis, 134
interesting objects, shooting, 41–42
Internet. See also e-mail; instant messengers (IMs); sharing images
    buying camera online, 23–24
    digital minilabs and, 264–265
    photo album images from, 195
    photo kiosks and, 264–265
    printing and, 264
    prints, ordering, 265–267
    readiness of images for, 14
    slide show images from, 195
    uploading images, 16
Internet Explorer
    FTP folders, accessing, 261
    HTML with, 257
intrigue, shooting for, 52

invitations, 218, 219
iPhoto, 198
iPrint Web site, 204
iron-on transfers, 278–279
ISPs (Internet service providers), 250
iVillage.com, 251

J

Jasc Software Paint Shop Pro. See Paint Shop Pro
JavaScript, 257
Jaz drives, 103, 104
Jiggle filter, 171
jigsaw effect filters, 175–176
jigsaw puzzles. See puzzles
JPEG format, 6
    charts, exporting, 245
    compression in, 63–64
    for Internet readiness, 14
    Kodak Picture Disk files, 72
    for online picture service, 266
    uploading JPEG images, 260

K

keywords. See image management
kids' projects, 218–222
    birthday party invitations, 218, 219
    coaches, images for, 221
    flyers, 218–219
    fun pictures, creating, 219–220
    sports cards and posters, 222
kiosks. See photo kiosks
Kmart, 268
Kodak
    digitization services, 71–75
    EasyShare printer, 274
    kiosks for sending pictures, 25–26
    photographic papers, 275
    Picture Disk, 71–72
    Pro Photo CD, 71, 74–75
    Quick Print Service, uploading digital image files with, 265
Kodak Photo CD, 71, 72–73, 73–74
    multiple resolutions of images with, 106
Kodak Picture Center, 71
    ordering prints from, 266
    sharing images with, 247
Kodak Picture Maker, 26, 77
    local photo labs with, 268
KPT Effects
    background images with, 164
    digital imaging techniques with, 137

L

layering objects, 141–142
LCD screens, 9
    selecting camera and, 20–21
Lens Flare filter, 166
lens flare filter, 155
lenses
    adding lenses, capability for, 21
    focal length of, 20
    quality of, 5
    speed, 20
letterhead images, 200–205
letters. See also personal letters
    business letterhead, images for, 200–205
Lexmark photographic papers, 275
light
    best possible light, using, 32
    capturing, 30–31
    interesting objects and, 41
    low-light situations, 12
    position of, 32
Lightning filter, 172
Liquify filter, 168
Little Fluffy Clouds filter, 172
local photo labs. See photo labs
long-distance photos, 12
lossless formats, 63
lossy format
    AutoEye, fixing with, 123
    compression, 63
low-light situations, 12
Lycos Angelfire, 251

M

Mac OS X
    iPhoto, 198
    scanners supporting, 69
    screensavers with, 192
macro capabilities, 20
Macromedia Dreamweaver, 259
Magic Wand tool, 115
    damaged photos, fixing, 119
    parts of image, selecting, 138
magical images
    mushroom garden image, 148–150
    North Sea light, 150–152
    rainbow image, 146–148
mail-order photofinishers, 77
management. See image management; storage
manufacturers' Web sites, 22
Mask Pro, Extensis, 134–135

masks, 145
    with personal letters, 211
megapixels, 5
memories, photos for, 28–29
memory cards, 9
    CompactFlash memory cards, 9, 21
    selecting camera and, 21
Mesh Warp filter, 162
MGI Software. See PhotoSuite
Microsoft. See also PowerPoint
    Access, project catalog pages with, 206–207
    Excel, 205
    FrontPage, 259–260
    Outlook, 233, 235
    Visio, 245–246
    WinZip, 235
    WordPad, 246
Microsoft Backup, 86–89
    as scheduled task, 87
Microsoft Office
    documents with images, sharing, 245–246
    personal Web pages, creating, 258
Microsoft Word. See also personal letters
    HTML-based e-mail, sending images with, 238–239
    97/2000 Viewer, 246
    project catalog pages with, 206–207
Midnight Blue Software. See also SuperJPG
    Screen Saver Toolbox (SST), 191–193
models, selecting, 22–23
monitors
    changing resolution, 59–61
    resolution, 59–61
morning light, 32
Mosaic filter, 166
Motion Trail filter, 166, 171
mouse pads, 228
    online print services printing images on, 267
multimedia effects, adding, 196
mushroom garden image, 148–150
mystery, shooting for, 52

N

Natural-Media filters, 160–161
Netscape Navigator, HTML with, 257
networks, Extensis Portfolio for, 99–100
night-time photography, 12
Noise filter, 168
nonglossy papers, 275
North Sea light image, 150–152
notebook computers, accessing images with, 16
number of color bits, 61–62

O

objects. See also digital imaging
    interesting objects, shooting, 41–42
    layering objects, 141–142
    removing objects from image, 144
Offset filter, 162
OFoto, 247, 249
online portfolio, creating, 252–256
online print services
    for business cards, 204
    postcards, printing, 208
    sharing digital images with, 246–249
    specialty printing, 267
optical character recognition (OCR) software for scanners, 70
optical resolution in scanners, 68
optical zooming, 5, 20
organizations, projects for, 228
Origami filter, 166, 172
Osco Drug, 268
Other filter, 168
Outer Bevel filter, 171
oversampling, 62

P

Paint Alchemy, Xaos Tools, 137
Paint Shop Pro, 93, 112
    as advanced consumer/business use editor, 132
    plug-ins with, 133–137
    rainbow image, creating, 146–148
Painter, 112
    filters, 160–162, 170
    Natural-Media digital technology, 131
    plug-ins with, 133–137
    as professional image editor, 131–132
panoramas
    creating, 225–227
    shooting, 47
papers
    for calendars, 278
    costs of, 11
    fine-art papers, 275–276
    for greeting cards, 277
    nonglossy papers, 275
    photographic papers, 275
    for posters, 279
    quality and, 6
    specialty papers, 277–280
    for stickers, 280
    types of, 274–276
partial focus, 38–39

http://www.muskalipman.com

288 Index

parts of image, selecting, 138
Patchwork, 173
PCs, 24–26
    suggested configuration for, 26
    types of, 26
PCX format
    compression, 63
    storing original images in, 86
PDF format. See also Adobe Acrobat Reader
    with Photoshop Album, 101, 188
perfect pictures, 109
personal letters, 210–213
    holiday letters, 212–213
    images, adding, 210–212
personal Web pages
    authoring, 257–260
    e-mail with URL pointer to image, 237
    free or low-cost space, 251
    FTP clients and, 260–262
    image size and, 62
    with Microsoft Office, 258
    online portfolio, creating, 252–256
    personal space, obtaining, 250–251
    posting images to, 235
    shooting for images for, 49–50
    software for automatically creating, 251–256
    with ThumbsPlus, 102
    uploading files to, 260–262
personality, shooting for, 49
Perspective Shadow filter, 171
photo albums, 179–180
    applications for, 197–198
    book-like picture albums, 185–188
    with database capabilities, 181–184, 197
    file size for, 195
    freeware and shareware, 198
    multimedia effects, adding, 196
    objects, adding, 196
    paging through, 187
    printed copies of, 195
    searching for images, 195–196
    sharing images, 194–195
    sorting images, 195–196
    sources for images, 195
    text, adding, 196–197
    uses of, 180–181
Photo Express Platinum 2000
    certificates, creating, 208–209
    as consumer-level editor, 133
Photo/Graphic Edges, 136
    filters, 166
photo kiosks, 25–26, 268
    Internet connections, 264
    using, 76–77

photo labs. See also custom photo labs
    digital images from, 75
    prints from, 267–269
    sharing digital images with, 246–249
Photo-Paint, 112
    distorting filters, 162
    filters, 169
    plug-ins with, 133–137
    as professional image editor, 131
photo proportions, shooting for, 51–52
photofinishers, 106
    mail-order photofinishers, 77
PhotoFrame, Extensis, 133
PhotoImpact
    as advanced consumer/business use editor, 132
    batch processing with, 126–128
    filters, 170–171
    flyers with, 218
    North Sea light image with, 150–152
    presets in, 152
PhotoImpact Album, 181–184
    editing with, 113
    hands-on use of, 182–184
    image management with, 101
    searching database, 184
    slide shows with, 189–190
    using, 198
Photomerge, 227
photomontage
    creating, 213–215
    shooting for, 47
Photoshop, 112
    Album application, 79–80
    batch processing with, 125–126
    filters, 167–168
    imaging techniques in, 137–145
    lens flare filter, 155
    plug-ins with, 133–137
    as professional image editor, 131
Photoshop Album, 100–101
    book-like picture albums, 185–188
    online portfolios, creating, 254–255
    paging through albums, 187
    slide shows with, 189–190
    titles for album, 186
Photoshop Elements, 95–96. See also Shutterfly
    for business cards, 200–205
    as consumer-level editor, 133
    editing with, 113
    filters, 167–168
    flyers with, 218
    image management with, 95–96
    online portfolios, creating, 254–255

Photoshop Album integrating with, 101
    postcards, creating, 207–208
    stitching software, 227
    Web Gallery, 14
PhotoSuite, 94–95
    for business cards, 200–205
    editing with, 113
    flyers with, 218
    image management with, 94–95
    mushroom garden image with, 146–148
    online portfolios, creating, 256
    for photo albums, 197
    photomontage, creating, 215
    Platinum edition for consumer-level use, 133
    for slide shows, 197
    stitching software, 226–227
    wine bottle labels, 217–218
PhotoTapestry effect, 215
PhotoWorks
    sharing images with, 247
    uploading images to, 248
picture-taking approaches, 31–40
Pinch filter, 162
pixel resolution, 5
Pixelate filter, 162, 168
pixels. See also resolution
    filters moving, 154
    image size and, 62
    resolution and, 58–61
Plug and Play scanners, 66
plug-ins
    filters, 171–176
    professional level plug-ins, 133–137
point-and-shoot cameras, 19
polarizing filters, 154
portfolio, online, 252–256
poses, shooting, 42–43
postcards
    business postcards, creating, 207–208
    electronic postcards, 240–242
    paper for, 278
Poster Edges filter, 115, 116, 155, 164, 165
Poster filter, 164
Posterize filter, 164
posters
    paper for, 279
    sports posters, 222
PowerPoint
    sharing images with, 246
    uses of, 197
    Web-page based slide shows, 258
practicing, 55
print size, 6
print-to-the-edge greeting cards, 277

printers. See also inkjet printers; papers
    adjustable printer head height, 272
    for business cards, 203
    desktop printers, using, 270–274
    dpi (dots per inch), 61
    features of, 271–273
    I/O interface, 272
    ink cartridges, 273
    maximum print size, 271–272
    for panoramas, 226
    paper-feed path, 272
    in PC-less environment, 16, 274
    quality and, 6
    resolution, 271
    speed of, 272
    types of, 270
printing
    business cards, 203
    costs of, 11
    future of, 263–265
    photo albums, 195
    slide show images, 195
The Print Shop Photo Organizer, 197
procreate. See KPT Effects; Painter
product catalog pages, 206–207
project quote sheets, 205
PSD format, 86
Punch filter, 162
Puzzle filter, 166, 172
puzzles
    filters for jigsaw effect, 175–176
    images on, 228
    online print services printing, 267
    paper for, 280

Q

quality of pictures, 5–6

R

rainbow image, creating, 146–148
red-eye removal, 101
removable storage media, 80–81
    copying images to, 85
    hot-swappable hard disks, 87–88
    saving images to, 103–106
    selecting, 103–104
removing objects from images, 144
    with Clone Brush tool, 146–147
renaming files with ThumbsPlus, 99
Render filter, 168
researching digital cameras, 17–18
reshooting, 55

http://www.muskalipman.com

resolution, 58–61
    changing display resolution, 59–61
    display resolution, 58
    image size and, 62–63
    monitor resolution, 59
    printers, resolution of, 271
Resurface filter, 173
retail stores
    buying camera from, 23–24
    prints from, 268
    scanners, buying, 71
Right Hemisphere. See Deep Paint
Ripple filter, 162
Ritz Camera/Wolf Camera chain, 268
Rotate command, 113
rotating, 113
    for slide show images, 122
Rounded Rectangle filter, 172
Roxio's PhotoSuite. See PhotoSuite
Rubber Stamp tool, 114–115
    damaged photos, fixing, 118–119
    painting with images, 142–143
    removing objects from image, 144
rule of thirds, 33

S

Safeway, 268
saturation of color, filters changing, 160
saving
    original images, 85–86
    to removable storage media, 103–106
scanners
    advantages of, 65–66
    automatic document feeders, 70
    batch scans, 70
    brands, selecting, 70
    bundled applications, 70
    buying tips, 70–71
    color depth and, 62, 68
    digital images with, 65–75
    dynamic range, 68
    features of, 68, 70
    imperfectly scanned image, fixing, 116–118
    interface for, 69
    Kodak digitization services, 71–75
    models, selecting, 70
    oversampling, 62
    software, 69
    speed of scan, 69
    storage requirements, 82–83
    tips on buying, 66–71
    transparency adapters, 70
    types of, 67–68

school projects, 222
Screen Saver Toolbox (SST), 191–193
Screens Filters, 174
screensavers, 16, 190–193
    applications for, 197–198
    creating, 191–193
    freeware and shareware, 198
    installing, 193
    objects, adding, 196
    sharing images, 194–195
SCSI scanners, 69
searching
    for photo album images, 195–196
    PhotoImpact Album database, 184
    for slide show images, 195–196
Seattle FilmWorks, 247
selecting digital cameras, 17–24
sepia filters, 154
sequences of images, shooting, 46
serial interface, 21
series of images, shooting, 46
settings, learning about, 54
shape of camera, 19
shareware, 198
sharing images, 14, 16, 231–262. See also e-mail
    accessibility and, 233–235
    choices for, 29–30
    documents containing images, sharing, 245
    equipment requirements, 232–233
    online services and, 246–247
    photo albums, 194–195
    photo labs for, 246–247
    practice and, 55–56
    screensavers, 194–195
    slide shows, 194–195
    viewing attached images, 234
Sharpen Edges filter, 159
Sharpen filter, 159, 168
Sharpen More filter, 159
Shatter filter, 172
Shear filter, 162
short stories, images for, 224–225
Shower Door filter, 172
shutter speed, 20
Shutterfly, 11
    ordering prints from, 266
    sharing images with, 247
silhouettes in pictures, 35
single-lens reflex (SLR) cameras, 6–7
size. See also file size
    of camera, 19
    image size, 62–63
    print size, 62
Sketch filter, 168

slide shows, 16. See also PowerPoint
    applications for, 197–198
    creating, 189–190
    file characteristics for, 121–122
    file size for, 195
    freeware and shareware, 198
    image management and, 97
    multimedia effects, adding, 196
    objects, adding, 196
    with Photoshop Album, 101
    printed copies of, 195
    searching for images, 195–196
    sharing images, 194–195
    sorting images, 195–196
    sources for images, 195
    viewing images with, 189
slides, scanners for, 67–68
SmartMedia memory cards, 21
Smoke filter, 171
software
    for scanners, 69
    Web pages, automatically creating, 251–256
sorting images, 195–196
sounds, adding, 196
special effects. See also filters
    with Eye Candy, 136
    shooting for, 48
specialty papers, 277–280
specialty printers, 269–270
speed
    lens speed, 20
    print speed, 272
    scan speed, 69
    shutter speed, 20
Sphere filter, 162
Splat
    digital imaging with, 136
    filters, 173
sports
    cards and posters, 222
    coaches, images for, 221
    photos, 29
Squint filter, 166, 171
Stain filter, 172
Stamper filter, 172
standalone digital picture makers, 24–26
Star filter, 154, 166, 171
stickers, paper for, 280
stitching software, 225–227
storage, 79–81. See also backup systems; CDs; DVDs; removable storage media
    amount of storage, determining, 81–83
    devices, 11
    ease of, 14

    estimating requirements, 81–83
    extra copies, creating, 89–90
    folder/directory system, creating, 84
    labeling images, 85
    for scanned images, 82–83
    selecting camera and, 21
    tips for, 84–90
storage space, 9
stores. See retail stores
stories, images for, 224–225
Strokes filter, 168
Stylize filter, 168
subject of photos, 29
SuperJPG, 92
    CDs, saving thumbnails to, 105
surprise features, 21–22
sweatshirts, 228
online print services printing images on, 267
Swirl filter, 162, 171

T

T-shirts, 228
    online print services printing images on, 267
Target, 268
television
    output capability to, 21
    viewing images on, 15
Television filter, 172
Terrazzo, Xaos Tools, 137
    filters, 174–175
text
    photo albums, adding to, 196–197
    wrapping, 212
Texture filter, 168
thermal inkjet printers, 270
thumbnails, 15
    CDs, writing to, 105
    grouping photos by, 83
    with Paint Shop Pro, 93
    with PhotoImpact Album, 181–182
    with SuperJPG, 92
    Windows Explorer window with, 91
ThumbsPlus, 98–99
    Automatic File Rename feature, 99
    online portfolio, creating, 252–254
    for photo albums, 197
    for slide shows, 197
    Web pages with, 102
ties, images on, 228
TIFF format, 6
    charts, exporting, 245
    compression, 63
    for online picture service, 266

for slide show images, 121
  storing original images in, 86
Tile filter, 162
tilt in image, fixing, 113
Total Xaos, Xaos Tools, 137
tote bags, images on, 228
transforming parts of images, 139–140
transparency adapters for scanners, 70
Tripod, 251
Twain, Mark, 5
24-bit images, 62
TypeCaster, Xaos Tools, 137

U

Ulead Systems. See Photo Express Platinum 2000; PhotoImpact; PhotoImpact Album
underwater photography, 31
URL pointer to image, e-mail with, 237
USB
  interface, 21
  printer connections, 272
  scanners, 66, 69
Usenet newsgroups, comparing cameras on, 23
UV-absorbing filters, 154

V

varying camera angles, 34
versatility of digital cameras, 4
vertical orientation of image, 109
video files, adding, 196
viewfinder, 20–21
Visio, Microsoft, 245–246
VistaPrint for postcards, 208

W

Wal-Mart, 268
Walgreens, 268
warming filters, 154
Water Drops filter, 171
Watercolor Edge filter, 161
Watercolor filters, 156
watermarks, creating, 211–212
Wave filter, 171
Web Gallery, 14
Web hosting sites, 251
Web sites. See also personal Web pages
  digitization services, 75

iPrint, 204
Kodak Picture Maker, locating, 77
for mail-order photofinishers, 77
for online services, 247
Ritz Camera/Wolf Camera chain, 268
Shutterfly, 247
visiting digital photography sites, 54
Web hosting sites, 251
Wet Paint filter, 162
Windows
  backup directories, 86–89
  original images, storing, 86
  screensavers with, 192
Windows Explorer
  FTP Explorer with, 261–262
  image management with, 90–91
Windows XP
  Backup, installing, 86
  screensavers with, 192
wine bottle labels, 217–218
WinZip, 235
workgroups, Extensis Portfolio for, 99–100
worm's-eye view photos, 34
wrapping text around image, 212
writing, images for, 224–225
writing image files to CDs, 104
WS_FTP32, 260–261
WYSIWYG editors, 258
  using, 259–260

X

Xaos Tools' Total Xaos, 137
Xenofex
  digital imaging with, 136
  filters, 172

Y

Yahoo! GeoCities, 251

Z

Zigzag filter, 162
Zip drives, 9, 11, 103
  for e-mail attachments, 235
zooming
  focal length and, 80
  optical vs. digital zooming, 8, 20
  settings for, 19